S0-BYT-329

Christology from Within

STUDIES IN SPIRITUALITY AND THEOLOGY 3

Lawrence Cunningham, Bernard McGinn, and David Tracy
SERIES EDITORS

CHRISTOLOGY FROM WITHIN

Spirituality and the Incarnation in
Hans Urs von Balthasar

MARK A. McINTOSH

University of Notre Dame Press
Notre Dame and London

BT
198
.M3996
1996

Copyright © 1996
University of Notre Dame Press
Notre Dame, Indiana 46556
All Rights Reserved

Manufactured in the United States of America

Library of Congress Cataloging-in-Publication Data

McIntosh, Mark Allen, 1960–
    Christology from within : spirituality and the Incarnation in Hans
Urs von Balthasar / Mark A. McIntosh.
        p.   cm. — (Studies in spirituality and theology ; 3)
    Includes bibliographical references and index.
    ISBN 0-268-00815-9 (alk. paper)
    1. Jesus Christ—History of doctrines—20th century.
    2. Balthasar, Hans Urs von, 1905—Contributions in christology.
    3. Spirituality—Catholic Church—History—20th century.
    4. Balthasar, Hans Urs von, 1905—Contributions in Catholic
spirituality.   5. Catholic Church—Doctrines—History—20th century.
I. Title   II. Series: Studies in spirituality and theology series ; 3.
BT198.M3996   1996
232'.092—dc20   95-50918
                                                                       CIP

∞ *The paper used in this publication meets the minimum requirements of the
American National Standard for Information Sciences—Permanence of Paper
for Printed Library Materials, ANSI Z39.48-1984*

TO ANNE

CONTENTS

PREFACE

This book emerges from a fairly early stage in what I hope may turn out to be, for many of us, a long period of reflection about the relationship between spirituality and thought. Having made the unsettling discovery that reason does indeed have a history, our era has become more sensible of the cultural and linguistic contexts from which all ideas are born. No one, it seems, has ever had a "pure" idea, quite untinged by the glorious but desperate struggle of ordinary life. And this awareness has reminded us of something well known to the ancients as well as to many non-Western cultures today: the patterns and practices by which we live our lives will also shape our thoughts.

Spirituality as a technical term is a notorious fugitive from definition, but at least one could say it involves a form of practice, a pattern of life in search of ultimate meaning. For Christians this practice most usually involves the belief that communion with Jesus Christ is the way of encountering ultimate meaning. The story of Jesus becomes in various ways the story within which Christians seek to live their lives, discovering in this particular unsubstitutable path the transforming companionship of God.

For Christians as late as the Middle Ages it would have seemed peculiar at best to engage in much reflection about God or the mystery of God's presence in Jesus without in some sense attempting to participate in the spiritual journey marked out by Jesus himself. Theology is, in this setting, a reasoned consideration of the implications of spirituality. And of course there is a reciprocal movement as well; what theology is able to draw into discursive understanding becomes a source of guidance (usually helpful, sometimes not!) on the spiritual journey. For some while now, my hunch has been that what we usually think of today as "spirituality" and "theology" are both anemic versions of themselves, much in need of rejuvenating communion with each other.

The book that follows originated in a dissertation that was written to track down the source of a curious anomaly. I was trying to make sense of various modern restatements of the doctrine of the Incarnation. In particular I was comparing the efforts of those two formidable denizens of Basle, Karl Barth and Hans Urs von Balthasar. What puzzled me was that while Barth clearly was working very hard to answer the usual post-Enlightenment critiques of the Incarnation, von Balthasar seemed at first glance perilously tantalized by a quite different vision altogether. Whereas Barth unfolded the exhilarating prospect of human fulfillment and exaltation in the Incarnation, von Balthasar spoke relentlessly of self-humbling, kenosis, and abandonment. It sounded as if Jesus' humanity might be in danger of a kind of oppressive half-existence in favor of the divine Word's cosmic self-emptying. And so I set out to see if this were really true, if such a "high" christology as von Balthasar's inevitably failed to connect with an authentically human Jesus. I discovered along the way that the key to interpreting von Balthasar's approach is the integrity of spirituality and theology in his thought. This discovery leads one to an understanding of the often startling, sometimes deeply moving, always profoundly thought-provoking vistas that von Balthasar opens before his readers.

After I completed the dissertation I began a year or more of reflection and revision (how that first year of undergraduate teaching does sharpen a sense of the questions!). In what follows now, I have reframed the whole in terms of this fundamental question about the relationship between spirituality and theology. It is still an examination of von Balthasar's treatment of the Incarnation, but the work has become a consideration of how spirituality and theology might function together today in the task of constructive theology. How von Balthasar draws on the spiritual sources, how they weave themselves together in his understanding of Jesus—these are now the focal questions. The book, I hope, may now become part of this larger conversation about the role of spirituality in our (post-)modern attempt to live and to understand at least something of what it means to live.

I am enormously indebted to the scholars at the Divinity School of the University of Chicago who guided the dissertation: Anne Carr, Bernard McGinn, and especially David Tracy. Without the great ongoing McGinn project of studying the history of Christian mysticism I would certainly never have had the equipment to undertake this project. Of particular importance is his concern to examine Christian mystical texts in search of their actual teaching and their connection to the history of Christian thought. David Tracy has provided not only the always-longed-for encouragement that only a dissertation director can give, but also the marvelous breadth of vision which inspires the best in all the rest of us. Of particular importance during this period has been his own reconsideration of various spiritual traditions in his great project on naming and thinking God.

Many friends and colleagues have afforded me the kind of stimulating conversation which fosters much thought, in particular my colleagues of the theology Department at Loyola University of Chicago. Especially important has been the continuing dialogue with old friends from Oxford: Stephen and Diana Evans, Gabriel Everitt, O.S.B., and Anders Bergquist; and friends from the University of Chicago: Matthew Ashley, Paul DeHart, John Kevern, Steffen Lösel, Lois Malcolm, Joy McDougall, and Aristotle Papanikolaou. I am immensely grateful to them all.

Above all I thank my family who give me so much, especially my daughter Liza, who has more or less grown up along with this book (and who by her example has inspired much mirthful energy in me), and my dear wife Anne, who bestows delight, grace, and patient wisdom, and to whom this work is dedicated.

1

FINDING ONE'S WAY IN
VON BALTHASAR

Why did Jesus of Nazareth do the things he did? What was happening
to the world when he sat down to eat with a sinner or gave himself
over to the cross? Christian theology ruminates over such questions
because they are so richly and imponderably mysterious. The theologian who explores the full reality of Jesus Christ is journeying through
strange country. There are hidden springs of meaning whose sources
seem to evade academic explanation, even while they beckon the mind
into the unknown. Theology has always had a way of searching into
these deepest dimensions of the Christian mysteries. For alongside the
official teachings and experiences of the Christian communities, next
to the critical and creative tools of the historian, biblical critic, and
philosopher, there has run a parallel resource: the sensibility and intuition of mystical knowledge.

There are a number of questions one might want to ask about the
use of such a resource in constructive theology today—questions about
its legitimacy, warrants, criteria of evaluation, and so on. One way of
answering those questions (perhaps the best way in the end, though
not the most direct!) is simply to offer a demonstration. This book is
such a demonstration. It is an attempt to show how one theologian,
working with the insights of spiritual theology, was able to explore
deeply into the mystery of Christ. The test, of course, will be to see
what kind of Christ emerges from such an approach: Is he recognizably continuous with what we *think* we know about the historical Jesus of Nazareth? Is he available for modern critical scrutiny at
all or has he been spiritualized into the ethereal? Is he an authentic
human being?

Over the vast range of his works, Hans Urs von Balthasar (1905–88)
consistently pursued what I would call a mystical christology. It is a

christology "from within." Although it would undoubtedly rank as a "high" christology, one that always assumes the full divinity of Jesus, it is not a standard christology "from above"; that is, its center of gravity is not really the eternal life of the divine Logos. Nor is it a christology "from below," focusing on the critical examination of Jesus' earthly sayings or ministry or sociocultural milieu. Rather von Balthasar develops a christology from within, an analysis of Christ from the perspective of those women and men who have mystically entered *within* the life of Christ.

Here then is a concrete example of christology that arises out of dialogue between spirituality and theology. The understanding of Jesus that emerges is disturbingly lifelike. This is a Jesus whose passionate desire, whose struggle and commitment have suddenly been rendered theologically accessible and significant. It is a christology that has found in spirituality a creative matrix for theological reflection, a matrix in which Jesus' divinity and his humanity no longer seem like mutual contradictions only reconcilable by complex metaphysics. It is above all a christology in which the spiritual pilgrimage of an authentic human being is not only present but salvific.

THEOLOGICAL LOCATION

Interpreting Hans Urs von Balthasar on the Christian doctrine of the Incarnation requires a certain agility. Categorizations and compartmentalizations of his achievements are already hardening, threatening to obstruct an unprejudiced, wide-ranging perspective. Von Balthasar's style is by turns allusive, poetic, combative, oracular, dense, and always idiomatic. It is easy enough for theological camps to claim him, most probably against his own will, as their champion or their foe. In such cases the insight of his christological vision might well be overlooked.

What were his own aspirations and concerns? Describing the group of young theologians who had gathered round the French theologian Henri de Lubac in the 1930s, von Balthasar writes:

> it was clear to us from the beginning that the bastions of anxiety which the Church had contrived to protect herself from the world would have to be demolished; the Church had to be freed and open to the whole and undivided world for its mission.[1]

Two of von Balthasar's most fundamental impulses are on display here: his "missionary" concern for the whole public realm of life, and his conviction that Christianity is only fruitful for the world if it lives as a freely available sign of costly discipleship. Herein lies much of the tension in von Balthasar's effort and the source of many puzzles in placing him theologically. On the one hand, he is universal in his hope for humanity and insistent on theology's vocation to speak from and to the very heart of secular life. But on the other hand, he can be relentless in his critique of any expression of Christian existence that might obscure the concrete form of discipleship: Christ's active self-giving.

To gain some sense of the difficulty in placing von Balthasar theologically (and therefore in knowing how to "read" his christology), we should note that he was deeply concerned that his attempt to reintegrate spirituality and theology might be mistaken for "integralism," which he opposed.[2] Von Balthasar is fully conscious of the frailty of human traditions and forms. His strong commitment to them, to their living expression, is due to his search for the Whole which alone can animate them and make sense of them. It may be that what finally preserves von Balthasar from becoming uncritical or rigid in his thought is his willingness to allow himself and his sources to be questioned radically by the Whole beyond themselves. As Rowan Williams has acutely observed of analogous circumstances: "The greatness of the great Christian saints lies in their readiness to be questioned, judged, stripped naked and left speechless by that which lies at the centre of their faith."[3]

CHRISTOLOGICAL APPROACH

Von Balthasar's sense of his own mission in life determined his approach to christology.[4] He never thought of himself as a systematic theologian, and even his work as a publisher, translator, and spiritual writer could only be secondary in his life. At the center of his work is

the task of renewing the Church through the formation of new communities which unite the radical Christian life of conformity to the evangelical counsels of Jesus with existence in the midst of the world, whether by practising secular professions, or through the

ministerial priesthood to give new life to living communities. All
my activity as a writer is subordinate to this task.[5]

Whatever he wrote, therefore, would need to serve this purpose of
nourishing conformity to Christ in the midst of the world. It is not surprising then that his treatment of Christian doctrines should always
seek to show their inherent connection with the practice of Christian
life. Life according to Christ takes place within the vast drama of salvation which the community's doctrines sketch out epigrammatically,
and the doctrines themselves are expressed in terms and patterns
drawn from the spiritual life. So there is a kind of correlational theology going on in von Balthasar's christology (though not perhaps of the
expected academic kind), in which human journeying and Christian
faith are connected.[6] In its own fashion this correlation seeks to display
the Incarnation's intelligibility and its coherence with the fundamental
patterns of Christian life.

These fundamental mystical and spiritual patterns are so much a
part of von Balthasar that he draws on them with great frequency,
sometimes overtly, but often seemingly unconsciously. He employs
the schemata and the imagery of the spiritual life as a framework and
vocabulary within which he can make prominent in Christ's journey
certain features which, apart from the language of spirituality, might
remain inexpressible or even unrecognized. Von Balthasar uses mystical patterns as a lens to see more deeply into the mystery of Christ.
Thus, for example, he develops a profound treatment of Jesus' human
consciousness of God in terms drawn from the apophaticism of the
Cappadocians and the Carmelites.

How does von Balthasar's christology work? We could say, very
crudely, that his christology is Chalcedonian in its structure and ani-
mated by the thought of Maximus the Confessor and Ignatius of
Loyola in its spirit. From the Definition of Chalcedon, von Balthasar
draws together two crucial insights.[7] On one side, he is unvarying in
describing the personal identity of Christ as the eternal Son of God; for
von Balthasar, that is *who* Jesus of Nazareth is. On the other side, he
takes Chalcedon's assertion that Christ is recognized "in two natures"
as far more than a simple negation of the Eutychian extreme opposed
at the council. This means that the existence of the human being Jesus
of Nazareth, as the historical existence of the Person of the Word, is a
definitively complete *human* existence whose every human characteristic, including a human mind and will, is actually preserved and

perfected, not circumvented or supplanted, by coming into existence in the eternal Person of the Son.

This is the underlying structure of von Balthasar's approach to the Incarnation: Christ is the divine Word existing humanly. But with the aid of mystical theology, he has been able to shift the central categories for envisioning the reality of Christ from ontological to obediential terms. Where Chalcedon speaks of a union of divine and human *essences* in Christ, von Balthasar will speak of a union of divine and human *activity* in Christ. He does this by radicalizing a suggestion that Maximus the Confessor had drawn from trinitarian theology and applied to christology. Maximus speaks of how the eternal Son possesses the divine essence according to his particular *mode* of existence as the Son. So Christ's humanity, while remaining perfectly human in its essence, is lived out according to that particular pattern of life or mode of existence which is the perfect enactment in human terms of the Son's eternal mode of existence.[8] Von Balthasar adopts this christological insight wholeheartedly, for it allows him to speak of the divine in Christ precisely in terms of the very human pattern and activity of Jesus' life.

This becomes almost an organic impulse in von Balthasar's christology. While he does not simply ignore the two natures in Christ, he readily points to the extreme difficulty of conceiving of a conjunction of divine and human essences. Instead he speaks of the eternal Word as the expression of a particular filial dynamic within the divine life, and of the human being Jesus as perfectly enacting this very same pattern of sonship in human terms. Two points need underlining here. First, by transposing christological discussion from essentialist to actualist terms, von Balthasar is attempting to alleviate the metaphysical discomfort with essentialist language in christology which theologians have felt since Schleiermacher.[9] He is also in this way following Karl Barth in trying to capture the historical movement, the *eventful* quality, of Jesus' existence. Barth and von Balthasar both want to "actualize" the doctrine of the Incarnation because, as Barth put it, the older christologies began with an event and moved to an event, but too often in the center "there ruled the great calm of a timeless and non-actual being and its truth."[10] This could never convey the striving, passionate self-giving which is the heart of von Balthasar's understanding of Christ.

Second, by conceiving the Incarnation in terms of a particular divine pattern of activity which takes place in analogical human terms in Christ, von Balthasar is ensuring that his christology does not become separated from its trinitarian basis. In other words, he wants to emphasize that it is not undifferentiated divine self-communication which results in the Incarnation, but rather it is that particular mode of existence of the eternal Son which Jesus lives out in his human sonship. Besides its trinitarian strengths, this approach has, in von Balthasar's view, the advantage that it does not threaten to transmute Jesus into a quasi-divinity; it is not Godhead per se which must—impossibly it would seem—be translated into human terms, but the activity of perfect sonship.

Because this line of thought is absolutely central to von Balthasar's christology, it is worth illustrating it here, even at some length, in the lucid words of the Anglican Thomist Austin Farrer, who develops an exactly parallel argument in his own works, stated in this instance more comprehensively than in any single place in von Balthasar:

> If Jesus was God, it seems he could have no soul to save, no lessons to learn, no destiny to make, no surprises to meet, no temptations to resist; and without such experiences, he would not be a man at all. Whereas, if he was fully human in all these ways, then what can be meant by saying that he was God? . . . The trouble is, that we have taken a false starting-point. We cannot understand Jesus as simply the God-who-was-man. We have left out an essential factor, the sonship. Jesus is not simply God manifest as man; he is the divine Son coming into manhood. What was expressed in human terms here below was not bare deity; it was divine sonship. God cannot live an identically godlike life in eternity and in a human story. But the divine Son can make an identical response to his Father, whether in the love of the blessed Trinity or in the fulfilment of an earthly ministry. All the conditions of action are different on the two levels; the filial response is one. Above, the appropriate response is a cooperation in sovereignty and an interchange of eternal joys. . . . Below, in the incarnate life, the appropriate response is an obedience to inspiration, a waiting for direction, an acceptance of suffering, a rectitude of choice, a resistance to temptation, a willingness to die. For such things are the stuff of our human existence; and it was in this very stuff that Christ worked out the theme of heavenly sonship, proving himself on earth the very thing he was in heaven; that is, a continuous perfect act of filial love.[11]

Here we can see exactly these crucial modes or patterns of activity which von Balthasar will mark as constitutive of Jesus' humanity and therein of his identity as the eternal Son. Von Balthasar will argue that the radical self-emptying of Jesus is not merely forced upon incarnate divine love by the brutality of a fallen world but also reflects the utterly kenotic reality of trinitarian self-giving.[12]

Von Balthasar, however, is not content simply to translate the Chalcedonian structure into more existential language about the Son's activity. He takes the further step of interpreting that filial mode of existence in the framework of Ignatian election and obedience to mission.[13] By casting the divine-human activity of sonship in terms of an Ignatian concept of mission, von Balthasar accomplishes a number of theological goals.

First, the emphasis on mission (*Sendung*) allows him to strengthen even further his christology's trinitarian correlation. For von Balthasar, the trinitarian persons are identified by their eternal processions, and their processions are understood as including their historical missions; the eternal Son *is* the activity of total loving response and obedience to the Father. This eternal mission includes, but is not identical with, its perfectly analogous human enactment in the filial mission of Jesus.[14] So every conceivable moment in Christ's life is always seen by von Balthasar as a trinitarian event, and he uses this trinitarian dimension to give his christology a dramatic multidimensionality, a cosmic sense of light and darkness that he finds (pregnant) in Jesus' every human act.

Second, by speaking of Jesus' filial activity in terms of mission, von Balthasar is able to focus sharply on the actual struggle and tension of Christ's human existence: the metaphysical concept of trinitarian mission is translated into the ascetic-mystical contours of a human life actively giving itself to the divine will. Von Balthasar's first step, as we noted above, is to recast christology from a discussion about divine and human essence into a study of the Son's mode of divine existence and its human embodiment in Christ. Now he takes the further step of interpreting that human form of filial existence in terms of a distinct pattern of calling, acceptance of life-mission, struggle of obedience, radical self-giving, and so forth.[15] This also gives von Balthasar a way to correlate the Incarnation with the great range of human experience: a life of self-abandonment to one's mission finds numerous analogues in Christian and non-Christian existence.

Third, the effect of this is to allow a very "high" christology, which strongly emphasizes the divine identity of Jesus at every turn, to find complete expression in terms of a very human life. Because Jesus' divine personhood is identical with a concrete mission of response to the Father, von Balthasar is not forced to make Jesus into a little divinity; what Jesus' divine identity/mission requires is not that he have a perfect, divine knowledge about himself or world history, but only that he know how to love the One whom he called Abba.[16] Indeed von Balthasar argues that for Jesus a certain ignorance about his true destiny, an ignorance growing ever darker as he makes his way into the extreme reaches of his alienated fellow humans, is a necessary feature of the Son's particular mission.

QUESTIONS AND CRITIQUES

There is, however, a massive question which looms disquietingly in the background of von Balthasar's effort, one moreover which clearly nags at him since he frequently rails against it: in spite of all his intentions to the contrary, does von Balthasar's christology, which speaks of Christ's humanity so unremittingly in terms of self-abandonment, kenosis, and death, lead ineluctably to a docetic Christ? Is the human Jesus forced by his mission to become so utterly transparent to the eternal Son as to vanish altogether, leaving only a created cipher, a picture frame through which one stares directly into heaven? Does Jesus' human existence give expression to the divine Word only by being silenced into nonexistence?

It is not a question in von Balthasar as in certain ancient christologies from above, such as we find in some gnostic texts, of the eternal Son never quite making real "contact" with created human life— merely hovering phantom-like above the suffering human being. The question is rather whether von Balthasar interprets the filial mission of Jesus in such a way that *his very humanity itself is significant for salvation*. What becomes of Jesus' humanity when it is intepreted as the human translation of the infinite divine filial kenosis? Is it a human existence which is emance empoweringly human, human in a way that is generative for an understanding of what it is to be human at all?

Because the final segments of von Balthasar's work (notably the last volume of *Theologik*) were only published in 1987, not a great deal of criticism has had time to develop on this subject. Yet we may note a sampling of the angles of inquiry which, eventually, lead to the questions asked above. Peter Eicher, for example, stands for several scholars when he asks about von Balthasar's commitment to the historical reality of Jesus.[17] His concern is that von Balthasar tends too much toward what Eicher terms an "*eidetic* reduction," a dissolution of the historical Jesus in favor of the theological *eidos* or form of revelation, which is the great object of the first massive, multiple-volume segment of the Balthasarian trilogy.[18] The result, fears Eicher, is that Jesus' historical existence is robbed of its weight and significance.[19]

A rather more profound question is put by Karl Rahner. An interviewer once asked Rahner to respond to the criticism that his own christology lacked a sufficient theology of the cross, a charge made by von Balthasar in particular. He responded with a brief explanantion of his human transcendental starting point, and the concept that real death is the ultimate fulfillment of the human person's fundamental opening toward the incomprehensible. One could thus regard "the death of Jesus as the exemplary achievement of such a real leap into the indeterminability of God."[20]

Here already we can note the quite different approaches of Rahner and von Balthasar, at least in their fundamental impulses, to the death of Jesus. Von Balthasar does not at all object to interpreting Jesus' dying as "a real leap into the indeterminability of God." Indeed we shall see that he often interprets Christ's passion precisely in imagery borrowed from the dark night tradition in mystical theology, that classic theme of the soul's encounter with the incomprehensible God. But for von Balthasar this tension between the finite, transcendentally open creature and the infinite, unknowable God is completely subsumed within the far greater abyss between the sinful, antagonistic creature and the holy, loving God. And it is exactly von Balthasar's working out of God's response to this predicament that Rahner finds questionable:

> If I wanted to launch a counterattack, I would say that there is a modern tendency (I don't want to say a theory but at least a tendency) to develop a theology of the death of God that, in the last analysis, seems to me to be gnostic. One can find this in Hans Urs von Balthasar and in Adrienne von Speyr, although naturally much more marked in her than in him. It also appears in an independent form in Moltmann. To put it crudely, it does not help me to escape from my mess and mix-up and despair if God is in the same predicament. . . . From the beginning I am locked into its horribleness

while God—if this word continues to have any meaning—is in a true and authentic and consoling sense the God who does not suffer, the immutable, and so on.

Rahner concludes by wondering about the polarity of any such christology: "Perhaps it is possible to be an orthodox Nestorian or an orthodox Monophysite. If this were the case, then I would prefer to be an orthodox Nestorian."[21] The implication here is that a Nestorian tendency in christology would above all emphasize the "without confusion, without change" formulas of (in) Chalcedon, so as to avoid threatening the impassibility of God and robbing the inner-trinitarian life of its mystery. By contrast, a theology of the cross that seems to overstress the kenotic implications of the cross for the inner-trinitarian life is perhaps in danger of monophysite tendencies, since all the weight is inevitably on the perfect suffering of the divine Son. And this, of course, is exactly the question which von Balthasar's undeniable emphasis on the dereliction of the eternal Logos must raise.

Rahner's concern is whether such a theology inevitably claims to know too much about the inner life of God and so risks a certain mythological tincture of an almost gnostic quality; and that such a theology therefore finds itself in thrall to a docetic Christ whose humanity counts for nothing in the work of salvation because this is entirely a function of the cosmic, inner-divine drama.[22] This is the question that must be put to von Balthasar's treatment of the Incarnation.

INTERRELATIONSHIP OF WRITINGS

Because it is my aim to illustrate the significance for christology of the cross-pollination which takes place between spirituality and theology in von Balthasar's thought, it may be useful to end this orientation chapter with a basic map of von Balthasar's work, noting the different categories and genres, so that when I draw christological threads together from various works the reader may have a sense of their interrelationship.[23]

In very rough terms we can distinguish three principal categories of work that are germane to our project: historical studies in Christian spirituality, constructive or devotional writings in spirituality, and constructive theology. This of course leaves aside his enormous efforts in the translation and editing of historical and contemporary writings, above all the spiritual-theological-exegetical works of his spiritual colleague, the Swiss physician and mystic Adrienne von Speyr (1902–67). I must leave to others the important but perplexing task of discerning the details of von Speyr's influence in von Balthasar's own works.

In the field of historical studies in spirituality, especially crucial for my purposes, are three early patristic studies on Origen, Gregory of Nyssa, Maximus the Confessor,[24] and two later works on Thérèse of Lisieux and Elizabeth of Dijon.[25] From the early patristic studies von Balthasar's christology draws a number of significant impulses: from Origen, spousal and connubial themes; from Gregory, emphasis on the divine being as an infinitely dynamic, not a static, life; and from Maximus, as we have already seen, even more directly christological insights. Working with the two French Carmelites, von Balthasar develops an acute sense of how to read the contours of a spiritual mission and how to assess its impact on a human life. Also in this category are the several historical studies, some nearly book-length in themselves, which appear in the volumes of *Herrlichkeit*.

In the field of theoretical and devotional writings in spirituality, I will be drawing particularly on the early and remarkable *Herz der Welt*,[26] in which his first patristic studies and his initial five years of contact with Adrienne von Speyr bear fruit in a penetrating "dialogue" with Christ. In this highly dramatic and allusive work many of the central themes of von Balthasar's treatment of the Incarnation are already in formation. Among many other works in this field, two are especially significant: his theology of prayer, *Das betrachtende Gebet*,[27] in which the Incarnation is interpreted as an archetypal framework for prayer; and the mature study of the nature and integrity of the different vocational states of life, *Christlicher Stand*.[28] In this latter work the theme of mission is explored in terms of the Christian's location within the mission of Christ.

As can be seen even from such a cursory profile, von Balthasar's mystical and spiritual studies are strongly theological in focus, and conversely his constructive theological works are deeply informed by the questions and perspectives of the spiritual life. Among all his theological works certainly his great contribution is the triptych *Herrlichkeit*, *Theodramatik*, and *Theologik*. Much will be written in years to come on the interrelation of these volumes, their presentation of theology in the light of the three transcendentals of beauty, goodness, and truth, and the intriguing possibility that they ought, each in its own way, to be seen as new theological genres and *not* as idiosyncratic attempts at systematic theology. All of that is beyond the present work.

It will be helpful, however, to note the different approach each panel of the triptych takes to the Incarnation. In *Herrlichkeit* there are elements of a fundamental theology; the aim is to draw the reader into an awareness of the process of perception, of the enrapturing power of beauty, and then to see how it is Christ who in his living, dying, and rising fulfills and surpasses all earthly forms in revealing the glory of God. For von Balthasar, however, it is *Theodramatik* which is of greatest importance; he attends to the actual dramatic encounter of divine and human freedom, and their respective roles in the cosmos-constituting drama. "What I am trying to do is to express this in a form in which all the dimensions and tensions of life remain present instead of being sublimated in the abstractions of a 'systematic' theology."[29] It is in this work that von Balthasar's most central christological tract is found, the interpretation of Jesus in terms of his great "role" or mission. Finally, in *Theologik,* the author offers a "reflection on the way in which the dramatic event can be transposed into human words and concepts for the purposes of comprehension, proclamation and contemplation."[30] Here the emphasis is, not surprisingly, on the incarnate Word as the basis of human speech and truthfulness.

In light of the foregoing introduction to the issues and problems at hand, let me now offer a succinct statement of the argument to follow. The key to von Balthasar's profoundly incarnational christology is the continual dialogue in his thought between theology and spirituality. In this light, one discerns a doctrine of the Incarnation which, while very Chalcedonian in orientation, avoids the docetic tendencies of some christologies from above, and in fact accords truly determinative salvific significance to the historical humanity of Jesus Christ. In the succeeding chapters I will take up in turn the dialogue between spirituality and theology in von Balthasar and its implications for his method; the consequent structuring of his christology; the four states into which his christology can best be analyzed (self-abandonment, obedience to mission, passion and death, and ecstatic communal life); and finally a synthetic overview of the role and significance of Christ's humanity.

2

A MYSTICAL CHRISTOLOGY

THE RELATION OF SPIRITUALITY AND THEOLOGY

As von Balthasar worked his way through the classics of Christian thought, the uneasy sensation settled over him that a tragic divorce had occurred between doctrine and practice, between theology and spirituality. As early as 1948 he began to address himself to the problem, and over the years the question returns again and again in his works.[1] He struggled to understand what he saw as the fatal consequences of this separation—the desiccation of dogmatics and the self-absorption of spirituality. Interestingly, he does not offer an easy, "no-fault" interpretation in which the severing is simply the unfortunate but inevitable result of trends in the history of ideas. The separation has in von Balthasar's mind a more grievously concrete cause: an absence of men and women with the grace to unify theology and spirituality in their own lives.[2]

Von Balthasar sees the first real impetus for this separation in the church's need to challenge false teaching and schismatic tendencies, and therefore to demarcate the limits of authentic Christian faith. It is at this point that he finds among the church fathers "a dualism developing between a polemical theology which threatens to lose itself in conceptual subtleties (though these are surely unavoidable), and an inner-churchly, non-polemical theology, which unfolds from the fullness of covenant-reflection."[3]

In the patristic era this dualism is not yet a threat to the unity of theology and spirituality, at least in the great doctors and teachers.[4] Commenting on the harmony between Gregory of Nyssa's life and thought, von Balthasar argues that this harmony is the very basis of mystical theology. "Far from opposing each other," he continues, "dogmatic and mystical theology are, if one conceives of theology as a

13

dynamic realization, even identical. It is thus that all the church fathers understand things, and most particularly Origen and the Cappadocians."[5]

What von Balthasar finds most suggestive in the patristic and monastic figures is their ability to find "straightaway the appropriate dogmatic clothing for their very personal experience."[6] The mystical *experience* is not in itself the proper object of much attention. The unity of theology and spirituality is best served when personal experience is the *aid* in comprehending and appreciating the content of revelation. Von Balthasar's nuptial-Marian perspective comes into play here, for he interprets spirituality as "the subjective aspect of dogmatic theology, the word of God as received by the bride and developing within her."[7] We could think of spirituality as the contemplative, environing matrix in which the infinite mysteries of Christianity can be received and bear fruit within the church's understanding. This fruitfulness, always a key notion in von Balthasar, is found at two levels: the existential liveliness of the mystery for the believer and the elucidation of the objective teaching of the church.

Following approvingly Leclercq's famous *Love of Learning and the Desire for God*, von Balthasar notes the unraveling of this existential-objective synthesis with the rise of scholasticism; nor does he overlook the antagonism sown by monastic theology in its opposition to the early scholastics.[8] With the new Aristotelianism and development of a scientific method, he argues that philosophical ideas, norms, and methods became a rigid structure imposed upon the content of faith.[9]

The result was an increasing isolation of dogmatic and mystical theology from one another, each becoming more inaccessible and unattractive to the practitioners of the other. Von Balthasar's sarcasm and his sensitivity to the pain of this state of affairs take turns in governing his depiction of succeeding eras. Post-Tridentine neoscholasticism loses all feeling for the mystery and glory of God and works with intentional independence from a developing "spiritual theology."

> The "mystic" is now identified increasingly in terms of his subjective experience of glory and is stamped as an exception, while the "rule" is represented by the strictly logical and intellectualist metaphysics of the Church. Those who are concerned to restore the lost unity (Gerson, Nicholas of Cusa, Petavius, Gerbert, etc.) remain outsiders and often pursue paths which lead to speculative Idealism.[10]

Von Balthasar's point is that the church's theologians had willingly adopted forms of thought that left them *outside* the deep mystery of theology's object, and that, conversely, those who retreated into a distinct "affective" theology presented material which "often degenerated into unctuous, platitudinous piety."[11]

He is clearly far from assigning blame only to the scientific theologians. The saints are more and more called to offer descriptions of their inner states and experiences; they are "required to describe the way in which they experienced God, and the accent is always on experience rather than on God: for the nature of God is a subject for the theological specialist."[12] It is as if the taste of spiritually inclined persons becomes so subjective and rarified that the objective mysteries of Christianity only manage to obstruct their view. The saints, therefore, "are not taken seriously in theology because they themselves did not venture to be theologically minded."[13] Von Balthasar describes with growing discomfort the sliding focus of writers like de Sales; imperceptibly the emphasis shifts from a pure Godwardness to a study of human transcendence. He concludes with humorous tartness:

> The devout mind is self-conscious and paradoxically takes self as its object in the very process of transcending and escaping from itself. . . . This tendency to introspection rests upon the celebrated spirituality of the *Grand Siècle* like mildew (or should we say, talcum powder?).[14]

The preciously coiffed and powdered faces only betray the self-preoccupation of much seventeenth-century spirituality.

One senses that the dilemma for von Balthasar is very real: both good scientific theology and clear teaching on the life and experience of the spirit are to be welcomed. His fear is that the church, in accepting this division, has almost without noticing it lost access to a vital way of understanding and teaching Christian faith. It is as if a particular language skill had been left to atrophy, and therefore a whole realm of life, custom, and reality for which this language was the medium has become lost. It is a realm in which existential awareness of the mysteries of faith and objective, catholic (in the sense of trans-personal, trans-communal) teaching about the mysteries can cohere as one life, and can, indeed, only find their respective fullnesses as they are united. It is a realm of theological discourse in which God is always the free

and active subject and never a fixed object (whether remote or immanent) of human deliberation.

THEOLOGICAL ROLE OF THE SAINTS

This brings us to von Balthasar's positive response to the dilemma
he so forcefully describes. To be sure, he is not about to overleap
present circumstances.[15] Rather we might describe his goal in terms of
the formation of a new matrix for theological discipleship, in which
participants "long to discover the living organism of the Church's doctrine, rather than a strange anatomical dissection."[16]

> What impedes the reintegration of dogmatic and spiritual theology
> so disastrously is the loss of the objective spiritual medium. . . .
> [This] spiritual dimension can only be recovered through the soul of
> man being profoundly moved as a result of direct encounter with re-
> vealed truth, so that it is borne in upon him, once and for all, how
> the theologian should think and speak, and how he should not. This
> holds good for both the estranged disciplines, dogmatic theology
> and spirituality.[17]

Von Balthasar is clearly pointing to an existential basis for theology, a
resource upon which he wishes to draw for the construction of his
own positions. In the life experience and teaching of holy women and
men one can find that essential "spiritual medium" in which a theology alive to the divine springs of faith can flourish.

How does he envision the theological role of the saints? What is
most crucial in these figures? He speaks of finding in the saints "the
source, ever flowing, ever fresh" of a theology of Christ's redeeming
existence, especially his passion.

> Their charism consisted in the ability to re-immerse themselves,
> beyond everything that convention might dictate, in a "contempo-
> raneity" with the Gospel so as to bequeath the legacy of their inti-
> mate experience to their spiritual children.[18]

Von Balthasar, just as much as liberal theologians from Schleiermacher
on, refuses to view redemption as purely a past historical event. But
the way in which redemption becomes an existential reality for the
present-day believer differs quite significantly between von Balthasar
and other thinkers. Some theologians (Kant or Troeltsch, for example)

might place the emphasis on the believer's present personal and subjective appropriation of the saving truth, which is itself symbolically represented in the historical events. Von Balthasar, by contrast, speaks of a contemporaneity with the Gospel; not so much a bringing forward of the past into the present experience of the believer, but a participation of the believer in the eternal aspect of definitive historical saving events. For von Balthasar, saving and revelatory events are never really "the past"; yet by no means is the concrete historical form of these events jettisoned for some more elemental core. Rather in his view these events, because of the effulgence of divine agency at work in them, are always open, communicable, and extensive realities. Therefore he resists any approach that would "look on historical revelation as a past event, as presupposed, and not as something always happening, to be listened to and obeyed."[19]

Von Balthasar defines the saints precisely as those who have ceaselessly "immersed themselves in the actual circumstances of the events of revelation."[20] For the saints the gospel narratives become a threshold over which the believer may pass prayerfully into the original and eternal presence of the saving events themselves. One notes here the strongly Ignatian perspective, particularly the instructions throughout the *Spiritual Exercises* to enter meditatively and imaginatively *into* the scenes of the gospels, seeking especially for an "interior knowledge of our Lord."[21] It is in this "interior" experience of the historic redemptive events that von Balthasar will seek fresh springs for theology.

Scientific theology, in von Balthasar's view, has not sufficiently unfolded the images and intuitions in the "implicit theology" of the saints; their contribution was too quickly channeled into a purely "spiritual theology" or else it was "taken captive by anthropocentric schemata of ascent and purification, still dominant in the doctor of the Church John of the Cross himself."[22] This is one of the dangers of turning to the saints for theological material, namely, that the subjective-existential medium of the saint's teaching will itself become the object of theoretical study. Instead, theology should focus on the powerful divine life which, acting like a magnet upon the saint, has drawn forth the teaching or life experience in question. Von Balthasar views the theological task in these cases as perilous but exhilarating. The aim would be to discern something of what God must be like through the effect of God upon the life of the saint, much as an astronomer attempts to calculate the mass of an unseen body by analyzing its gravitational effect on an object that can be seen.

What is the nature of the saint's "contemporaneity with the Gospel" and contemplative exposure to God? Von Balthasar's prime metaphor here is nuptial and Marian. The saint within the community of the church enters the ecclesial role of the bride in communication with Christ the Bridegroom. "The purpose of contemplation is to cause the life of the bride to be transformed."[23] The saints by their attentiveness to the Word begin to be transformed, in the classic terminology, from image to likeness; and it is their receptivity and transformation that provide the model form for Balthasarian theology, just as their teaching is its primary matter.[24] Von Balthasar sees this gift of openness and availability to the Word as first a gift of the church, but it often becomes manifest

> in a saint, whose soul has gazed so long and deeply on the light of God that it has come to hold within itself an almost inexhaustible store of light and love, and so can offer lasting force and sustenance.[25]

Here again we note the nuptial pattern: the adoring and praying saint becomes the fruitful matrix, the medium of human availability for God, in which divine reality can become reciprocally available for humanity in very human terms and concepts. For theologians in particular, the saints "are a new interpretation of revelation; they bring out scarcely suspected treasures in the deposit of faith."[26] Von Balthasar suggests in this passage an additional theological role for the saints, namely, the beckoning puzzle which their lives set for theology. "Their sheer existence," in addition to any teaching they might offer directly, attracts theology's attention, luring it into deeper acquaintance with the inexplicable radiance to which these unlikely figures gesture.

In spite of his ardor for the reunion of spirituality and theology, von Balthasar is not without rules for the discernment of spirits: not every spirituality is a fit medium for the theological task. Indeed he is conscious that the very inadequacies of some forms of mysticism have caused them to be ignored by theology. Authentic mysticism has a verifiable *ecclesial orientation* that von Balthasar believes distinguishes it from other phenomena. It must be recognizably an "explicitation and interiorisation of the revelation of the Logos by the divine Spirit."[27] In other words, mysticism which is not in some way in the service of the whole church's ever deeper appropriation and understanding of life in Christ is not an appropriate theological matrix.

Von Balthasar is harshly critical of any naiveté which "uncritically accepts as genuine every alleged or authentic vision, audition, stigmatisation, and so on" without discerning whether it has any "integral connection with the total Church."[28] Yet he is also concerned that such sensible phenomena not be ruled out automatically. What must be discerned is whether one has surrendered all personal claims to "experience" in favor of making oneself available to share in the experience of Christ, which itself is then to be shared with the church: "The individual with his experience is ever an expropriated member of the whole and must feel and behave accordingly."[29] On this question von Balthasar formulates what he calls the "determinative maxim":

> it is not *experience* of a union with God which represents the yardstick of perfection or the highest stage of ascent, but rather *obedience*, which can be quite as tightly bound to the experience of abandonment by God as to the experience of union with God.[30]

Authentic Christian spirituality is already communally oriented, for it is a spirituality ordered primarily to obedience, which always involves community.

We find an interesting concrete sense of these criteria in an interview with two members of the Community of St. John, the secular institute founded by von Balthasar and Adrienne von Speyr. They stress two criteria as characteristic notes of the founders' intentions for the community: "obedience as following the crucified Lord" and "the ability to disappear into the Church."[31] This latter quality is described as modeled upon a notion of John as the beloved disciple who unites the hierarchical church of Peter with the church of love (Mary). "John is the one who brings both together and who disappears with his love into Peter." Von Balthasar and von Speyr stressed again and again "that, at all costs, the Community [of St. John] likewise should not present itself as a community or even as an ecclesiastical institution." The emphasis is on the practical anonymity of the community, which should act as a hidden channel of grace: the most important idea is "that something of the grace given to us could be communicated to our environment through the presence of one of our members without anyone being conscious of it, not even the person concerned."[32] So the central criterion of authentic spirituality would be a sharing in Christ's total availability to serve God's work in the world, a sharing which is in no way self-seeking or even self-conscious.

What is ruled out therefore are spiritual manifestations marked by an especially introverted focus, more concerned with the "progress of the devout, pious self" than a living participation in the biblical revelation.[33] The great founders of orders were never so concerned with "Franciscanism" or "Dominicanism" as with Christ and the world he came to save. Any spirituality, therefore, which is constantly measuring its own particular features, comparing them against others or other states of life, betrays "an infallible sign of decadence."[34]

Clearly von Balthasar is concerned to find the right criteria by which to avoid mystical writings and experiences that are merely bizarre, but to his mind the Gospel itself is likely to foster in the saints something which will always seem outrageous to the eyes of the world, and this radicality in his view has an important place. What he is more anxious about is the kind of subtle, pervasive orientation of entire generations of spiritual writers which, precisely because it is commensurate with the contemporary culture's concern with self and inner experience, will go unchallenged.

Discernment in this regard requires a judgment regarding whether the saints or mystics in question are more interested in Christ or in detecting their own progress toward Christ, and whether they are willing to give over to the church all their experiences or teachings with a certain anonymity and complete freedom from self-regard. For von Balthasar the best test of the theological fruitfulness of mysticism is its transparency to Christ, its complete unwillingness to be the subject of people's attention or to distract them from a deeper following of the Gospel. The ultimate criterion by which von Balthasar judges the helpfulness to theology of a mystical teaching is simply the authenticity of that mystical path as a Christian way of life. What counts is not visions or lack of visions, but the measure of a believer's love of God and neighbor.[35]

Whether von Balthasar's criteria of discernment are sufficient in judging the theological fruitfulness of mystical writing remains an open question; he does not at least rule out further criteria such as intelligibility or coherence with what is otherwise believed to be the case about reality. Though of course for von Balthasar the final criteria of truthfulness and adequacy to reality are found not so much in general philosophical judgments as they are in a living fidelity to the self-giving existence of Christ.

His aim in drawing on the saints is best understood as analogous to theological works of the patristic and monastic periods. He wishes to interpret central Christian mysteries in a manner capable of drawing readers closer to participation in the mysteries themselves. Early medieval Cistercian writings on Christ afford an interesting analogy. In discussing these works Bernard McGinn has noted that what is most vital about any such christology is not so much its treatment of metaphysical details, "but rather how it makes use of inherited material to form a language about Christ's redeeming work that can serve as the basis for a program of ascesis and religious formation."[36] Much the same effort is suggested by von Balthasar's own words: "true theology, the theology of the saints," is concerned with "bringing human beings and their whole existence, intellectual as well as spiritual, into closer relation with God."[37] Von Balthasar believes that theology should be suited to the work of religious formation. His own commitment to this requirement is plain when we recall that one of the great efforts of his life was the establishment of the secular religious institute, the Community of Saint John, a cause for which he was required and willing to sacrifice his own membership in the Society of Jesus.

CHRISTOLOGY FROM WITHIN

We come now to the heart of von Balthasar's notion of the peculiar access to the inner reality of Christ that the saints and mystics give to theology. It is an approach to theology which thoroughly bridges the usual distinction between christology "from above" and "from below." Von Balthasar does indeed have a very high christology which certainly presupposes a doctrine of the Trinity, yet he also constructs this christology with constant attention to the historical human reality of Jesus. But again he does not do so in a strictly academic, historical-critical manner, beginning with an attempted unearthing of one candidate or another for the role of "historical Jesus." Instead he explores the participation of the saints and mystics in the life of Christ in order to understand Jesus' divine-human reality "from within."

Von Balthasar sees the saints as the concretizations in each age of that particular unfolding of Christ most needed by their contemporaries. By the activity of the Holy Spirit, "the individual historical existence of Christ can be so universalized as to become the immediate norm of every individual existence."[38] It is crucial for von Balthasar that this mediation of Christ through his faithful people *not* be limited to a mere following or external imitation, but rather that it includes a profound sharing of Jesus' own consciousness. In one of his most significant and programmatic statements, von Balthasar writes: "The saints are not given to us to admire for their heroic powers, but that *we should be enlightened by them on the inner reality of Christ*, both for our better understanding of the faith and for our living thereby in charity."[39] Because of their communion with Christ, the saints bear within themselves the marks of his own experience. How does von Balthasar explain this participation in Christ? First, humanity itself is ordered to fulfillment in Christ and this is actualized by sharing in the obedience of Christ's own mission; and second, Christ is a uniquely open and inclusive being, always drawing his fellow humans into his own life.

On the issue of human orientation to Christ, it is clear that von Balthasar sees the whole of history as a space opened by God for human freedom and interaction with God.

> [This is] in no sense an empty space but one that is shaped and structured and completely conditioned by certain categories. The framework of its meanings is constructed of the situations (the interior situations) of Christ's earthly existence. Man cannot fall out of this space which is Christ's, nor out of the structural form created by his life.[40]

The theme of this "acting space" will be developed later in *Theodramatik*, but even in this earlier work we can see von Balthasar moving toward a nonessentialist reading of human participation in Christ. We might interpret his imagery this way: because of the creation of all things in Christ, certain patterns of self-giving love are inherent foundational structures in historical existence—rather like the way gravity necessarily structures physical existence; to live according to these habits of life is to live freely, unencumbered by fighting against the grain. But Jesus Christ is the true identity of these structures of existence; they turn out to be not abstract laws but the historical dimensions of a personal being. Therefore, human obediential love has a predisposition for self-fulfillment in Christ.

Jesus is a Thou to his fellow humans, the other whom they join themselves to in faithfulness, but he is this not as one marked off in simple contradistinction; rather Christ is "the origin and ground in which our whole being with all its roots is fixed, from which it draws its sustenance and derives all its best and characteristic features."[41] To recur to our metaphor of a language which gives access to a particular world of existence, we might say that von Balthasar understands loving fidelity and obedience to be the forms of speech which put believers in communication with the deep reality of their ongoing and usually hidden life in Christ. The saints can and do gain access to the "interior situations" of Christ as they live according to the rhythms of self-giving love and obedience that constitute Christ's own existence.

Perhaps the most obvious basis for this perspective of von Balthasar's is his deep immersion in the *Spiritual Exercises*. The task of the exercitant, as Ignatius repeatedly urges, is precisely to ask for this sensitivity to Christ's inner life "that I may love him more intensely and follow him more closely."[42] This spiritual directive von Balthasar transforms into the basis for an understanding of human fulfillment in Christ. Conformity to Christ includes within it the possibility of an inner sharing of Christ's own experience.

Von Balthasar's second approach to this question of how the saints come to participate in Christ is focused less on the christomorphic structure of the believer's existence (Maximus and Ignatius), and more on the inclusive nature of Christ's own personal existence (Bérulle). We need to stress here not only the openness of Christ's life to participation but even more the capacity of his divine-human life actively to generate related situations in the life of the believing community.[43]

This is no passive experience in which the believer is simply lost in the overwhelming reality of Christ—as is made clear in an amusing way by von Balthasar's description of Thérèse. While it is true that Thérèse grows into total selflessness, in another sense it is her very self which is the chief object of her considerable spiritual activity: Thérèse as new translation of the Word of God. She labors ceaselessly to enter the shareable mysteries of Jesus' life, above all, of course, his fresh, spontaneous, and innocent yet utterly demanding childhood. Jesus attracts her relentlessly into conformity with himself by his beguiling love, but von Balthasar also highlights the degree to which Thérèse responds by working away upon all her acting, willing, thinking, so that in everything she may "embody the Word of Love in her life."[44] Thérèse's new Christ-self is precisely the self she so self-consciously fashions from the quotidian details of her life.

Drawing on Bérulle, von Balthasar argues that this kind of participation in the stages of Christ's life is grounded in the eternal presence of those historical moments for Christ himself:

Like Eckhart, Bérulle especially emphasises the fact that the incarnate love of God is always Now, grounded in the eternal Now of the Trinitarian processions. In this eternal Now of the God-Man "the actual enjoyment, the living disposition, by which Jesus effected any given mystery [of His earthly life] is always living, actual, present for Jesus."[45]

What happens, according to Bérulle, is that Christ's inherent capacity to include souls within himself makes it possible for those whom he draws to himself to share in his own living experience of his earthly life.[46] So the believer's participation in the ever-present interior reality of Jesus' life is completely based on Christ's fundamental personal inclusivity. And in fact it is exactly this participation in Christ that grounds the fullness of human historical existence, namely, the capacity to be for and with another in freedom and love.

Von Balthasar gives a multihued account of this inclusive capacity of Christ. It is not simply an untroubled sharing of divine delights, for there is no more accessible state of Christ's existence than his suffering. Von Balthasar reflects on the church's invitation to "co-suffering" in terms of John's story of Lazarus,

> where Jesus deliberately lets "the one whom he loves" die, and sends no news to anxious sisters, but leaves them in a forgottenness with the pitch of a dark night, lets this night (brought down on them through him!) submerge himself also (Jn 11.33ff), and thereby gives them a part in his God-abandonment which pre-figures that of the Eucharist.[47]

The Bérullian metaphysics of capacity achieves in von Balthasar a grave and more historically grounded depth from his reading of Christ's earthly life. We see that this inherent capacity or opening out of Christ is grounded in the momentum of Jesus' self-giving—a momentum so powerful that it impels him to the cross and begins to sweep others into his own destiny. Jesus is accessible to the saints and faithful who seek him precisely because he chose always to give others (the disciples, Magdalene, above all Mary his mother) a share in his mission. Therefore each moment in his earthly life, for all its Bérullian eternality, is in von Balthasar's reading already structured to include others; each state bears within it a fundamental orientation towards companionship and self-sharing.

So what exactly does von Balthasar hope this participation of the saints in Christ will contribute to theology?

> What is necessary today, after long experience of the history of theology, is an effort at an authentic *theological* deepening of the particular mysteries of salvation in their incarnationally concrete character.[48]

Von Balthasar wants to explore the great theological loci by taking them back into their christological-trinitarian depths. Every doctrine is replete with the tension, passion, and drama of a human life because it emerges from the community's experience of Jesus. Like Karl Barth, von Balthasar is not ultimately fastened to a particular dogma or theological principal; neither the triumph of grace nor the glory of self-giving love could be the real object of their theology, but only the living person Jesus Christ. And the saints have been granted a capacity to witness to the ever-new, ever-deeper dimensions of Christ's living, dying, and rising. In fact, as he surveys the whole range of Christian doctrines, von Balthasar suggests that it is christology that stands to gain most "from what the saints experienced."[49]

Von Balthasar inevitably turns to "passiology" as his most potent example.

> There are the graces of participation in the passion given to the Church, the experiences of the saints, which are quite inexplicable except as participation in Christ's states. These experiences constitute the vast, limitless field of the "dark nights". . . . To my knowledge, no theology has seriously undertaken the task of seeing them as a whole and evaluating them from the point of view of dogma. . . . Why should we persist in ignoring the detail of these sufferings, making not the least attempt to use, for a better understanding of the faith, these experiences so valuable for the Church?[50]

Through the saints, each moment of Christ's existence is made continually and newly present in his Body, and it is von Balthasar's aim to enlist these experiences in deepening the Body's understanding of what has taken place in the Head. Sometimes von Balthasar will develop features of Christ's life in direct conversation with mystical theology, as for example is the case with Christ's passion and the mystical dark night. In other areas the correlation is not directly stated;

nevertheless the analogue is always there, subtly shaping the frame of reference, lending the transcendent trinitarian mission a homely, earthly, human basis. As he remarked of Thérèse of Lisieux's own theological insights, von Balthasar is not merely drawing inferences from mildly parallel experiences in the saints back to the inner reality of Christ. No, von Balthasar is claiming the right to draw on the saints' own grace of participation in Christ as a direct source for theological construction. And so he aims for a christology "from within."

GENERAL METHODOLOGICAL IMPLICATIONS

One of the most fundamental methodological impulses in von Balthasar is his preference for concrete historical event and encounter over more universal metaphysical claims, and this precisely for the sake of conveying the stunning, often enrapturing, reality that is theology's source. He is not going to ignore the work of fundamental theology, but his principal concern is always that the living heart of Christianity be presented in a theological manner that is truly expressive of its native dynamism and pattern. So for example the phases and struggles of a saint's life may provide an invaluable counterpart to more scientifically abstract descriptions of Christ's person and work.

This is not simply a personal preference of von Balthasar's; he believes that the largest and truest category for interpreting the divine-human encounter is not metaphysical but covenantal. Theology is truly *Christian* for him when reflection on the philosophical incomprehensibility of God, often expressed in terms of some form of "negative theology," is transformed into reflection on the incomprehensibility of God's love for creation.

> It is radically incomprehensible that absolute love, utterly fulfilled in the plenitude of trinitarian life, should be able, for the sake of sinners—which I am—to divest itself [*se dépouiller*] of divine traits in order to die in deepest darkness. In the face of this laughable absurdity, all negative theology is only an innocent naivety. But it is precisely this laughable absurdity, in the figure God offers me in his revelation, which rushes upon me with an irresistible and literally mortal force.[51]

For von Balthasar the problem of understanding and knowing God is always a subsidiary of the far more radical problem of the confrontation of human sin with the love of God. The issue for him is not so much a question of thought as an actual encounter with love "which rushes upon me." For this reason the analysis of the divine-human encounter is going to find a theoretical basis not in an experience of absolute dependence (Schleiermacher) nor in a transcendental apprehension of being (Rahner) but in concrete acts of loving obedience which participate in Christ, who is himself the hurtling incomprehensibility of divine love.

In his early work on Origen, von Balthasar had examined an understanding of truth and knowledge which is primarily a *relatio rationis*, leading to a science of "essences." Following Origen he leaves this aside in favor of an alternative:

> If, on the contrary, truth resides above all in the assimilation of an existent being to its Idea, that would consequently mean a life, a tension, something secret; the being would have to abandon itself in order to be caught hold of.[52]

In this conception, truth is very personal indeed and is disclosed through an actual existence of self-abandon, of being drawn into the life of the Idea. For von Balthasar and Origen, of course, the archetype is the Logos, *the truth of whose divine reality becomes known primarily as one is caught up into Christ's own life of self-abandonment to the Father.* There is always this double abandon in von Balthasar's search for truth: the believer's self-abandonment to Christ so that the believer is caught up in that overwhelming disclosure of truth which breaks open upon the cosmos in Jesus' self-abandonment to the Father.

For this reason von Balthasar resolutely avoids any forms of metaphysical and theological reflection that might in any way pass beyond the sharp relief of the actual historical existence of Christ. He eschews extreme Origenism and later spiritualizing tendencies such as are found in Boehme and Schelling: "The aim of one and all is to reduce the historical character of Christianity to the general, pre-historical relationship between God and man, between a time which passes and an eternity always latent in it and above it."[53] The fear is that in the concern of scientific theology to ground itself in transcendental or universal correlates, it may dissolve the very features of concrete reality which are most disclosive of truth.

A strong case in point is theological interpretation of the crucifixion. How does one draw the line, von Balthasar asks, between a genuinely theological reading and one which tips over, transforming death-and-resurrection "into a universal and generally knowable philosophical truth detachable from faith"?[54] He is not opposed to discerning the cosmic dimensions of the cross, or even to setting it within a framework of analogies, provided always the similarity is recognized only within a yet greater dissimilarity.

> What that theology [of the cross] must do is to discern whether the universality which confronts it belongs to the unique historical fact of the Crucifixion and Resurrection of Christ, or to a general idea. In the latter case, emphasis may fall either on the symbolic, imagistic form, or on the concept, conceived as a law of history or of existence, but in any of these versions the Cross of Christ is regarded as a particular instance of something, if perhaps a remarkable one. That is theologically unacceptable.[55]

Von Balthasar's concern is that when this happens, the supervening concept which becomes the rule for the actual mysteries of Christ's existence will not be able to afford a sufficient exposure to the truth of the saving events. If a general rule could ever grasp the true depths to which God's love extends itself in Christ, there would have been no need for an actual historical redeemer. Von Balthasar's view, I suggest, is that far from benignly bringing the true meaning of the historical symbol to intelligibile consciousness, abstraction towards a general rule actually homogenizes and distorts the shocking profile of the Crucified—which alone could really grip the believer with some sense of the truth of what is involved.

Alongside all these concerns there is a genuine opening in von Balthasar to the impulses of fundamental theology. Indeed this is closely related to the point I just made, that the powerful impact of the actual historical reality of revelation, and the force of that impact registered in scripture and the fellowship of the church, is arguably the most capable of bearing witness to the truth—precisely by drawing one into a response. So, for example, the plausibility of divine love is conveyed best not so much by correlation with what has all along been recognized as love, but by the capacity of the actual life of that love, Jesus Christ, to draw one into communion with himself.[56] To be sure this builds on some pre-understanding (*Vorverständnis*), without which even the ability to discern the presence of a sign of divine love would be impossible; yet even so the progress from human analogy to divine reality always requires personal conversion.[57] So truthfulness and understanding come about through concrete historical acts of fidelity and self-abandon to the reality one desires to know. And this of course strongly parallels the Balthasarian hagiographical method generally, i.e., to seek for the plausibility and intelligibility of theology in correlation with the believing, obedient self-giving of faithful men and women.

We find both a descending and an ascending impulse in von Balthasar's fundamental theology. As each aspect of the divine-human encounter makes contact with human experience, that contact brings about a conversion and enrapturing of the human knower, drawing her or him into a far deeper and more existential understanding of truth than the general law or human correlate could on its own have provided.[58] Human desire, law, or expectation point in the direction of the divine reality but are more than fulfilled by the utter kenosis of grace; one could never, on the basis of the human correlate alone, have predicted or characterized the final reality of grace. To return to von Balthasar's Origenian perspective, it is always the conversion, the transformation, and the fulfilling of human existence that discloses the truth about God's relationship with creation.

EXEGETICAL IMPLICATIONS

Few aspects of von Balthasar's theology are more in need of a carefully nuanced analysis than his approach to scripture. In any given instance, his treatment of biblical materials is likely to earn him dismissal by modern biblical scholars. Harmonization of gospels, importation of later ecclesial standpoints, frequent inattention to underlying forms and sources—such examples of seemingly blatant disregard for the historical-critical science blithely follow one another across the Balthasarian oeuvre. Yet is von Balthasar really only clinging vainly to long-forsaken precritical modes of exegesis?

I want to suggest that in fact von Balthasar is very knowingly challenging contemporary scholarship, in both the theological and biblical fields, to consider the powerful *theological* assumptions at work, though they often go unrecognized or unadmitted, in the task of contemporary scriptural exegesis. As Hans Frei and Brevard Childs have made us increasingly aware, the underlying assumptions of modern biblical criticism are not theologically neutral.

The practical theological implication of some historical critical exegesis is that the privileged meaning of scripture is discovered in the historical background of the text. Von Balthasar by no means denies the presence or significance of this moment in the formation of the text's meaning, but he sees it as just that, one stage in the maturation of meaning. As we have seen above, *the significance and meaning of biblical events is for von Balthasar ultimately predicated on the living presence of those events in the living Christ.* The interpretation of biblical texts, therefore, must include an awareness of the original historical "presencing" of certain events in the matrix of the earliest community (the concern of modern biblical critics), but it must also take account of two other stages: the developing understanding of those events as that is depicted in the final form of the New Testament canon, and *also* the continual deepening of that understanding as the church is drawn into a living enactment of the text through participation in Christ. For von Balthasar, the theological and spiritual life of the church is crucial to any complete interpretation of scripture.

Brian McNeil, one of the translators of *Herrlichkeit*, has argued that the aim of von Balthasar's critiques of historical critical method is often misjudged:

> Balthasar often fights the battle against what he sees as aberrations of contemporary exegesis, but this is not in order to retreat to a secure conservative stronghold, untroubled by the questions of exegetes: it is precisely in order to *harness* scholarly exegesis for the greater battle in defence of the fundamental insights of the Christian faith—a defence that must be undertaken against secularisation, but also against an untheological Catholic conservatism that is equally deadly for the Church.[59]

This is not the place to argue a case about exactly what theological presuppositions are legitimate in a scriptural hermeneutic, but it would seem naive to imagine that there could be none at work at all.[60] Our job here is to discern how someone doing christology "from within" is going to interpret scripture and to assess how adequately that form of exegesis is likely to render the figure of Jesus: Is he a historical human being whose earthly life is determinative for salvation, or only a stained-glass image of the church's imagining?

By way of orientation we might simply say that von Balthasar, who is very thoroughly read in modern biblical studies, develops his exegetical christology in two stages: first he works with a form of historical critical exegesis in order locate Jesus within the constraints of history, to "pick out," as it were, or locate the real Jesus. Then he seeks to move closer, to seek an interior knowledge in the Ignatian sense, and for this he adopts a more figural or typological reading, though even here elements of redaction criticism continue to play an important role. We will consider his approach in these two stages.

A key example on the historical side would be von Balthasar's interpretation of Jesus' historical self-understanding. So for example he suggests that even if one disagrees with the fundamental presuppositions of "demythologization," there might be an important and legitimate "depaschalization" to be undertaken in order to assure a realistically historical human Jesus. Faced by the overwhelming reality of the Resurrection, the community attempted to convey some of that postpaschal sovereignty even in the lowliness of Christ's mortal state. The disciples "were sometimes tempted, while doing this, to trespass over the boundaries of the strict hiddenness."[61] Here we can see the effort to balance between the legitimacy of the church's developing understanding of Christ and the importance of Jesus' historical reality.

Von Balthasar accepts the inauthenticity of many sayings ascribed to Jesus, especially regarding titles of messiahship.[62] He argues instead that Jesus himself had begun to forge a link between his sayings and his deeds; von Balthasar claims this on the historical grounds that if such a connection had been established later by the church it would have likely been made much more on the model of the Hellenistic sage.[63] Von Balthasar would find significant backing in biblical scholars like E. P. Sanders and Adela Collins when he suggests that Jesus probably did have an apocalyptic view of his own mission, and that such a view is if anything likely to have been toned down by later sources and redactors. From this von Balthasar goes on to posit some historical kernel in the passion-resurrection predictions; he fully grants that their present state is inauthentic, but argues that some dark awareness of an approaching apocalyptic "hour" would be historically conceivable.[64]

In his most complete consideration of the issues in *Theodramatik* II/2, von Balthasar offers an illuminating and judicious survey of the exegetical issues in christology from the early nineteenth century to the present. He notes the increasing recognition of a theological or dogmatic apprehension of Christ in the New Testament. Near the end of this section he asks: "Anyone who regards this dogmatic 'overlay' in the New Testament as something superimposed on Jesus' supposedly straightforward human life . . . must ask himself whether, once the said overlay has been removed, he can still present a plausible picture of the historical Jesus."[65] The question is telling because it highlights von Balthasar's own principal concern to locate a plausibly historical human Jesus by means of theologically informed historical criticism.

He goes on to suggest that there are two issues on which every interpretation hangs. The first he terms the more "dogmatic" issue of how the historical Jesus could have understood his life as in some sense being accomplished "for us"; and on this he follows Martin Hengel's view that the sense of the *pro nobis* is so developed, at such an early stage, that at least some germ must be traceable to Jesus. The second hinge is the more "apocalyptic" issue of Jesus' eschatological expectations; and on this he is in a large company of historical critics who hold that to see this apocalypticism as later accretion is not warranted and that to existentialize it away is anachronistic. Von Balthasar proposes that these issues not be seen as mutually exclusive; their weighty presence in the texts suggests that any adequate interpretation of the historical Jesus must hold the two tendencies in tension, allowing them to interpret and set the bounds for each other.[66]

There yet remains the question of how this strand of more historically oriented exegesis is woven together with von Balthasar's spiritual reading. Does the latter threaten to lose touch with the historical humanity delineated by the former? This is a profoundly christological issue for von Balthasar. The literal historical reading is no more left behind than Christ's humanity.

> The human nature we come into contact with first; it is the medium covering yet revealing the divine element, becoming transparent in the resurrection, but never, in all eternity, to be discarded or disparaged. The spiritual sense is never to be sought "behind" the letter but within it. . . . And to stick to the literal sense while spurning the spiritual would be to view the Son as man and nothing more. All that is human in Christ is a revelation of God and speaks to us of him. There is nothing whatever in his life, acts, passion and resurrection that is not an expression and manifestation of God in the language of a created being.[67]

The key here is the conviction that the historical humanity of Jesus is in no way an encumbrance which merely masks the divine life, but is in its most humbly human details, and precisely therein, the immediate expression of God. In the same way, von Balthasar's figural (and Ignatian) strand of exegesis is never a leaving behind of the historical figure of Jesus, but an attempt to enter into the deepest possible communion with him.

In a contemplative reading of scripture, God employs each scriptural mystery of Christ to draw the believer into the melody of Christ's own existence; "the possible variations on the theme of self-giving divine love and of invitation into the depths of divine meaning are endless."[68] But this event of scriptural reading leading to participation in Jesus is not spiritual in the false sense of somehow being rarified and unearthly; the contemplative reading must rather seek the "blossoming" of the scriptural narratives in profound personal appropriation: "Everything [in scripture] is concrete and must be represented with the senses and the imagination, without which a mere intellect would not even be human and would not correspond to the Word made flesh."[69]

When this mode of exegesis is translated into von Balthasar's more strictly theological efforts the same rubrics are observed. The presence of the risen Jesus in the church becomes, through the Holy Spirit, the source of a theological transposition from the historical situation of Jesus to the post-Easter situation of the community.[70] The aim is never to submerge the historical humanity of Jesus but precisely "to preserve the identity of the person of the historical Jesus and the historic Christ present in the Church."[71]

What does this look like in practice? We have noted how von Balthasar ranges between historical-critical "locating" and spiritual-figural "participating." At the risk of over-schematizing this, one might discern three exegetical modes which he adopts as needed to accomplish his exegetical objective, namely, a portrayal of the developing impact which Jesus has upon the understanding of the church. So when von Balthasar wants to point to the historical "seed" of Jesus' earthly existence he adopts a recognizably historical-critical approach (with a certain emphasis on source and form critical analysis). When he wants to show how this preliminary stage of Jesus' reality begins to impress itself on his followers, he draws on an interesting Balthasarian hybrid—a kind of redaction criticism in which the different redactional viewpoints are treated almost as spiritual types (for example, a particular view might reflect not only an ancient community closely linked to Peter but also a continuing Petrine element in the church's life). Finally, and only in the larger context of the first two approaches, von Balthasar will interpret the narrative patterns and other images in a figural reading designed to bring out what he takes to be their inner spiritual and theological meaning.

One intriguing example of von Balthasar's first, more historical-critical, mode of exegesis is his interpretation of the Son of Man problem in the gospels. Von Balthasar accepts the historical likelihood that Jesus may not have had any developed understanding of his work: "We should not expect to find Jesus giving a full theological treatment of his 'hour' prior to undergoing it."[72] Nor does he insist that Jesus necessarily identified himself with the Suffering Servant of Isaiah 53 or the apocalyptic figure of Daniel 7. Rather he argues that more ambiguous Son of Man statements, such as Mark 8:38[73] and Luke 12:8,[74] are likely to have some connection to authentic Jesus material.

Then comes von Balthasar's interesting move: he suggests that the obvious distinction between Jesus and the Son of Man is traceable not to any real divide between Jesus' self-identity and the coming Son of Man in Jesus' thinking but rather to his sensitivity to the utter "hiatus" which stands before him, the abyss between the sinfulness of the people with whom he identifies himself and the holiness of the coming Kingdom of God, an abyss toward which he is moving and *in which his own future status remains unknown to him.* Von Balthasar argues for a hidden identity between Jesus and the Son of Man "which can only be expressed indirectly."[75] His self-identity and the apocalyptic consummatory figure of the Son of Man remain separate in Jesus' thinking because he always leaves in the Father's hands every interpretation and validation of his own earthly struggle.

Von Balthasar develops this theme, drawing on the work of such biblical scholars as E. Schweitzer, Hengel, and Kümmel to show that unless there were at least some implicit *possibility* of linking Jesus and the Son of Man in Jesus' own teaching it would have been unlikely for his followers to have made so much of the figure. If Jesus spoke of the future impact of his earthly work by speaking of the Son of Man instead of "I," says von Balthasar, this shows

> how stupendous and unimaginable he found the relationship between the two sides of his own self: on the one hand, he was someone living on earth with a particular mission that, humanly speaking, he could carry out; and, on the other hand, he was plunged into a mis-

sion that had been eschatologically stretched to the breaking point through the experience of the "hour" (Passion-Resurrection), with an outcome that, at present, was quite unforeseeable.[76]

This example shows how seriously von Balthasar takes the findings of historical critical exegesis as matter for theological reflection, without of course allowing the necessary silences of historical criticism to impede an elucidation of the theological implications of its own findings. Indeed in this case the fundamental historical finding, i.e., the extremely tenuous linking, at best, between Jesus' self-understanding and the Son of Man, becomes the crucial insight by which von Balthasar unfolds the extremity of Jesus' position and his precarious existence on the edge of a future which is his own and yet utterly beyond him.

Next we turn to von Balthasar's depiction of the gathering power that Jesus' earthly life has for his followers. Here again he draws on the discerning eye of the historical critic to illuminate the shifting historical context of Jesus' words and the community's realization that these words are not past but present and powerful. So for instance with reference to Jesus' parables, von Balthasar takes as gain the critical insight that the church has modified Jesus' teaching, precisely, he argues, in order to express the living presence of this same Jesus in the community. The *krisis* which rears up in Jesus' parables must now be aimed directly at the present community:

> The horizon of the Cross which stood before Jesus as the end of the world becomes for the Church the horizon of the second coming of Christ (for only so could she enter Jesus' horizon), and Jesus' words to the scribes and Pharisees become an address to Christians. . . . In this process, a text with an eschatological emphasis (e.g. Lk 12.58) can change into a text with a paranaetic emphasis (Mt 5.25f.).[77]

Von Balthasar is far from insisting that every word in the mouth of Christ in the gospels is authentic Jesus material. The fact of ecclesial interpretation and reception is not a problem for him but a germ for theological growth, a sign that here, in such a place, one should look for an example of Christ's followers being formed by his living impact.

Sometimes as he attempts to flesh out this "entering of Jesus' horizon" by the church, von Balthasar will pay attention not only to the more "objective" side of this process (the form which impresses itself) but also the subjective coloring which a given community or spiritual

stance of the church will give to things. Following Marxsen's interpretation of the more genuine "short" ending of Mark, von Balthasar
highlights the community's sense of journeying *toward* the resurrection and parousia (both as one for Mark). "The vision of the Risen
One thus remains for preaching something in the future, and with a
marked eschatological slant."[78] Von Balthasar contrasts this with the
Johannine account in which the risen Jesus is encountered *in the act*
of resurrection ("do not hold me").[79] These perspectives—journeying
into an ever-greater horizon of life (Mark), and the life-changing experience of that Ever-Greater in the present (John)—are very far from
being distinctions which von Balthasar would want to flatten out and
harmonize. They remain enduring and crucially interacting perspectives within the church.[80]

As much as source, form, and redaction criticism are given a role in
von Balthasar's exegesis, they can never disclose the entirety for him;
they establish certain limits and orient theology in the direction of important realizations, but given this historically grounded orientation
von Balthasar reflects on the spiritual meaning: usually the interior
meaning for Jesus himself of some word or deed and the shared meaning for Jesus' contemporaries and his present followers. Examples of
this mildly figural (rarely allegorical) exegesis are widespread indeed,
and sometimes their luxuriance would seem to work against their
theological gravity, but they can be deeply thought-provoking in the
best sense.

A case of the latter kind is the Balthasarian notion of Christ's
"saving absences," a meditation on Jesus' withdrawal of himself at
various points in the gospels. Among other instances he considers the
various degrees of physical and spiritual distance which Jesus allows
or even creates between himself and his disciples during the time of his
agony in Gethsemane, ranging from the extreme of Judas to the rela-
tive proximity (even though in sleep) of Peter, James, and John: "no
one on his own can lay claim to any specific perceptible nearness of
the Lord, but it is a great thing to persevere, watch and pray at the distance accorded by the Lord."[81] But then von Balthasar moves to a yet
more interior perspective. Noting how the gospels depict Christ as intentionally withdrawing from his mother Mary, he proposes that in
these acts of distancing

> Jesus is admitting Mary into the same godforsakenness that he him-
> self is experiencing in his separation from the Father. The intimacy

of one's share in Jesus' destiny and mission is gauged by the intimacy of one's share in his central salvific experience. Here the degree of inner participation is the degree of the experience of his *absence*.[82]

As believers are initiated by Christ into this communion-in-absence with himself they enter analogously into his own communion-in-absence with the one he calls Father. Further, von Balthasar interprets John's story of Jesus' delay in coming to Martha and Mary at Bethany as another image of Jesus bestowing upon those who are dear to him a share in his own struggle. So Jesus' grief at Lazarus's grave is due to the "inner anguish of having to share eucharistically in anticipation his godforsakenness with the very people whom he especially loves."[83]

Instances of this figural exegesis are not necessarily dependent for their validity, in von Balthasar's view, on historically verifiable authentic Jesus material. What is required is an understanding of the power of the living Jesus to initiate his followers into the crucible of his own life, and an interpretive awareness that this inclusive and participatory dimension of Jesus' existence is all along part of his earthly existence.[84] In this case it is, very characteristically for von Balthasar, not some triumphal experience of Christ's glory streaming upon his people, but the drama of his sharing in the world's bitter separation from God. Most significantly, von Balthasar achieves these kinds of insights not by reflecting on some static, eternal verity about the nature of Christ but by meditating on the concrete, dynamic, interactive patterns of the gospel narratives. For all von Balthasar's concern to foster communion with the divine in Christ, it is clear that this communion is always and only found in very human mediations: the historical humanity of Jesus in encounter with the human discipleship of believers.

3

THE STRUCTURE OF BALTHASARIAN CHRISTOLOGY

TWO MAJOR HISTORICAL RESOURCES

In his most concentrated christological tract, *Theodramatik* II/2, von Balthasar deals with the classical christological issues of the two natures of Christ and their union in the one Person of the Word. But even in discussing these questions he is inspired to move toward a more historically concrete Jesus, considered in all the tension and drama of salvation. In the very wide field of von Balthasar's christological material, which is present virtually everywhere in his work, one can discern a successor structure to the old nature-person model. Now I want to uncover the principles which animate this new model.

In his extensive study of Maximus, von Balthasar concluded that one of the most significant contributions the Confessor had made was his nurturing and employment of a growing philosophical distinction between the order of being (*einai*) or essence (*ousia*) on one hand, and the order of actual existence (*hupostasis*) or personal existence (*huparxis*) on the other.[1] Von Balthasar points out that Christian thought had by no means already arrived at the medieval scholastic clarity of the "real distinction" between essence and existence. Nevertheless Maximus was pushing towards a crucial new dimension beyond the fixed philosophical categories of nature and essence.

For Maximus this was a dimension of reality revealed in the free relationship of God to the radically contingent world. Beyond the necessary *natures* of things there is the gratuitous fact that they *exist*. Maximus sees a polarity between the true, unchanging essence, on one side, and personal, actual, freely-acting existence on the other side. In Maximus's view it was the inability to recognize this polarity that had led to the continuing confusion and argument after Chalcedon. The problem was not that the Nestorians united the reality of Christ too little and the monophysites too much. Rather the problem was in conceiving the union solely on the level of nature, a union therefore which could only be imagined in spiritual terms for the Nestorians and utterly physical terms for the monophysites.[2]

> The unity of God and the world in Christ could not be expressed by a pure philosophy of "essence." All [such] "physical" and "ontic" union (*henōsis ousiōdēs, henōsis physikē*) becomes a mixing of two poles in a new "nature" (*ousia, physis*) [the monophysite conception]; but if one wanted to avoid this mixing, one could only conceive of an accidental, exterior, "moral" union, by means of a "spiritual relation" (*schesis*) between both natures [the Nestorian conception].[3]

To unlock this puzzle Maximus unfolds his developing category of existence.

Drawing on earlier trinitarian theology as developed by the Cappadocians and Amphilochius, Maximus proposes "mode of being" (*tropos tēs hyparxeōs*) as a dimension of reality quite distinct from essence. In trinitarian terms this "manner of existing" is what distinguishes the Three from each other. It is therefore a category which is distinct from the divine nature per se (otherwise there would be three gods), but not in the sense of being another item in the category of nature (otherwise the Trinity would be a quaternity). Rather, as von Balthasar puts it, the notion of mode of existence is a kind of miraculous theological and philosophical quantum leap—it hints at a developing awareness of another category of reality—existence—irreducible to the category of essence.

I would explain the impact as follows. When this trinitarian conception is transposed into christological terms, one has arrived at the level of reality at which one can discuss the unity of Christ. The unity is *not* at the level of nature, which would either undermine the divine and human natures by producing a *tertium quid*, or else regress to a merely external union of wills. Instead, both natures are preserved in their integrity and fullness, and the union is at the level of existence; that is, the divine and human in Christ are united in enacting together that particular pattern of self-surrender, obedience, and love which is the mode of existence of the eternal Son, i.e., the pattern which distinguishes the Son from the Father and the Spirit. A human being living according to this pattern would be existing in every respect as a fully human *person*, in the modern sense of that term; but this very same pattern of life would identify this human being as the Person of the eternal Son.

This is the very discovery of Maximus which von Balthasar appropriates in his own treatment of the Incarnation. Maximus's sense of wonder in considering the human features of Jesus and seeing in all of them the characteristic marks of the Word—this is what captures von Balthasar's imagination. Following Maximus, he asks:

> Are we not invited to a kind of phenomenological glimpsing of the appearance of Christ, who shows us a being whose whole manner down to the last word, the least gesture, betrays a human nature, yet a human nature transposed in its entirety to another mode of existence?[4]

For von Balthasar the key in this is Maximus's sense that *the humanity of Christ reveals the divine precisely by being so human.* Every human feature of Jesus' existence is translated (*übersetzt*) into a divine mode; the least human gesture enacts the most characteristic traits of the eternal Son's existence. Or as von Balthasar puts it in another place:

> That which distinguishes the Word from the Father [the Son's mode of existence] is no longer distinct, after the union, from that which distinguishes the humanity of the Word from the rest of humanity [Jesus' pattern of life]. With this formula, christology attains its summit.[5]

The very same mode of existence, or hypostasis, which is the distinguishing identity of the Son, is the hypostasis which identifies the human being Jesus and causes him to be a living, historical person, distinct from other human persons.

Von Balthasar also emphasizes that for Maximus this event takes place in the creation, preservation, and fulfillment of Christ's human nature, and not at all by its circumvention. The humanity of Jesus can be actualized according to the mode of the Son's existence, but it is actualized precisely as a human nature. This hypostasis which divinizes the humanity also "confirms and consolidates it in its natural humanity."[6] So in Maximus von Balthasar has found a way to transpose christology from the category of fixed and unchanging essences to the category of dynamic and historically actualized existence, a change which better suits his concern for christology in terms of the concrete events of Jesus' living, dying, and rising. And von Balthasar has also found in Maximus's theory of hypostatic union, as opposed to union at the level of natures, a way to talk of the divine identity of Jesus without at all threatening his full humanity.

In taking up Maximus's insights into his own christology, however, von Balthasar works quite a transformation upon the patristic heritage. The depth of his commitment to learning from the saints about Christ causes him to fuse and reinterpret the Maximian hypostatic structure with an Ignatian structure of mission and election. Von Balthasar wants to take very seriously what is learned when one examines the participation of the saints in the interior and apostolic life of Christ. And for him the absolutely preeminent model of this participative inner knowing is given by the *Spiritual Exercises* of Ignatius. That is, what one discovers in identification with Christ is the overwhelming role of divine mission in his life: his total and complete election of this mission, his perfect availability for it, his loving obedience to it. In short, the mission of Jesus is the truth of his identity.

What has happened, I believe, is that the Maximian hypostasis, or mode of existence, is rendered even more concrete and more historically present by being transposed into an Ignatian concept of mission.

Von Balthasar believes very strongly that Ignatius initiated a sea change in spirituality. Ignatius reinterpreted the focus of the spiritual journey: *the purifying ascent of the soul to its divine archetype becomes the obedient descent of the disciple into the "ever greater" love of Christ's own mission*. In one of his most quintessential and crucial summaries, von Balthasar writes:

> Patristic, and even medieval spirituality . . . takes eternal happiness, the contemplation of God, as man's goal; consequently the supernatural end of human nature can serve, under the elevating influence of grace, as man's sure compass throughout his spiritual journey. For example, man only needs to gaze upon his own "restless heart" in order to realize where his path lies to "eternal rest in God." The emphasis shifts as soon as Ignatius fixes on the "praise, reverence and service of God" as man's end, and subordinates everything else, the contemplation of God and one's own happiness, to this end. Once this is accepted, human nature, even when it is elevated by grace, cannot act as the guide for man in his praise, reverence and service of

God; ultimately such guidance can only come from God and revelation of his will. Therefore Ignatius builds his whole spirituality upon the concept of choice; that is, upon God's choice, accomplished in eternal freedom, which is offered to man to choose for himself. This new "identity" and "fusion" between the Creator's choice and that of his creature begins ever more surely to replace the classical ideal of identifying their essences, the ideal of "deification." If this identity is to be achieved, man must strain every nerve to clear aside all obstacles, and by means of the "spiritual exercises" become entirely "disposed" to receive God's will.[7]

This Ignatian model of the spiritual journey plays a crucial role in von Balthasar's mission-structured christology. Several key points are present in this passage. First, the yearning neo-Platonic heart, seeking assimilation to its divine ideal, is "Ignatianized" to become the obedient apostolic servant, abandoning self to the divine mission; and hence what was a kind of necessary and inevitable process of ascent becomes, in von Balthasar's mind, a free and historical activity of choosing. Second, unity with God is attained not by an identification of essences but by a fusion of the divine choice of mission for a person and that person's own free choosing and enactment of the same mission.

And here the link with Maximus is especially clear, for if we transpose back into more directly christological language, we have almost exactly the Maximian discovery, that the union in Christ is on the basis not of essence or nature but mode of existence. For von Balthasar the eternal Son's mode of existence is identical with his being *sent* by the Father, his *Sendung* or mission. By analogy with the Ignatian spiritual journey, then, the humanity of Christ comes to fulfillment and unity with the divine as Jesus humanly chooses and enacts the mission of divine sonship.

Von Balthasar often mentions how the highly imaginative meditations of the *Exercises* are designed above all to draw the exercitant into a concrete awareness of the loving choice *and* struggle, inherent in the fiber of Christ's life, and to hear therein a personal call of God to oneself.[8] In this context von Balthasar highlights how each individual human person comes to fulfillment expressly by being given a share in Jesus' own mission.

> [Christ gives us] a mode of existence. It is no mere "supernatural elevation" of a vague, general nature that is imparted to us by grace, but a share in the personal existence of the eternal Word of God. . . . This

"form" of the Christian . . . may be called his "mission." To this he should constantly apply all his natural capacities, so that in this surrender to God's service he may find his own supreme fulfillment as a person in a manner surpassing his natural and imperfect potentialities.[9]

Mission fulfills, even in a sense creates, identity. For Ignatius "mystical union with God sacramentalized, or incarnated, itself in apostolic service. This union remained incomplete until it was expressed in all the dimensions of life."[10] If we draw on this as an analogy to help us understand the nature of the union in Christ, we return to the idea that Jesus' humanity is fulfilled and united to the eternal Son precisely as Jesus incarnates the Son's mission in his own living, dying, and rising.

CHRISTOLOGICAL PROBLEMS AND MISSION-STRUCTURED CHRISTOLOGY

Now how will von Balthasar put to work this new understanding of person-mission (adapted from Maximus and Ignatius)? His aim is to focus entirely on the actual divine-human life of Jesus, rather than on a series of more scientifically abstract notions which, in more standard approaches, set out Christ's reality seriatim. He intends by the concept of mission to answer christological questions in a way that conveys something of the dynamic actuality of Jesus' existence. We can now take up these problems in turn: (1) the union of the two natures and Jesus' self-understanding, (2) the reality of Jesus' humanity as brought to fulfillment in the person of the Son, and (3) the relation between the incarnate Word and all humanity.

The first problem is the possibility of union between the two natures of Christ: we have to acknowledge two natures but how to do so without turning Christ into a "mythical chimera"?[11] As we noted in the last chapter, the usual procedure for von Balthasar in questions of being is to locate the ontological difference between divine and human being within the even deeper abyss of the creature's sinful antagonism towards the Creator. In the present instance this move forces von Balthasar to face not just the being of Christ but the even more difficult issue of Jesus' consciousness. For if human existence is not merely an analogy (within a greater dissimilarity) of divine existence, but is also sinfully alienated from divine existence, then to be truly human

Jesus' consciousness must be expressive of this. Von Balthasar concludes that it might be possible to make "credible" some notion of the union of two natures in the more neutral, "more abstract," ontological terms.

> But in the aspect of consciousness it becomes acutely difficult. How can there be an identity between the consciousness of a (divine) person in his assumed humanity and his inherent divine consciousness, particularly if the nature that has been adopted exists in the mode of alienation from God?[12]

As we might expect, von Balthasar sees the basis for the possibility of this union of nature and consciousness in the concept of mission. In his proposal, "Jesus experiences his human consciousness entirely in terms of mission."[13] But von Balthasar is concerned to avoid treating this issue in abstraction from the historical concreteness of Christ's life: the theoretical problem (the union of two natures) must be grounded in a realistic exegetical survey of Jesus' self-understanding.

Von Balthasar sets the scene by examining what he calls the elliptical structure of christology, deriving as it does from the interaction between the objective historical figure of Jesus and the community's testimony of faith about him. Historical critical scholarship has made us more aware of the implications of this interaction, and von Balthasar insists on the need to take this analysis into account.[14] He quite thoroughly traces the shifting attitudes to the *Bild* of Christ and the historical Jesus from Schleiermacher to Ritschl, to Herrmann's discovery that his carefully nurtured picture of the "historical" Jesus' inner life had become untenable, to Bultmann's conviction that the living object of faith is found in the kerygma alone, to Käsemann's important turn away from this view in 1953 and the developments of his view in Fuchs, Bornkamm, Conzelmann, and Ebeling.[15] In all of this careful account, von Balthasar is working his way toward the question: "How did Jesus understand his mission within the span of life granted to him? Was he only the 'witness to faith,' or did he know that he was more?"[16]

As we noted in the previous chapter, von Balthasar's exegetical proposal is to answer such questions about Jesus' self-consciousness by allowing two strands of what he takes to be authentic Jesus material to interpret each other, the "apocalyptic" strand of Jesus' expectation of the Kingdom, and the more "dogmatic" strand of Jesus' sense of living on behalf of others. After a careful development of each of these strands (with extensive reference to pertinent historical critical studies), von Balthasar allows the two strands to confront each other in this crucial passage:

> Might not Jesus' consciousness of his mission have been that he had to abolish the world's estrangement from God in its entirety—that is, to its very end—or, in Pauline and Johannine terms, deal with the sin of the whole world? In that case, *after* his earthly mission, the decisive and (humanly speaking) immeasurable part was still to come. . . . It cannot be denied that his earthly work, prayer and toil was the integral part of his entire task, that is, it cannot be said that the redeeming act was solely concentrated in the future, in the coming Cross. . . . However, the awareness that his life is moving toward a "baptism," toward that "cup" he will have to drink (and which, when the hour comes, will prove humanly unbearable, stretching him beyond all limits, Mk 14:34, 36), means that his life cannot proceed along "wisdom" lines but must follow an "apocalyptic" rhythm. His life is running toward an *akme* that, as man, he will only be able to survive by surrendering control of his own actions and being determined totally by the Father's will (Lk 22:42 par). . . . If we can define the core of apocalyptic as the imminent expectation of God's final judgment of the old world, and therefore the change of aeon to a new world, we can say that this apocalyptic dimension—if Jesus lives within this horizon of expectation—is most definitely concentrated in him. . . . [Yet] he cannot attain the goal and end of his task by means of his human activity, but . . . must hand *himself* over to the Father for that purpose.[17]

Two determining themes come to light in this passage.

First, von Balthasar's attempt to cross-pollinate the apocalyptic and the redemptive strands yields an interesting result: the decisive *krisis* into which Jesus travels on behalf of his fellow humans is none other than the apocalyptic moment. In other words, the quite early Pauline sense of Christ's death being "for us" may indeed find its source in authentic Jesus tradition, namely Jesus' commitment to the coming "hour"—the moment when, perhaps at the cost of his own life, the Kingdom would begin to come in power for his people.

Second, von Balthasar sees Jesus as approaching this hour of apocalyptic judgment and re-creation with a mounting awareness that he can only attain this goal, for himself and his people, insofar as he is willing to hand himself over to the Father. This means that Jesus' salvific journey into the apocalypse is accomplished precisely by his utter self-surrender to a mission which takes him beyond the limits of his own life. It is key here that Jesus' saving activity consists in a kind of momentum of love which literally carries him beyond himself. In no sense is this simply passivity in Christ:

> His suffering and dying is not a mere Passion but a superaction. The difference between it and his earlier deeds emerging from his active spiritual center is that now his Yes to God is stretched beyond all finite proportions.[18]

By placing himself at the disposal of the Father under the direction of the Spirit, Jesus accomplishes a kind of super-eminent act of loving, an enactment in human terms of the eternal Son's mode of existence.

In the exegetical groundwork of his christology, von Balthasar is working toward a conception of Christ's mission as that which effects an actual change in the relationship between God and humanity. He insists that Anselm had pondered this understanding of the atonement deeply and was on the right track, but had formulated things "in a decidedly narrow way" (einer gewissen Engführung).[19] Even more, however, does he criticize modern exemplarist theories of atonement in which cross and resurrection are handy visual aids which God merely adopts to convince humanity of what has always been the case anyway.

Instead, von Balthasar points to the pungency and drama of Jesus' actual struggle, to the sense of infinite and eternal matters being truly at stake in the details of Jesus' life. Von Balthasar envisions the self-offering, in love for God and humanity, of this particular human being, Jesus, to be of infinite value to God. His exegesis is designed to locate Jesus in a credible historical setting: the total self-commitment of this Jesus of Nazareth to his mission, i.e., his active and self-conscious self-bestowal into God's hands for the inauguration of the judging and saving reign of God.

Moreover, von Balthasar has sought to establish in this exegesis, primarily by accenting the apocalyptic dimension of Jesus' life, an openness in Jesus' self-understanding to that which is beyond himself—to the Kingdom, the Father, the ultimate immeasurability of his own mission. In so doing, von Balthasar has attempted to describe a credible human expression of the mission and mode of existence of the eternal Son.

He elucidates this human sense of mission in terms of four aspects of Jesus' self-consciousness. The first of these is the element of ultimacy which Jesus senses in his mission and its constitutive role in his self-understanding.

> In the individual human consciousness of Jesus, there is something that in principle always goes beyond the purely human horizon of consciousness. . . . If we could put into words Jesus' fundamental intuition concerning his identity, it would be: "I am the one who must accomplish this task." "I am the one through whom the kingdom of God must and will come."[20]

This is not theoretical knowledge for Jesus, but rather, von Balthasar makes clear, an almost intuitive sense of a "practical" imperative. It is not in any sense heteronomous, "because of the identity of person and mission affirmed at the very outset."[21] In this connection von Balthasar wishes to steer a middle way between opposing extremes on the relation of Christ's human self-consciousness to his divine self-consciousness; neither, on one hand, a docetic super-historical self-awareness nor, on the other, a chimerical two-story consciousness. He grants that for Jesus, self-consciousness and God-consciousness must coincide, but only within the limits of his mission, namely his awareness that he is utterly the one sent, the one who is entirely child and word:

> The task given him by the Father, that is, that of expressing God's Fatherhood through his entire being, through his life and death in and for the world, totally occupies his self-consciousness and fills it to the very brim. He sees himself so totally as "coming from the Father" to humankind, as "making known" the Father, as the "Word from the Father," that there is neither room nor time for any detached reflection of the "Who am I?" kind.[22]

Von Balthasar intends this awareness of Jesus to be understood in very human terms. In order to be the human incarnation of the eternal Word, Jesus certainly does not, in von Balthasar's view, have to understand himself to be the humanity of the Second Person of the Trinity, he only has to desire and know how to be word of the Father to the last fiber of his being. On the basis of this Balthasarian approach we could say that any awareness Jesus has of the uniqueness of his filial relationship with the Father is not an innate theoretical knowledge but is progressively discovered in practice as Jesus becomes painfully familiar with the alienation from God in which others live.

This brings us to the second aspect of Jesus' self-consciousness, the degree to which it is historically mediated. Von Balthasar pokes gentle fun at pious pictures (deriving from scholastic approaches to Christ's omniscience) of the child Jesus knowingly playing with pieces of wood to make a little cross, etc. Von Balthasar grants that as part of Jesus' mission he would have had a special sensitivity for the lovableness of his fellow humans in God's eye, and also for the pain of their antagonism towards God. But he also insists that "Jesus undergoes a historical learning process with regard to his fellow humans."[23] Quite interestingly, von Balthasar develops the idea that Jesus' mission would in fact have especially disposed him to a deep interior knowing of others. His desire to be with and for them grants Jesus a profound "readiness to be affected by the inner constitution of his fellow humans," and a lodging of their destinies in his own heart.[24] In the end Jesus' increasing disappointment may have "triggered the inner unveiling of the mystery," transforming his readiness and willingness to give all into a darker and darker sense of the yawning abyss between the divine desire for human love and the human unwillingness to love, the abyss into which his mission leads.[25]

The third aspect of Jesus' self-consciousness which von Balthasar wishes to consider is the role of the Holy Spirit. For our purposes it is enough to note the importance of von Balthasar's theory of "trinitarian inversion." In the eternal trinitarian life, the Spirit proceeds from the Father and through the Son, and in the state of exaltation Christ "sends" the Spirit with the Father. But during the time of his earthly ministry, von Balthasar explains, the Spirit as the bond of freedom and love of the Father and Son becomes the One who "sends" the Son into the world and continues to send and direct him. What von Balthasar wants to make clear from this is that the Spirit's guidance and rule in Jesus' life is not a diminution of Jesus' freedom, because the Spirit remains "within" him; his predisposition to receive and send the Spirit ensures that his human experience of the Spirit is not heteronomous. At some points in Jesus' mission this experience is of a free consent and yearning, but at other points the Spirit presents Jesus "with the Father's will in the form of a *rule* that is unconditional and, in the case of the Son's suffering, even appears rigid and pitiless."[26]

Finally von Balthasar takes up directly the question of Jesus' knowledge. Critical of the patristic and scholastic portrayal of Jesus as omniscient, von Balthasar proposes that Jesus' knowledge should be conceived of as strictly limited to the changing horizons of his mission. His knowledge is of a more practical, "knowing how" variety—how to love and be obedient, how to be expressive of the Father and how to be immured in human darkness. Von Balthasar proffers a highly suggestive analogy by which to understand the changing shape and extent of Jesus' knowledge and experience of God:

> The equally great variations found in Christian mystical experience of God—ranging from moments of illumination to the constrictions of dryness and forsakenness—can give us an inkling of the possible variety of forms of knowledge experienced by the earthly Jesus.[27]

It is significant that unlike almost any other similarly "high" christologies, von Balthasar's proposal makes quite as much of the intensity of night, of suffering and unknowing which Jesus experiences, as of his positive knowlege and intuition. This reflects von Balthasar's concern to give full scope to Christ's deep immersion in the most realistic details of alienated human existence. The self-abandon of Christ's humanity is not just in aid of becoming transparent to the divine mission. Rather, Jesus' commitment to his mission brings about his full actualization as a concrete human being and so his full sharing in the extremes of the human relationship with God.

Now we turn to what von Balthasar perceives as the second thorny problem, ensuring the reality of Jesus' humanity as it is actualized in the person of the eternal Word:

> Here we have someone who is entirely human, an unabridged human being, who "became like us in all things but sin"; how then, when he uses the word "I", can he be speaking not as a human person but as divine? Or, if he *also* speaks with a human "I," how can there be two persons in him, be they ever so intimately united?[28]

It would be unfortunate to overlook the simple fact that von Balthasar does indeed see this as a major question which must be put to classical Chalcedonian christology. He assumes the full and undiminished, uncurtailed (*abstrichlos*) humanity of Christ. Given this fact, the question is how to understand that the identity of this human actor is the eternal Word. Von Balthasar suggests that the necessary task in answering such a question is to trace back into its christological and trinitarian roots the meaning of the theological term "person" and to note what philosophical explanations have made of it. He argues that the only way out of the puzzle is to reinterpret the concept "person" with the new concept of "mission." He hopes that by doing this he can provide a surer foundation for the historically actualized human life of Christ than sometimes seemed possible in older theories of hypostatic union.

Significantly, von Balthasar wishes to begin by examining what Jesus does, the impact that he has, and from there to ask the question, "Who *must* he be to behave and act this way?"

> In putting the question in this way, we are pursuing a "christology from below." We are not asking, for instance, about the contents of Christ's knowledge, let alone the kind of personality he had, but about the conditions that made it possible for what empirically took place in him. . . . [Could a mere herald or messenger] be "sent" (*Gesendeter*) in such an absolute sense that his mission (*Sendung*) coincides with his person, so that both together constitute God's exhaustive self-communication?[29]

If we look at the actual concrete history of Christ, von Balthasar asks, what kind of mission is it that would call for such a unity of one's mission and personal identity?

In fact, what von Balthasar develops is a notion of mission as *constituting* the person. He unfolds an analogy based on the maturation of an individual conscious subject who comes to know *who* she or he is precisely through interaction with others, and through the acceptance and fulfillment of commitments, goals, and acts of love. Ultimately, von Balthasar argues, this constitution of the conscious subject as a fulfilled person, secure in her or his own identity, can only be accomplished by interaction with God.

> It is when God addresses a conscious subject, tells him who he is and what he means to the eternal God of truth and shows him the purpose of his existence—*that is, imparts a distinctive and divinely authorized mission*—that we can say of a conscious subject that he is a "person." This is what happened, archetypically, in the case of Jesus Christ, when he was given his eternal "definition"—"You are my beloved Son."[30]

What makes the Son who he is from all eternity, says von Balthasar, is precisely the "uninterrupted reception of everything that he is, of his very self, from the Father." And this bestowal of the Son's "I" in turn establishes his own spontaneity and that mode of existence, sonship, "with which he can answer the Father in a reciprocal giving."[31] Von Balthasar proposes that if Christ's earthly existence is the *missio*, "the translation into creatureliness" of this eternal *processio*, then just as the Son's eternal life of receptivity and response establishes him as a person, so in human terms "it is the fact of being he who is open, he who receives, he who obeys and fulfills that makes him—*a* man, of course, but only by making him *this* particular man."[32]

Here we see a most critical move in von Balthasar's thought: it is not enough, in his view, to say simply that the ultimate self-communication of God to creation results in an incarnation, a divine-human life; for it is not undifferentiated divine self-giving which is the issue, but rather the earthly expression of that particular divine mode of existence termed "sonship." And the creaturely form of this sonship is not human existence per se, but the particular human individual Jesus of Nazareth. It is his concrete, unsubstitutable, human life which comes to fulfillment through the person-constituting mission of the Son.

What makes Jesus unique is that in him mission and person coincide perfectly, indeed are one; for his mission is *to be* the Son. He is definitively "person," and since all humanity is oriented towards fulfillment in him, each human being achieves her or his own personhood and stability of identity, expressly by sharing in Christ's mission. "This deepening or elevation of the conscious subject does not alienate the latter from himself but enables him to 'come to himself'."[33]

Looking at how human individuals come to blossom as persons by being known, loved, and given a purpose, we are able to understand something of how Jesus' full humanity can be actualized, personalized, by living out the mission of the Son in response to the Father's love. And then, reciprocally, once we have thus gained some sense of Jesus' unique mission, its person-constituting power, we begin to discern that the very sense of calling and purpose which fulfills other individuals as persons in fact derives from their participation in Christ's own mission. Jesus' destiny opens up an acting area, a *Spielraum*, in which the actions of each individual can have eternal significance, in which "each individual is given a personal commission . . . entrusted with something to do and with the freedom to do it. . . . This personal commission . . . is actually constitutive of the person as such."[34]

The themes of freedom and fulfillment in the act of self-giving to one's mission are absolutely central to von Balthasar. Again and again he underscores that this person-making grace of mission is no alien thing, but is the very form of life which the Creator knows will mean each individual's deepest joy and consummation. God's "Idea" for each individual is

> unique and personal, embodying for each his appropriate sanctity. . . . The fulfillment of God's will does not mean carrying out an anonymous universal law which is the same for all; nor does it mean the slavish imitation of some fixed blueprint. . . . On the contrary it means freely realizing God's loving plan, which presupposes freedom, and is, moreover, the very source of freedom. No one is so much himself as the saint, who disposes himself to God's plan, for which he is prepared to surrender his whole being, body, soul, and spirit.[35]

Here, then, is the basis not only for the existence of Jesus as a human individual but for his constitution as a particular historical person— for his freedom, joy, self-understanding, and willingness to give his all. The self-sharing of the divine sonship with creation is this Jesus Christ.

The third crucial christological problem which von Balthasar raises concerns

> the relationship between the divine Person of the Logos and the totality of human nature; since he seems not to be an individual in our limited sense, he must somehow have adopted human nature as a whole. If this is so, it becomes credible that his work of atonement has affected the whole of human nature.[36]

The question at issue is *how* exactly the humanly incarnate Word can be inclusive in this way, "adopt[ing] human nature as a whole," without thereby forfeiting his true, concrete, historical human existence. And once again von Balthasar intensifies the whole problem by not allowing the more ontological dimension of the issue (the relation of Christ's humanity to human being generally) to become separated from the soteriological dimension, namely, the fact that this relationship has to be accomplished in the context of human sin.

So Jesus must accomplish the Father's saving will in a way that fulfills and supersedes the highest human hopes, but because of the sinful framework of human existence he can do this only in a manner which carries him beyond the limits of human life. Von Balthasar notes that Israel's hope ultimately "required the bursting of the boundaries of death which as such belong constitutively to human being. This means not-death in death, word in what is not word, fulfillment in failure."[37] In other words, the human existence of Christ is accomplished salvifically for others precisely by being extended past the limits of what is constitutive of human existence: his true life is found in his death, his ultimate speaking is heard in his silence (especially of the tomb), and so on. Von Balthasar does not intend these simply to become rhetorical paradoxes. He recognizes keenly "the central difficulty that opens up here, in giving man his centre-point by locating him beyond himself, in his death."[38]

He carries this problem over into what he considers its deepest measure, the risk such an understanding of Christ's work runs of utterly detaching him from his co-humans. One way out of the problem, he suggests, is Karl Barth's idea of vicariousness (*Stellvertretungsgedanken*) in which one human being is rejected in order that the others may be accepted. This would mean that Jesus' beyond-human-limits-existence, far from being at a remove from humanity, is the integral factor implicit in every human existence—it is the suprahumanity which wins humanity the possibility of new life. But von Balthasar sets this option aside for the express reason that it still isolates Jesus to an unacceptable degree. Commenting on Barth's approach, he states:

> The fate of this one [Christ, the rejected one] remains the paradoxical and disturbing exception, and one no longer sees how it can be anthropologically significant, or how indeed "imitation" can be possible. If such an imitation is taken seriously, is that not something inhuman? And if the real thing has been accomplished by the one (who alone is God-man), is not imitation in any case superfluous and essentially defective?[39]

So von Balthasar seeks an interpretation of the Incarnation which guarantees the full, inclusive, and shareable humanity of Jesus. His solution will be a concept of mission which is ecstatic, which discovers the center point of human existence in an act of loving that always carries one being into communion with another.

FOUR CHRISTOLOGICAL STATES

In this chapter and its predecessor, I have been describing the script and directions, as it were, by which von Balthasar's christology comes to performance; in the chapters that follow I will be interpreting the play in action. By now it should be clear that von Balthasar's concept of the Son's mission has a very definite profile. Certain characteristic moments are absolutely essential to its realization. Preliminarily we may identify these as follows: *(1) the availability of Jesus for his mission; (2) his actual obedience to his mission; (3) the momentum of this mission which carries Jesus beyond human limits and so into the chasm between sinful creature and holy Creator; and (4) the resultant fulfillment of Jesus' existence as inclusive and participable.*

As ever, we have to remind ourselves that von Balthasar's christology is a more or less continuous performance, present to some degree in almost all his writings. Our task is to employ the pattern of christological moments or states (which emerged in his notion of mission) as a structure which can illuminate the diverse insights of his christology in the form of a coherent whole.

In approaching the task this way we are highlighting von Balthasar's own desire to avoid the more standard divisions of person and work in favor of a dynamic reflection of the historical drama of Christ's existence. So while each of the states that we will consider does make its presence felt in all the stages of Jesus' life, there is also a sense in which the pattern of these states develops in correlation with the progression of Jesus' destiny: his early life and the beginning of his public ministry coincide with the state of availability and self-surrender that is necessary for him to elect and choose God's mission as his own. The course of his ministry is shaped entirely by his obedience to his mission. His passion and death come to pass as he delivers himself into the extreme alienation of his people and so is carried beyond the limits of human life. And finally in his resurrection, ascension, and sending of the Spirit, Jesus' human existence is revealed in its fullness as enrapturing love, and therefore inclusive of all people.

In employing the concept of theological states as a means of interpreting von Balthasar's christology I am also drawing on themes he himself has appropriated from Christian spirituality, particularly from Bérulle and Ignatius. Von Balthasar frequently alludes to the great variety of christological states of being into which God draws the believer at various moments of life.

It is God who arranges the "theological states" of the believer, plunging him at one time into the deep waters of the Cross where he is not allowed to experience any consolation, and then into the grace given by resurrection of a hope. . . . No one is able or permitted to fit these "theological states" into a system that can be manipulated and surveyed to any extent by man. Their every aspect, even when they seemingly contradict one another, is christological and therefore left to God's disposition.[40]

The premise for this experience of Christian spirituality is, as von Balthasar says, the reality of these moments in Christ. It is because Jesus has experienced them that believers seeking to conform their lives to his will find their own experiences structured in this way; God bestows on them a taste of that particular state of Christ's mission most apt for their present situation. As von Balthasar puts it:

The definitive space in which we are at home is the space of the fulfilled mission of the Son, who has returned home to the eternity of the Trinity with all his earthly experiences. Here all the situations experienced appear in their definitive truth. As the multiplicity of the Son's "states" (to use Bérulle's basic word—"*états*"), they are all integrated into his eternal and unified state with the Father.[41]

Von Balthasar adopts this conceptuality from Bérulle, as we can see, because it provides a coherent account of believers' experiences of sharing in the mysteries of Christ's life. But he also makes use of it because the notion of christological states provides a way of envisaging the salvific import of each one of Jesus' inner stances and stages of life. It is a kind of elaboration for von Balthasar of the more traditional distinction of Christ's state of humility and state of glorification.

And as one might expect, von Balthasar makes this theme of the christological states his own by going back behind Bérulle to Ignatius, and with him to the classic traditions in Christian spirituality of *apatheia* and *Gelassenheit*, of apophatic ascent and the dark night of the soul, and finally of the *ekstasis* of love and nuptiality. Each of these themes comes into play as a mystical analogy (warranted by its origin in the mystic's participation in Christ) for the archetypal occurrence of these states in Jesus' own existence. And in the Ignatian *Spiritual Exercises* themselves, we can discern an interesting parallel to the states of von Balthasar's christology.

As he himself describes it, in the First Week the exercitant seeks the gift of indifference, detachment, and abandon to God which "enables [the exercitant], dispossessed of any self-constructed pattern of life, to enter into the imitation of Christ, to which he is introduced in the Second, Third and Fourth Weeks."[42] Examining the pattern of the *Exercises* further, we can see how the Second Week moves through a following of Christ in obedience, the Third Week includes the ultimate extension of that obedience in the meditation on Christ's passion and death, and the Fourth Week draws the exercitant into an awareness of the Risen Lord and his unlimited presence and activity in all creation. Von Balthasar nowhere declares that his christology is structured according to the *Exercises*, and I would not mean to imply any tight correlation. Nevertheless it is clear that von Balthasar's Ignatian interpretation of the spiritual life as readiness for and response to one's divine mission has provided him with an interpretive analogy for the dynamic pattern of Christ's life.

4

THE STATE OF SELF-SURRENDER

THE PHENOMENOLOGY OF INDIFFERENCE

I must now set the scene for the first christological "state," self-surrender or indifference, by considering von Balthasar's central range of interpretations of this spiritual stance. Running through his works one can discern a virtual phenomenology of self-abandonment which includes a general survey of the phenomenon in Christian experience, attention to its historical shading and development, and a particular focus on the theme in its Ignatian form.

The most fundamental prerequisite, in von Balthasar's mind, for participation in the Christian life, is willingness to renounce personal calculations and make oneself available for the mission in life that God intends one to enjoy. This stance of generosity towards one's mission has its basis in the prevenient intimacy that God offers. Humanity's surrender of itself to God always comes about through the recognition that life in God is humanity's intended vocation, that humanity is long-awaited and rejoiced over in heaven—this is where humanity most belongs: "We need not first pave for ourselves an approach to God on our own; already and always 'our life is hidden with Christ in God' (Col. 3.3)."[1]

Von Balthasar speaks of humanity's "place" in God in terms of the divine ideal, the true reality of each person in God. This notion should not be understood as implying a frozen and alien divine will to which the human person is pushed to conform, but is best conceived in terms of the *thelema* or wish of God for each person, which includes a strong sense of God's desire and love for the person. Describing this sensation from the soul's perspective, von Balthasar writes: "I'm being inquired after; my presence is desired, needed even—or so it seems. Somewhere there exists a bright image of me, an image of what I

could have been, of what I am still (but how?) capable of becoming."[2]
The activity of self-surrender to this divine idea is accomplished in
communion with the Word, in whom all true "selfhood" is hidden.
Yet, von Balthasar emphasizes, the human person's archetypal self is
not the *object* of human seeking and hunger; rather that self is the
consequent *result* of the creature's communion with God:

> In seeking and hearing God [the human being] experiences the high-
> est joy, that of being fulfilled in itself, but fulfilled in something
> infinitely greater than itself and, for that very reason, completely ful-
> filled and made blessed.[3]

Von Balthasar qualifies this interpretation of self-surrender to God in a
very significant way. Commenting on Catherine of Siena's description
of "indifference as 'desire', 'thirst', 'longing'," he says that this should
not be conceived in an Augustinian sense of the "ontological love of
the creature for the absolute God. What matters here is not attaining
and possessing God, but *the ardent desire to correspond with God's
requirements and expectations.*"[4] The yearning which draws the soul
beyond self, and so into an indifference toward particular earthly
choices, is for von Balthasar an eros of being which has taken on an existential, even evangelical, hunger and thirst for righteousness.

   This note of gospel urgency in an apostolic life is highly characteristic of von Balthasar's approach. His call for strict adherence to God's
will for one's life is itself tempered by the conviction that such an act is
always undertaken as an act of love in response to divine love, as an
event of joyful homecoming. So, for example, speaking of Thérèse of
Lisieux's growing willingness to surrender even her most cherished
dreams of God, von Balthasar adds:

> If such an attitude is not to become abstract and inhuman, this state
> of indifference must preserve human desires and hopes in all their
> vitality . . . . There is no trace in Thérèse of the Quietism which
> simply allows a person to drown his own will in the will of God.
> The mystery of indifference is much more a mystery of personal
> love, and the exchange of wills, one which requires explanation in
> terms of the Trinity.[5]

The christological implications are near at hand: the humanity which
surrenders itself to its divine mission and true identity does not
become a hollow shell but finds its hopes and aspirations growing all

the more vital, active, and definite. The process of self-abandon is an act of personal love or communion, echoing the trinitarian perichoresis (and instantiating it in the case of Christ) in which one person comes to ever greater consummation in giving self over to the other, only to receive an ever greater return of love.

In its heart, then, the act of self-surrender is an act of fruitful love, but von Balthasar is acutely aware that the circumstances of human life often work against such an experience of the matter. So long as humanity is "subject to the law of sin," he writes, this act of indifference "will always have a painful aspect. We have to renounce what is our own since this encumbers the space in us to which God's Word lays claim."[6] With this awareness of the painful encumbrance of sin, von Balthasar's treatment of self-abandonment begins to take on a darker and graver tone.[7] He argues that because of the tenacious possessiveness of sin, true receptivity to God and availability to one's mission will always entail a sense of sacrifice and renunciation. The act of placing one's life in God's hands is (not inherently but due to the structures of sin) an experience of constraint, loss of freedom, or even of death. "Only when God is free to demand what he wants without reservations on the part of the believer, can the possibility of a Christian sense of mission arise."[8] So it is that the act of self-surrender seems in von Balthasar's reading to be colored by an incalculable element of risk, of unknowing, and of surrender to a God whose true visage is obscured by sin.

In his early meditative work *Das Herz der Welt*, von Balthasar offers an evocative and deeply characteristic description of this unsettling experience: God's repeated calling and the soul's continued wariness in response.

Soft it approaches, almost inaudible and yet quite unavoidable: a ray of light, an offer of power, a command that is more and less than a command—a wish, a request, an invitation, an enticement: brief as an instant, simple to grasp as the glance of two eyes. It contains a promise: love, delight and a vision extending over an immense and vertiginous distance. Liberation from the unbearable dungeon of my ego. The adventure I had always longed for. The perfect feat of daring in which I am sure to win all only by losing all. The source of life opening up inexhaustibly to me, who am dying of thirst! The gaze is perfectly tranquil, having nothing of magical power or of hypnotic compulsion: a questioning gaze which allows me my freedom. At the bottom of it, the shadows of affliction and of hope alternate. I lower my eyes; I look to one side. I don't want to say "no" in the face of those eyes. I give them time to turn away. . . . These "ghostly hours" recur more and more seldom, and the enveloping layers of everyday life grow stronger and thicker around me. . . . I seal myself off from God and this becomes my usual state—my second nature. Maybe this is the habit of sin, the habit of evil.[9]

This passage captures almost uncannily the conflict which von Balthasar sees at work in the soul between its fundamental desire for God's call and its sinfully fearful self-enclosure against this call. Especially notable is the vein of poignancy which runs through the writing: the tender possibility that the divine beckoning holds out is easily spurned, and yet it is the very thing for which the soul has unknowingly longed all along. And deep in the mysterious recesses of the divine gaze von Balthasar discerns not anger or judgment but "shadows of affliction and of hope." The soul's confused pain and yearning is only an echo of the same alternation of feeling in the divine depths as the offer of a mission is lovingly, almost shyly, made by God to the cold-hearted and mercurial soul. Throughout, the soul's "freedom" is never jeopardized by God's approach but is rather a yet-to-be-realized possibility, newly opened to the soul by this calling from God.

In cases where the divine call meets with some positive response, the enticement to self-abandon becomes stronger still. Even the desires and intentions seemingly integral to one's self-giving are "demanded" for sacrifice. Von Balthasar points to the crucial moment in Thérèse's development when she has acquired not only an availability but a taste for suffering as part of her mission. Suddenly she is "pulled back in a serene, mature recognition that her mission of suffering must become a unity with her indifference." All Thérèse's religious aspirations, which she had begun to cling to as her sole possession, are allowed to give way to the one active work of abandonment (Hingabe): "Just in time she remembers the whole point of her own little way: to leave the choice to God. She embraces the sacrifice God asks of her."[10]

This theme of the relentless momentum of self-abandon, in which each level of indifference is sacrificed to an even deeper self-surrender, bears significant fruit in von Balthasar's interpretation of Jesus' earthly ministry: Christ is forced to give over each of his accomplishments, until finally all his teaching and healing, his mission itself, is surrendered in apparent failure, and in Gethsemane even his *capacity to surrender* to God's will seems shaken and nearly stripped from him.

Von Balthasar's considerable knowledge of the historical paths which self-surrender has taken has already shown itself in his interpretation of general Christian experience. Here we may note some of his views on the historical permutations of indifference as these bear on his christology.

He interprets pre-Christian *apatheia* as including in the Stoics a certain practice of withdrawal from the world in order to achieve transcendence and, in the tragedians, self-transcendence through the suffering of an incomprehensible fate.[11] With the coming of the Gospel, says von Balthasar, this classical attitude of *apatheia* is illumined by the shape of Christ's self-surrender in love *for* God and humanity.[12] The difficulty, historically, says von Balthasar, has been that Christianity rarely manages to clothe this christological re-creation of *apatheia* in philosophical concepts that are adequate to its true dynamic. The crucial gospel intersubjectivity, renunciation of self in love *for* the other, is cloaked by Stoic or neo-Platonic systems of thought that von Balthasar believes are less dialogical and more concerned with self-transcendence per se.[13]

He goes on to explore a new intensification of self-abandon in the later Middle Ages. "Eckhart's *Gelassenheit* is one of the most beautiful illustrations of that unchanging Christian challenge of the saints."[14] Von Balthasar is particularly taken with Eckhart's position that true indifference requires one to hand self over to God so completely that God "takes over care and responsibility for him," even "takes over his suffering, which comes to him only by way of God and in that way is transfigured by God."[15] What is important for our purposes here is the theme of indifference as a means of divine presence in the believer. Eckhart, says von Balthasar, "completely transforms Indian/Greek/Arab apatheia: it is the opposite of a technique of preserving oneself from sorrow; it is not a question of pain or pleasure but of the total gift of oneself to eternal love."[16] In his reading of Eckhart, von Balthasar repeatedly underscores that this "total gift of oneself" renders one more and more available to the divine love, in the sense of becoming a living human medium of its expression.

Von Balthasar sees Eckhart at the crest of a new wave in Christianity's understanding of indifference, a wave which would pour itself out in Eckhart's followers such as Suso and Tauler. Whereas much of patristic and medieval Christianity interpreted indifference from an ontological itinerary (ascetic discipline followed by contemplative elevation from images and passions to pure being), the suffering of later medieval society confronted Christianity with a more tragic understanding of existence. Von Balthasar believes there was a crucial shift from a transcendental *despicere mundum* to a more tragic and christological *despici a mundo*. In this way an obscure meaningfulness can be recovered in the seemingly meaningless suffering of believers, which no longer accomplishes an ascetic contempt for the world but only endures contempt *by* the world.

Sharing in Christ's suffering lends a new, if hidden, hope and meaning to self-surrender because "in the night [of Christ's agony], in which God hid himself, there was the darkness of an extreme love, which could still be affirmed even in non-vision and the naked faith of indifference."[17] This is for von Balthasar always the secret and fruitful inner truth of self-surrender (even when it is obscured by sin), namely, that the human act of self-abandon to mission is always drawn into an encounter with a still greater act of trinitarian self-abandon for humanity's sake. Grace itself "is participation in a divine disposition, in the inner selflessness of God's threefold outpouring. Eternal happiness can thus only be an entry into the finality of God's selfless humility, into the bliss of not existing for oneself."[18]

What von Balthasar has traced in all this is a mounting sense in Christianity that a believer's act of self-surrender is in effect called forth and constituted by the descending reciprocal divine act of self-surrender. And just as this trinitarian kenotic momentum constitutes the divine persons precisely *as* persons for each other, so being drawn into this momentum at the human level brings about the constitution of the human individual. The aim of indifference is no longer the attainment of a putative, static passionlessness of divine being but participation in the person-constituting, self-giving activity of God. Even in putting it this way we have already alluded to the implications for christology; although the night of sin darkens and infects self-surrender with pain and anxiety, the apparent disappearance of the human individual Jesus into the mission of the Son is in fact the appearing of Jesus as an authentic person, fulfilled and consummated in this encounter within "the darkness of an extreme love." Jesus is not absorbed into a featureless divine *stasis* but liberated and made alive in the self-giving activity of the Son.

Something of this strange exchange is captured in von Balthasar's depiction of the "two" Thérèses. At the same time as one Thérèse is receding "ever deeper into the shadows," the true Thérèse is coming "forward into the light." The latter "comes to fruition in exact measure that the first wears away, blossoming ever more beautifully, more deeply conscious of the divine light."[19] What makes this picture so significant christologically is that unlike other saints, who come to fulfillment in terms of some work of objective teaching or ministry, "the mission in Thérèse's case, seems to be called 'Thérèse'." Her utter self-surrender and apparent loss of self does not simply give rise to some new hospital or weighty scholastic insight but to a new *person*, the true and vibrant Thérèse, a new reality of God's love come to be incarnate in the world by means of her self-giving.

We arrive at some final particularizations of von Balthasar's understanding of self-abandonment by noting the coloring which his Jesuit background lends to the theme. In his deeply considered work on *The Spirituality of St. Ignatius*, Hugo Rahner pinpoints a key development in Ignatius's understanding of indifference. Prior to the all-important mystical experience at Manresa, Ignatius was filled with extravagant penitential aspirations of entering a Carthusian monastery and making barefoot pilgrimages. But after Manresa Ignatius is granted a deeper level of self-abandon which takes him in a profoundly "worldly" direction. Quoting Nadal's account, Rahner suggests that once Ignatius "felt the total self-surrender of his soul become a living reality" he was "drawn and driven to devote himself utterly to the care of the salvation of souls."[20] From now on the emphasis in Ignatius's teaching would be that the "more" of self-surrender is always measured by its concrete activity on behalf of others in the world. Here we see the fore-echoes of von Balthasar's insistence that indifference is not in aid of a purificatory ascent to higher levels of being but that such an ascent itself is really only attained through evangelical commitment to one's mission in the world.[21]

We find a confirmation of the importance of this point in de Guibert's magisterial work. Commenting on Ignatius's growing self-abnegation and self-mastery, de Guibert adds that this

> was not in any manner a way of gradual disengagement from the sensible, nor a flight ever more complete from the corporeal. In this regard it was completely different from the type of mysticism which can be called "Dionysian."[22]

This understanding of Ignatius corroborates two of von Balthasar's most central perspectives: first, that union with God is always enacted in a concrete earthly mission, and second, that self-surrender is not the antagonist of human freedom but its great benefactor. In his own interpretation of Ignatius, we see him emphasizing both points. Ignatius, says von Balthasar, developed the idea of abandonment in all its "Christian radicalism," but he avoided doing so in a metaphysical formulation. Self-surrender in Christian terms never implies "the ancient hylemorphic model whereby God is form and the creature is matter."

> The practice of indifference, as understood by Ignatius, does not therefore mean the inevitable annihilation of man's own being and will. . . . No, the true mystery of Christian revelation is this: the perfection of the kingdom of God . . . can be pursued as the universal operation of God in the active co-operation of the creature—in abandonment, surrender, service.[23]

Consequently a certain determinative significance is accorded humanity in the work of God (above all the humanity of Christ), and God's human partner and agent is assured its reality.

Von Balthasar holds that Ignatian indifference and availability to God never in the least causes one to cease being "a spontaneous and free human subject."[24] Such a human agent for Ignatius always "remains a person, but his own person becomes as it were completely transparent to the person who sends him."[25] Here von Balthasar's language rather gives away his deeply christological basis in reading Ignatius—which for our purpose is all to the point, of course. Self-surrender to the divinely given mission (*Sendung*) renders the human being "transparent" to the "Sender." It does not undermine human freedom but installs it within a greater freedom, and draws it into a new and more complete unity with the very source of personhood.

THE STATE OF SELF-SURRENDER IN JESUS CHRIST

Now we are in a position to consider what shape von Balthasar's reading of self-surrender gives to his interpretation of the Incarnation. Although I alluded above to the christological significance of particular features in von Balthasar's reading of indifference, it will be useful here to draw together the decisive features which converge in his treatment of self-surrender as a christological state. First, self-surrender is always a response, a coming-out-of-oneself, to the prior self-giving of divine love. Second, it is therefore not a process of ever more perfect self-transcendence but inherently a dialogical, intersubjective act which is always oriented toward another person or persons. Third, this availability for others is the medium in which the provisional humanity and personhood of the subject comes to realization and vitality. Fourth, because of the structures of sin which pervade human existence, self-giving is experienced in terms of loss and constraint, even of ultimate disappearance of the self. And fifth, because of the infinity of the trinitarian self-abandonment, human self-abandonment, which is always an event of sharing in the divine form of self-giving, acquires a powerful momentum that carries the subject ever farther into self-giving love. These summary principles which we have seen unfolded above in von Balthasar's "phenomenology" of self-surrender, are, I believe, the idiomatic features that come to life in his depiction of the self-abandoned dimension of Christ.

Von Balthasar senses in the New Testament witness to Jesus a curious and seemingly irreconcilable confrontation between authority (*Vollmacht*) and poverty (*Armut*). These are the "distinguishing marks" of Jesus' existence, and von Balthasar ponders how the extremes of both could coexist in Christ. Yet the dynamic of the scriptural narratives continually points to this: Jesus' commanding presence, his power and authority for people, stem precisely from his poverty, his continual abandoning of himself—both to the people themselves, their needs, their hungers, their diseases, *and* to the One whom he called Father.[26] Jesus' claim and salvific power for others derives from his human readiness to express God's Word in every detail of his life, in his complete self-surrender to the filial mission.[27]

Christ's humanity is drawn, in its least detail, into existence precisely as it is given over to the mission of the Word. This is not a passive "suffering" of God on Jesus' part, but an active readiness and expressivity which shape his every moment. Christ's "handing-over of himself is no mere passivity but a form of action, which—humanly speaking—demands of the subject far more self-possession and initiative than the pursuance of self-imposed precepts and goals."[28] Von Balthasar sets the salvific significance of Christ's life in the framework of his self-surrender: this is the means of God's presence in the world and simultaneously the means of drawing human existence into fulfillment in God.

Jesus' early life, prior to his public ministry, reflects one dimension of his availability. In his readiness to place himself in the hands of his natural family, religious institutions, and his society, Jesus was in fact making himself available to God. Each of the earthly ties can be seen as a representative of the divine calling.[29] We might elucidate von Balthasar's somewhat schematic hint here by suggesting that in "abandoning" himself to the earthly structures around him, Jesus is drawn into deeper levels of maturity and personhood: from the infant who learns to smile by smiling back at smiling parents, to the young man whose capacity to love is shaped and exercised by the needs and sufferings of those around him. In every case the human structures of the world, which draw forth a self-giving response from Jesus, are the concrete means by which the Father begins to call him more and more deeply into his mission, and therefore into his own identity.

It is perhaps unfortunate that von Balthasar seems not to unfold this insight very often in terms of the narrative details of the gospels. There are a number of initiatives, however, which point us in the right direction. Von Balthasar notes that Jesus' public ministry has a certain prodigality, even "wastefulness" (*Vergeudung*), which is a definite sign of the unreserved self-giving of his existence. This unexpected lavishness pours itself out regardless of circumstances and "runs as a leitmotiv through so many of his parables" (the carelessly sown seed or the scorned banquet or the multiplication of loaves).[30] Von Balthasar chooses biblical imagery of gifts seemingly squandered or scorned, yet always fertile, rich, full of the possibility of new life. Here we see something of the theme of the "two Thérèses," of human potential apparently dissipated into hiddenness only to blossom in a new and startlingly public way. Jesus' self-giving means the ever more drastic expenditure of himself, and yet there is always coming to birth thereby something unaccountably new, divine, rich in love and mercy—and something engagingly, empoweringly human.

Von Balthasar speaks of the whole of Jesus' earthly life as a continuing struggle in which he works to yield more and more of himself to the coming apocalyptic deed of God's salvation. Jesus seeks to make his entire human existence into an "ultimate gesture (*Gebärde*), so that it may become something that God's hand can form in its entirety."[31] Von Balthasar often affirms the theoretically complete nature of the hypostatic union from the moment of Jesus' conception. It is clear, however, that in historical, existential terms he envisages a more progressive unfolding of the Incarnation. It is almost as if the Incarnation of the Word, always confirmed in the eternity of the Word's self-communication, nonetheless comes to a greater and greater fullness precisely through the very human struggle of Christ to render himself ever more available to the Father's will.

In his late writing on the subject in *Theologik* II, von Balthasar makes amply clear that he by no means considers Jesus' humanity in adoptionist terms, a pliant human subject taken up by stages into the divine plan. Rather, he emphasizes, quoting Rahner with approval, that the humanity of Christ is itself the living expression of the Word's self-communication, and has no other grounds of existence.[32] Yet it does seem that von Balthasar credits Jesus with a growing and not always easily won state of "surrenderedness," so that in a certain sense one could say that the Word does come to fuller expression through the historical course of Jesus' self-giving.

We might note two such examples that von Balthasar takes up. The first is the case of Jesus' exposure to temptation. The nature of human existence makes it plain that Jesus, like everyone else, must be faced with the necessity of "choosing" between good and evil. Jesus grows through these times of testing because, without surrendering his "freedom" to choose, he refuses to "choose with indifference between good and evil." Instead Jesus comes to "commend himself and all his freedom to the protection of love . . . he surrenders his freedom to the beloved [Father] in order to receive the law of love." Each instance of this testing causes Jesus to know and actualize this love within him which "wants to abandon itself, to surrender itself, to entrust itself, to commit itself to love."[33] So Jesus' attitude of self-abandon draws him into a fuller realization of his own being, in this case his love. And of equal significance, this personal realization correlates with Jesus' saving work; for central to the latter in von Balthasar's estimation is Christ's continual offering of love to the Father in all the circumstances where humanity has failed to love.

The other, more specific, example is Jesus' passion in Gethsemane. In this case the testing is intensified to the utmost because, von Balthasar holds, on the Mount of Olives Jesus abandons himself to the extremity of human alienation. It is precisely Jesus' self-abandonment to the needs and experience of his people that leads him into their suffering. "Jesus no longer distinguishes himself and his fate from those of sinners," and so he "experiences the anxiety and horror which they by rights should have known for themselves."[34] But for von Balthasar this availability of Jesus for the human other is always embraced within a still greater self-giving to the divine other.

And so paradoxically, but crucially in von Balthasar's understanding, the very attitude that leads Jesus into the depths of his fellow humanity's sinful agony also leads him beyond himself towards God. "The prayer-agony on the Mount of Olives has as its unique object a saying 'Yes' to the will of the Father."[35] We can interpret von Balthasar to mean that Jesus' self-surrender draws him out into the place where, faced by the frightful oblivion in which sin has hidden the Father's face, he must choose to give himself into the Father's hands. But in constrast to our first example, in Gethsemane the Father no longer appears to Jesus as the love to whom he longs to commit himself. Now he must struggle painfully to find within himself the availability and readiness for the Father's will. Von Balthasar recognizes this historical achievement on Jesus' part when he writes: "At the end of the prayer-agony, *disponibilité* in its fulness is re-conquered. 'It is enough' (*apechei*, Mark 14.41). Now Jesus is free from every bond, whether exterior or interior."[36]

We have seen now how Jesus' radical availability is the key to his saving power for people: it renders him transparent to the Word of life, and by means of it he accomplishes the loving self-surrender to the Father which humanity has been unable to offer. We have also seen how this pouring out of his own life on behalf of others leads to his historical development and fulfillment as the one unsubstitutable Jesus of Nazareth.

But perhaps even more significant, in terms of the Incarnation, has been the sense that Jesus' human life is a continual act of being drawn out into fuller existence *towards* the other—whether God or neighbor. It is as if the humanity of Christ, not just in metaphysical terms but in concrete historical ones as well, were the direct, moment-by-moment result of the magnetic self-giving of the Word. The idea would certainly not be foreign to von Balthasar, for it is a constant and central theme in Maximus:

> this reciprocal gift which deifies humanity for God through the love of God, and makes God human for humanity through [God's] love of humanity; making through this wonderful exchange God to become human for the theosis of humanity, and humanity to become God for the humanization (*anthroposis*) of God.[37]

It is the last phrase which is especially significant in the present instance—humanity becomes God *so that* God may exist humanly: humanity is drawn to give itself over entirely to God so that God can reach into the depths of human life. This is very much the idea which von Balthasar is trying to trace out in terms of Jesus' historical existence. So for instance when he speaks of Jesus' "growth in the clear self-conscious comprehension of his mission," he points out that this intensification

> displays no corresponding taking over of the control by Jesus, but precisely the opposite: an increasing self-abandonment to the control by the one who alone can draw out of the whole lived existence the definitive word that God needs to complete his new and eternal covenant.[38]

In other words, the more Jesus comes to a mature personal realization of his mission and identity, the more he is self-abandoned to the Father, and consequently all the more expressive of the Father's definitive Word.

Von Balthasar develops this theme in a radical fashion by stressing the ecstatic structure of Jesus' self-giving. This theme reaches its acme in von Balthasar's treatment of Christ's resurrection, ascension, and sending of the Spirit. But even in Jesus' earthly life von Balthasar stresses the degree to which the humanity of Jesus is continually drawn into existence and even beyond the limits of human existence by the attractive force of the Father. Jesus' human readiness, mirroring Mary's *fiat*, becomes the medium in which the Son's eternal mission comes to human expression.[39] The archetype of all created availability to God

> is found in the way Christ's human nature stands out—ecstatically—in relation to his divine person, from which he draws his human existence; the mission he receives from the Father forms not only his office and destiny as Redeemer, but the essential traits of his individual nature.[40]

One might say that, for von Balthasar, the drawing near of the Father's love in the person of the Word initiates a reciprocal *ek-stasis* of created existence, and in the consummation of this encounter the Incarnation takes place. In terms of Jesus' historical life, his self-surrendering existence is a ceaseless act of ecstasy, of existing in the beyond-human-limits mission of the Word.

Viewed through this dimension of self-surrender, von Balthasar's christology attempts to interpret the Incarnation not only as meta-physical event but as a constant historical activity that is as much the "work" of Christ's humanity as it is of the eternal Word. It is the supremely active work of self-giving. Yet it is always a work which is elicited by the Father's love.

> It is the Father who draws him, as it were, out of the world—out of the world not only of his family, his relatives, his country (Mk 6.4), but also out of the world of his human nature and its laws, out of the world of his memory, his understanding, his will. In the dark night of his redemptive Passion, the Father demands of the Son and the Son freely offers the Father all the inner resources of his humanity. . . . In the Cross, the full ecstasy (that is, the total self-abandonment) of the Son is oriented toward and consummated in the Father.[41]

It is essential to underscore here that this *ekstasis* of Jesus "out of the world of his human nature" is not meant at all by von Balthasar as a denial or loss of Jesus' humanity. As the passage suggests, in the context of the ultimate self-giving of the cross, Jesus does not some-how cease to be human, but in his suffering and death he does cross the spiritual and historical barriers erected by sinful humanity be-tween itself and God and pass beyond them into that consummation of human self-giving which is trinitarian self-giving. Von Balthasar also emphasizes that as Christ is drawn through self-surrender into unity with God, he does not thereby become removed from the world and people around him:

> By thus fulfilling the plan of the triune God for the world, Jesus does not flee the world and go to God; he goes, rather, to the very foun-dation of the world—or, more precisely, he reveals himself as the innermost foundation of the world.[42]

In the human self-abandon of Jesus the world has its true heart re-stored, a human existence which is fulfilled, liberated, made available to all in being given over to God.

THE TRINITARIAN GROUND OF SELF-SURRENDER

Much of von Balthasar's writing has an undeniable scent of the sanc-tuary, a tendency to view everything in heavenly terms. As a result of this latter day *theo-logia* (in the original patristic sense of the term), one might conceivably form the impression that von Balthasar's christology has been cut to fit a heavenly model imposed on it from above. But he is entirely aware of this danger and works to avoid it. He is quite critical of what he sees as gnosticizing tendencies in atonement theories which make so much of the eternal heavenly "sacrifice" that the historical event of Golgotha seems a pale and unnecessary shadow.[43]

Von Balthasar certainly assumes the basic Christian belief in the Trinity, but he is concerned to face the full concrete profile of Jesus' historical existence, and then to ask how that causes us to understand more deeply the inner life of God. One may of course have doubts about the degree to which the earthly life of Christ can inform about the eternal life of the Trinity, yet a very positive assessment of the trinitarian implications of Jesus' human existence (such as von Balthasar's) is quite the reverse of a gnostic overlay of cosmic congeries upon the historical details of Jesus' earthly life. In other words, von Balthasar is undeniably bold in reading the pattern of Jesus' life back into its trinitarian source. But the fact that this trinitarian transposition must therefore stand as a claim about the eternal life of God does not mean that von Balthasar actually *begins* with an assumption about the minutiae of the heavenly household and then constructs a christology to fit.

When he considers the ultimacy of Jesus' self-giving to God and neighbor, von Balthasar can suggest that the Incarnation itself is not a demand that the Father places upon the Son but is rather the Son's own "idea." And when he considers the apparent acceptance by the Father, in raising Christ from the dead, of the Son's sacrifice, von Balthasar goes on to write:

> It seems to me that this proposal of the Son [to give himself away for the world] touches the heart of the Father, humanly speaking, more profoundly than even the sin of the world; that it opens in God a wound of love. . . a wound identical to the procession and circumincession of the divine persons in their perfect beatitude. . . . I do not think that this interpretation, which Moltmann and myself proposed at about the same time, is gnostic or otherwise rash, but rather I believe that it alone achieves an interpretation of the gospel facts without distorting them: *ut non evacuatur crux Christi* (1 Cor. 1.17).[44]

The emphasis is not on any alleged inner-trinitarian "speculation" but on the importance of rendering a faithful interpretion "of the gospel facts." What we find in von Balthasar is an attempt to account in trinitarian terms for the possibility that is only known by virtue of what takes place in Christ; i.e., the reality of Christ's divine-human self-surrender finds its condition of possibility in God's "wound of love," that opening and outpouring of divine life which is the triune perichoresis.

By no means does the historical fact, however, imply an eternal necessity:

> Even if it is true that the coming to light of the inner-trinitarian mystery in the dispensation of salvation lets us see something of the law of the immanent Trinity, it is nevertheless impossible to deduce from the inner law that this going-forth was necessary.[45]

So von Balthasar wants to suggest that God is an eternal life of mutual self-surrender. It is this divine self-positing as "other" which makes possible a created other, and indeed the possibility that the creature may share in divine union *without* losing its otherness.

> It is exceedingly good . . . that an otherness exists in God himself, by virtue of which God is first of all an infinite inner life of self-giving. Because of this he is also the freedom to create something different from himself, which now acquires from him the property of being other.[46]

Here, finally, we can see the trinitarian basis which von Balthasar posits as the possibility for Jesus' self-surrendered union with the Logos. If the basis of union were simply divine essence per se, Jesus' self-abandon would lead to his absorption into the divine and to the loss of his humanity. But von Balthasar argues, following Bulgakov, that Christ's self-giving suggests an infinite "selflessness" of the divine persons as characterizing the relations within the Godhead.[47] And this eternal self-surrender is the condition for the possibility of the eternal Word communicating self in what is not-Word, sinful human existence, even in death.

5

THE STATE OF OBEDIENCE

THE NATURE OF CHRISTIAN OBEDIENCE

This chapter follows very closely on the heels of its predecessor. For what we have to consider here is the translation of self-surrender and availability into an active pursuit of mission. We have seen how much prominence von Balthasar gives to the "ever more" momentum of self-abandon, and how, following Ignatius, he measures and tests this continually deepening self-giving by its actual commitment to the needs of God and neighbor which a given mission discloses. Now we want to see how the dimension of obedience shapes Christian existence, and what light this sheds on von Balthasar's understanding of the Incarnation.

At the heart of von Balthasar's myriad discussions of obedience there lies his belief in the forward momentum bestowed with every mission. He sees every disposition to authentic self-surrender as bearing within it the seeds of certain charisms which must come to fruition if the mission is to thrive. In von Balthasar's view, one's mission is only made known by revelation, that is, by finding one's place in the mission of Christ. As we saw above, a mission is never, therefore, adequately pursued by a purely self-transcending ascetical ascent toward higher levels of being but comes to fulfillment in a concrete historical apostolate; its direction is not to be found purely in an inspection of the unquiet longings of one's own heart but in obedience to externally manifested counsels and guidance. Indeed von Balthasar specifically credits Ignatius of Loyola for the evolution of *apatheia* into active obedience. The self-surrendering availability of the believer "can no longer remain at the level of indifference in the sense of *merely* letting things happen; no, the particular will of God, which is to be actively grasped and carried out, must also be actively pursued."[1] He points out that whereas the Rhineland mystics place abandonment at the end, "Ignatius transfers it to the beginning"; it becomes more and more a prelude and a prerequisite for the active cooperation of humanity in God's work.[2]

What must be made clear is that self-abnegation finds no completion "in renouncing one's environment in order to grasp the absolute (in ecstasy or absorption), or in renouncing one's own personhood or God's."

> Rather, it [renunciation] lies in faith itself, which, instead of a self-designed plan of life, accepts a commission from God, a divine piloting in commandments and counsels, and carries out these directives through every temptation from without and within.[3]

Right away, however, this description of obedience needs to be taken along with two fundamental corollaries in von Balthasar: obedience always includes a divine gift of interior freedom and energy, and it is always a response of love.

The first of these points derives from the close intimacy with God that obedience to a given mission affords. As believers carry out the details of the work God calls them to, they begin to share, von Balthasar argues, in God's own sense of fulfillment and delight—in their words and deeds the coming Kingdom declares itself, stretches its sinews and comes to life. "The person who faithfully and perseveringly carries out" her or his mission, experiences "something of God's joy in seeing his salvific will accomplished on earth as in heaven."[4] Von Balthasar seems to be reflecting here not only upon the cooperation of wills which is brought about through obedience but on the possibility of a real human sharing in the trinitarian bliss. Moreover he holds that such a possibility is open beyond a merely external knowledge that what one does is in accord with the divine plan:

> This [sense of God's joy] is not an event exterior to man: in living faith that includes hope and love, the germ of divine life is implanted in him and grows along with his practical, lived fidelity, assuring him in a mysterious way that he is on the right road to the Father and indeed is his beloved child.[5]

One can note here the implication such a perspective would have for christology: Jesus' human acts of obedience are themselves the seed bed in which the "germ of divine life" can come to consciousness within him, "assuring him in a mysterious way" of the rightness of his course, strengthening and confirming in him a sense of the intimacy of his filial relationship with God.

Along with this sense of sharing in God's joy and a consequent growth in the stability of one's own identity, von Balthasar sees an outright gift of divine energy and strength.

> Far from being just a gift received passively . . . it [the sense of calling] is a commission entrusted to man, a transfer of power from archetype to image, a task man must perform in the freedom of his non-identity with the archetype, and for which he has been given the necessary power and means. By relieving man of the feeling of being always a recipient, this active side of his calling justifies him in a corresponding sense of having been called to a "state of life."[6]

Especially noteworthy in this passage is its concern that obedience not be seen as constituting a position of passivity. It is just the reverse that an attitude of obedience brings about: a sense of worth and dignity, of having been entrusted with something unfathomably (if not always recognizably) significant to God, and the personal freedom and strength to see the commission through. From this standpoint, obedience to mission is an essential contributing factor in the integrity of the human person.[7]

The second crucial specification of obedience is its curious atmosphere of liberty; obedience is only true, von Balthasar believes, when it is undertaken not out of fear or servitude but in joyful response to the Beloved. "Neither is obedience mechanical; it results from understanding in love, and has to be one in sentiment with the will of the person commanding."[8] In his extensive work on the different vocations within the one calling to follow Christ (*The Christian State of Life*), von Balthasar precedes his interpretation of obedience in the different religious states with his understanding of the role of love. Fundamentally for von Balthasar, love is the only authentic core of obedience. It transforms every "obligation" into a "choice," and every (external) desire of the beloved becomes the (interior) desire of the lover. In this state, "necessity and freedom are conjoined."[9] It is only love which preserves obedience from being oppressive, and when love is allowed to grow cold then the desires of the beloved revert to commands, set among many other, possibly more appealing options. Love is also what gives life and permanence to obedience:

> Love can never be content with an act of love performed for the pre-
> sent moment only. . . . As a pledge of love, it wants to lay its
> freedom once and for all at the feet of love. . . . Every true love has
> *the inner form of a vow*: It binds itself to the beloved—and does so
> out of motives and in the spirit of love.[10]

Von Balthasar thus suggests that what makes something an act of obedience is love's desire to place its own freedom in the hands of the
beloved as a kind of trophy of love, a token of love's aspiration to have
no desires but what the beloved desires. By taking the beloved's desires
as its commands, love makes its vow and binds itself to the beloved.

But clearly the world is not unfamiliar with distorted and un-
healthy forms of love, the very suggestion of which must inevitably
raise questions about the adequacy of von Balthasar's view here. Still,
he is consistently aware of this danger, and always refers to the Gospel
as the norm of every authority.[11] Formally at least, von Balthasar is
clear enough: by speaking of love as the inner commitment and drive
which bind someone to obedience, he intends to interpret obedience
as that which does *not* diminish human selfhood but is the strongest
expression of its own ability to choose freely, to love.[12]

From the nature of the relationship which inspires obedience, we
turn to the impact of such a life upon the obedient person. In von
Balthasar's thinking, the interior assent which lies at the basis of true
obedience is much deeper than a simple upsurge of passion or zealotry.
Rather, we could say that inherent in the freedom of obedience there
lies a recognition of one's truest self. As we saw in the passage from
Heart of the World in the previous chapter, the call to mission is so
breathtaking for the soul precisely because it is the revelation of the
"adventure I had always longed for," it is the sudden and almost
heartbreaking recognition that here, finally, is the soul's true meat and
drink.

In other words von Balthasar never conceives of obedience, at least
in itself, as a response to an alien command. Christ as Word calling
the believer to share in his mission speaks of something previously ungraspable and yet hauntingly familiar.

> [The Word] is *my* truth as the truth about me and my own truth;
> the Word that reveals me and gives me to myself. In this Word were
> we created, and in it lies our entire truth, our idea, one so unexpect-
> edly great and beatifying that we should never have claimed or
> believed it.[13]

This is not for von Balthasar a formulaic expression of humanity's creation in Christ, but an attempt to express a sense of the wonderfully surprising discovery of self which he discerns in the obedience of the Christian faithful. It is the recognition of selfhood as one's own and yet as wholly a gift. For von Balthasar therefore, obedience is so crucial because apart from it, and from the pilgrimage it entails, Christians might never claim for themselves what is truly theirs: the particular form of cooperation with God which they were created to enjoy.

With the examples of Simon Peter and Thérèse, von Balthasar illustrates his sense of the matter: that obedience is a means of a self-discovery far beyond what the believer might find "by scrutinising his own dispositions, aspirations, talents and potentialities"; for only "the man obedient to his mission fulfils his own being."[14] In the gospels, Simon is less than a roaring success as a fisherman, and von Balthasar interprets this as suggestive of Simon's inability to discover his true mission in life.

> The form "Peter," the particular mission reserved for him alone, which till then lay hid in the secret of Christ's soul and, at the moment of this encounter, was delivered over to him sternly and imperatively—was to be the fulfilment of all that, in Simon, would have sought vainly for a form ultimately valid in the eyes of God and for eternity.[15]

Two points are worth noting. It is Simon's encounter with Jesus which brings "Peter" into existence, which delivers him from remaining only a shadow of what he might truly have become. In the same way, of course, von Balthasar envisions Christ's humanity being delivered, quite literally, from mere potentiality precisely by his obedience to the calling of the Father which grasps him in the Word. But second, what becomes real in Peter is that which was really there in Simon but which, apart from obedience, could never become real, concrete, and incarnate. So analogously with reference to Jesus' humanity, his obedient life of ultimate filial love "incarnates" not only the eternal Word but his own humanity.

In the case of Thérèse, the self-discovering journey of obedience begins with the move into Carmel. Only in this way, says von Balthasar, could the *potential* dynamic in her life grow into an "infinite movement."

> What Thérèse needs is that her *personality* should die, and that she should be reborn as a *person* at a level where she has to draw upon

all her latent possibilities. . . . Through entering this new state of life Thérèse is given the opportunity to shed her personal limitations and acquire the stature which is hidden for her in God and is only to be revealed through her mission to the Church.[16]

Especially significant here is von Balthasar's imagery of *death and rebirth as a means of bringing into existence the full truth of one's being*. As we noted in the last chapter, the structural effect of sin is to darken and harden the experience of self-surrender or obedience, so that what in itself should be a pattern of freely willed and joyful discovery necessarily becomes a far more drastic expenditure of oneself. The paradox enforced by sin is that the latent possibilities of one's being are only forged into incarnate life as one is led by obedience through the fire of the passion.

Actual obedient participation in Christ's own living, dying, and rising is of course, for von Balthasar, the crucible in which believers' true selves come to fruition. By his "obedience unto death," Jesus withdraws his "personality" in order to enact and make manifest his mission; "each withdrawal takes him towards death, each manifestation to the *Parousia*."[17] In Christ, believers share the same pattern: their "personality" is withdrawn "behind the pure veil of objectivity and obedience" so as to be given a share in Christ's saving sacrifice; but the fullness of their existence reappears, in some cases not until the Parousia, "in others their following of Christ leads them to appear again in this world, as Christ appeared for forty days after the Resurrection."[18] The significance of this pattern for von Balthasar's understanding of the Incarnation is intriguing. Let us turn directly then to the role of obedience in Christ.

OBEDIENCE AS A CHRISTOLOGICAL STATE

Von Balthasar's reading of believers' participation in the obedience of Christ suggests that he has conceived, analogically, what might be termed a historical-existential basis for the Incarnation. The true human stature and reality of Thérèse only come to expression as a result of her seeming disappearance into a hidden life of obedience to the rule of her order. But she is forced by this costly obedience to grow into a deeper person, "to draw upon all her latent possibilities"; and so this death of her "personality" leads her into a new resurrection-identity, the full personhood she was created to enjoy. What is suggestive for our understanding of Incarnation in von Balthasar is the fact that this full manifestation of the believer's humanity is always the result of an arduous journey of obedience. It is a historical-existential understanding of humanity, not an ontological one.

When von Balthasar highlights the historical pattern of Christ's obedience—life into death into new life—we may be justified in seeing this as the structure by which Jesus' full human existence comes to term, and thereby the Word becomes incarnate. The full potential of Christ's humanity is ever more completely realized in each act of obedience to the mission of the Word, climaxing even with his human death. Von Balthasar himself repeatedly adverts to the analogy with religious life when he describes the Holy Spirit as acting in Christ's earthly life as the "rule" to which Christ gives himself in obedience, much as Thérèse gives herself to the Carmelite rule.[19] Jesus' "obedience unto *death*" is thus *not* seen as the counter-argument to obedience; i.e., his death is not an event which might somehow reveal obedience as finally imperiling Christ's humanity beneath the crushing burden of his divinity; rather, his death is the forge in which his humanity, superheated by his divine mission, is brought to its fullest state of self-expression and reality—a fact necessarily obscured by the form (death and hell) which sin requires it to take, but a fact which von Balthasar nonetheless sees made manifest in Jesus' gloriously human resurrection state.

Perhaps the strongest evidence for this interpretation lies in the fact that von Balthasar emphasizes this event-full, developmental structure with reference not only to Christ's humanity but to his divinity. In a pivotal passage he speaks of human identity and being as emerging through God's gift to humanity of mission.[20] In the patriarchs and prophets, in John the Baptist and Paul, we can see, says von Balthasar, this awakening through the divine call to one's true nature and identity. "The final instance in this line, an instance surpassing all others, is when, at his baptism, Jesus is given his mission by the One who sent him."[21] But in von Balthasar's reading, the fulfillment of Jesus as a personal being is entirely bound up with his obedient fulfillment of his mission, and this is only underway but not complete at his baptism. For this reason von Balthasar is led to open up the ontological structures of Incarnation to historical development:

> A mission can only be carried out within a time span, and, particularly in the case of Jesus' mission, the final phase, the "hour," has the greatest significance for its execution. Consequently, Jesus' exis-

tence-in-mission manifests a paradoxical unity of *being* (and a *being* that *has always been*) and *becoming*. "God sent his Son" (Rom 8:3; Gal 4:4) fully and definitively in the Incarnation: he was "born of a woman," "in the form of sinful flesh"; but his task, although he adhered to it daily and hourly, could only be "accomplished" on the Cross (Jn 19:30). Since the Subject in whom person and mission are identical can only be divine, it follows that "God's being" really "undergoes development" (E. Jüngel); it follows that he who is born the Son of God has a nature that exhibits development.[22]

We can easily see the tension in this passage. Von Balthasar's loyalty to the classical metaphysical interpretation of the Incarnation is profound, but his commitment to the actual history of Jesus' destiny is no less so. And so in a rather fascinating way he is led towards the notion that Jesus' fulfillment (as the human being who is the eternal Son incarnate) is forged through the obedience that culminates in the final apocalyptic "hour" of Golgotha. Because mission and identity are one in him, Jesus' humanity comes to full existence only as he enacts to the end the obedience of filial love. It is only as the eternal Word comes to the last shuddering reverberation of God's meaning, in the human obedience of Jesus on the cross, that Jesus' humanity is brought to *its* consummation.

Does this mean von Balthasar believes that divine being experiences, analogically, a new level of "achievement"? He does indeed. Both the givenness and the to-be-fulfilled quality of Jesus' life find their ground in the procession of the Son:

> [This is] a single *being*, which, while we may not call it *becoming*, is the streaming-forth of eternal life, superevent. The dramatic dimension that is part of the definition of the person of Jesus does not belong exclusively to the worldly side of his being: its ultimate presuppositions lie in the divine life itself.[23]

The "superevent" (*Über-Ereignis*) of the Son comes to expression as the historically unfolded life of Jesus, whose own humanity to the same degree comes to expression through his concrete acts of filial obedience. In von Balthasar's reading of the Incarnation, each obedient act of Jesus carries him deeper into the mystery of himself. His self-surrender is no longer an interior stance but an active, external, interpersonal obedience which brings him into the midst of his peoples' needs; and it is precisely through his obedient, though fatal, loving of *them* "to the end" that Jesus exists as the human being God created him to be.

In the first part of this chapter we noted that a person's obedience might be seen as the forging of his or her full human stature. We also noted that this obedient existence is always for von Balthasar a response of love; indeed, the very sense of necessity so implicit in obedience is the result of a lover taking the beloved's desires as commands. This theme reaches an apex in von Balthasar's christology. But here he comes to a dilemma. On the one hand he certainly wishes to affirm the freedom of obedience; he refers to the efforts of Chrysostom, Anselm, and Thomas "to illuminate the perfect unity of the wills of the Father and the Son, and therewith the voluntary (*sponte*) character of all the Son's acting," which he admits "Thomas rates higher than obedience to an order."[24] But on the other hand, von Balthasar questions whether this entirely squares with the compelling urgency of Jesus' obedience and the ubiquity of the divine necessity (*dei*) in the gospels.

Von Balthasar seems to have developed two separate but related responses to this problem about Christ's freedom in obedience. One approach is simply to refer again to the trinitarian basis of Christ's existence. As we saw in the last chapter, von Balthasar takes Christ's identity as the eternal Word as sufficient warrant for a highly evolved theory of trinitarian kenosis. He understands Christ's divine-human obedience as possible only because it is the direct historical expression of the eternal "mystery of the Kenosis whose first result is the Incarnation, followed by the whole human existence of Jesus."[25] On this basis, then, he argues that the Son's "obedience presents the kenotic translation of the eternal love of the Son for the 'ever-greater' Father."[26] This argument is a kind of variation on the one we saw above regarding the possibility of a trinitarian ground for the historical "becoming" of the Son in his earthly human existence (this historical eventfulness argues no ultimate "change" in God if it is understood as being the historical projection of that "superevent" of the Son's eternal procession). Analogously in this instance, von Balthasar argues that the urgently necessary quality which pervades Jesus' life of obedience need not be seen as a lack of freedom once it is recognized as the historical projection of the Son's eternal freedom to serve the co-equal yet "ever-greater" Father in love.

It would be easy enough to grow troubled here, sensing a kind of speculation all too quickly transposable into oppressive ecclesial and social structures. Yet one could argue, more accurately I believe, that for von Balthasar, Jesus' human obedience is by no means to be taken as merely an example for humans, and a possibly oppressive one at that. Rather, all human understandings of obedience are to be tested and measured against the joyful and abiding freedom which is the ground of Christ's own obedience. An obedience, no matter how costly, that does not spring from a free desire to bestow upon another the gift of one's love and labor would not be an obedience commensurate with Christ's. Moreover, Jesus' obedience is always a free response to the costly and prior self-giving of his Father:

> If the one and undivided love of God takes on a filial, and hence its most obedient, coloring in the person of the Son, the love of the Son is not therefore to be regarded as inferior (subordinated) to the Father's love, but as none other than the eternal "expression" (Heb 1:3) of the perfect selflessness and self-giving of paternal love by which the Father determined, not to keep his divine essence wholly for himself, but to pour it out abundantly on the Son.[27]

In other words, Jesus' obedience is not simply a historical form of the Son's eternal obedience, it is the historical form of the *Father's* self-giving, which it is the Son's mission eternally to express. So every human obedience must also be tested for the presence of an "evergreater" self-giving on the part of the one to whom obedience would be offered; and absent such a prior and continual self-giving on the part of the "superior," any call for obedience would be liable to grave questions of legitimacy.

Von Balthasar traces out the implications for Christ's humanity of all these trinitarian arguments. He suggests, following Ignatius, that the obedience of a human will to the divine will is always understood as an installing of human willing in the divine freedom of choice itself; it is never intended as a sacrifice of human freedom but a gracious invitation to cooperate in the divine work.[28] "The freedom of Christ lies in the fact that he shares by obedience in the omnipotence and freedom of the Father."[29] Von Balthasar means by this that in Jesus divine will and human will no longer confront one another as alien and perhaps competitive forces. Jesus need not come before God "with petitions of his own designing," for his will is already "included in the trinitarian dialogue between Father and Son in the Holy Spirit"—and this not to the overruling of his human will but its infinite fulfillment.

> Here it becomes apparent that the surrender of human choice in favor of the divine call is by no means identical with the extinction

of the creature's function in favor of the divine function. The creature's act of obedience is not a quietistic renunciation of its own
nature, nor is God's act of love a suppression of the autonomy of
the one loved. . . . Nothing makes the human individual more autonomous than the divine mission that he accepts in free obedience
and with full responsibility.[30]

The incarnational implications of this view are powerful. Jesus' very
human obedience grants him an entrance into a realm of freedom and
possibility far beyond human conceiving; rather than oppressing him,
the attunement of his will with God's will means that his every desire,
every act, every word becomes the direct expression of God—with all
the power and authority of God.

Once again we see a pattern emerging in which a fundamental
state of Christ's historical human existence (in this case, obedience)
leads him beyond the expected limits of human life, not so as to short-
circuit the human reality but, rather, opening all his acts of human
obedience to a divine consummation and strength. And once again we
see a conjunction in which the fullest possible realization of Christ's
humanity coincides with the fruition through obedience of the divine
mission of the Son.

We may conclude this chapter by considering some instances where
this theme is brought out in von Balthasar's treatment of the narrative
of Christ's life. In each case we see the integrity of incarnation and
salvation; that is, Christ's human life achieves its fulfillment, as the
human presence of the Word, precisely as he enacts by his obedience
the salvation of his people. So for instance "when Jesus goes to meet
the prophetic *kairos* represented by the Baptist . . . this is a first act of
obedience."[31] What results from this is Jesus' initiation into the needs
of the people:

Jesus' descent into the river is at one and the same time solidarity
with all who confess their guilt and dive into the waters of judgment
and salvation, and—as solidarity—obedience to the voice of God
which sounds forth in the prophet's voice, and thus obedience incarnated in history.[32]

Note the theme of "obedience incarnated in history," for here writ
small is the great scheme of Balthasarian incarnational soteriology:
the concrete human acts of Jesus, by which he comes to his own
full stature, enact that perfect obedience which is the basis of his
people's reconciliation with God. Von Balthasar sketches a reading of

the gospel narratives in which Jesus' obedience takes the form of a positive movement towards the apocalyptic hour "of judgment and salvation"; this is savingly significant because Jesus obediently commits himself to this "hour" with a wholeheartedness which is avoided and even opposed by his people.

Another important example of the incarnational and salvific impact of obedience is Jesus' darkened "knowledge" of his mission. Von Balthasar argues that it would not be necessary for Christ to know the complete shape of his mission, for the precise reason that this knowledge is, as it were, surrendered in favor of an absolute obedience to God "in order to reconcile the world to God."

> With the word obedience, we immediately touch on the most intimate disposition of Jesus, and it is without doubt more important and more salutary for perfect obedience not to want to know the future in advance.[33]

Again we see that the very concrete features of obedience, in this case with regard to Christ's human knowing, have a powerful shaping effect on his historical human life—they "bring him into the world," as it were, in a very particular and savingly significant way.

Interestingly enough, these themes are also at the forefront of the incarnational soteriology of two of von Balthasar's most favored conversation partners: Maximus and Karl Barth. In Maximus, the obedience of Christ restores a harmony of heaven and earth which human disobedience had painfully disrupted. By enacting this perfect obedience in the pivot-point of all creation (human nature), Jesus creates a new synthesis between all the divided orders of the cosmos and achieves from *within* a renewal of human nature.[34] In the case of Barth, the linking of obedience, salvation, and incarnation is even clearer and provides a very helpful sense of the horizon of understanding at work in von Balthasar. For Barth, a large part of what is "the new and helpful thing" in Christ, and therefore significant for salvation, is precisely that in him

> sin is condemned by not being committed, by being omitted, by full obedience now being found in the very place where otherwise sin necessarily and irresistably takes place. The meaning of the incarnation is that now in the flesh that is not done which all flesh does. . . . Jesus Christ's obedience consists in the fact that he willed to be and

was only this one thing with all its consequences, God in the flesh, the divine bearer of the burden which man as a sinner must bear.[35]

It is exactly because Christ in his obedience does not flinch from doing what humans fail to do, or from bearing the guilt which humans refuse to face, that he works towards the reconciliation of humanity with God. And this, says Barth, is the very activity which identifies him as the Incarnate One, "God in the flesh."

What we have sought to show in this chapter is that von Balthasar has opened a new depth to approaches such as those of Maximus and Barth. He has done so precisely in unfolding a complex understanding of the very human dimension of Christ's obedience. Drawing on the insights of a spirituality which shares in Christ's obedience to his divine mission, von Balthasar has highlighted the interior freedom of obedience. He characterizes it not only as a response to love but as a discovery of one's truest self and therefore as a fulfillment of one's own being. In terms of the significance of this for his treatment of the Incarnation, von Balthasar has profiled a dimension of Christ's existence which brings into high relief the development of Jesus' full human stature through time. And he has shown how this obedience, paradoxically and savingly, leads Jesus simultaneously into the depths of his people's sin *and* into the union of his will and the Father's. As von Balthasar himself puts it:

> the absolute opposition between grace and sin could really only spring up in the total *disponibilité* of unconditional obedience. This obedience reveals itself now as the fundamental presupposition of christology: it makes possible both the event of the Incarnation and the human existence of Christ as its decisive work.[36]

Von Balthasar sees obedience as the motive force of historical existence. It is the pattern of spiritual being by which both Jesus' human existence and thereby the Word come to full historical expression.

6

PASSION, DEATH, AND HELL AS
CHRISTOLOGICAL STATES

In the last two chapters I have interpreted the spiritual states of self-surrender and obedience as constitutive dimensions of the Incarnation. My aim has been to see these states as concrete features of Jesus' mission and to show how, for von Balthasar, they are fundamental aspects of the spiritual and historical process by which the Word of God becomes fully incarnate in a human life. One may inquire whether the Word could somehow be less incarnate in Jesus' infancy and then somehow more incarnate in his maturity. Surely for von Balthasar and for the tradition generally, the incarnation "takes place" entirely at the Annunciation and Nativity? If the Incarnation were conceived in exclusively metaphysical terms, von Balthasar would agree. But the whole point of his christological endeavor has been to recast our thinking about the Incarnation into spiritual and historical terms, even communal and political terms, as an ongoing corporate event whose personal center is Jesus of Nazareth, and whose circumference is the ever-widening circle of the whole struggling and searching Body of his people. Jesus' encounters with others, above all with his Father, under the direction of the Spirit, are the very means whereby he is drawn farther and farther into his mission. And this process by which Jesus fulfills his mission in the world brings about his ever more concrete existence as the incarnation of the Word.

So we have discerned in von Balthasar a "reciprocal" dynamic of incarnation: *both* the eternal Word and the humanity of Jesus come to full historical realization through each other, through their common enactment of the one mission. In a manner analogous to the full blossoming of the real Thérèse (or any believer) through obedience to her mission, the humanity of Christ is drawn into ever fuller presence to God and to fellow humanity by carrying out the Word's mission; and the Word comes to ever fuller presence to humanity and history precisely through the continuing development and fulfillment of Christ's humanity.

When we turn now to the state of Christ's suffering, death, and presence in hell, we come to a paradox: at the very point where Christ's humanity would seem to be least "fulfilled" and to be suffering actual extinction, here, says von Balthasar, is the point at which Jesus is most completely human and the Word most fully incarnate.[1] As Herbert McCabe has very insightfully said, the mission of the Son is precisely to *be* human; so the fulfillment of Jesus' humanity and the fulfillment of the Word's incarnation necessarily intersect, but because of the human state of separation from God this point of intersection is the cross.[2] For it is in crucifixion that Jesus enters most utterly into alienated human existence and so shares completely in concrete and not just theoretical humanity.

In von Balthasar's treatment of Christ's passion we see perhaps the clearest example of his attempt to integrate the often separated dogmatic loci of "Person" and "Work" in christology: the Incarnate person who is Christ comes to existence through the work of the cross. As we have noted before, there is an illuminating parallel to Karl Barth's effort to reframe christology according to the narrative pattern of Christ's saving work. In answer to the question, in what sense is Christ's death "the goal of his existence and therefore the new beginning of ours"? Barth writes:

> This is all true of his death because it is the clear and complete and consistent fulfilment of his human abasement, and therefore the human complement and repetition of the self-humiliation, the condescension, in which God himself became one with us in his Son. . . . The cross was and is the crown of the life of the man Jesus because it came about conclusively in his crucifixion that he genuinely took to himself the situation of man as it is in the judgment of God and therefore in truth, making it God's in his person.[3]

Note here Barth's emphasis that it is in the crucifixion that Jesus most completely enters and embraces the deepest reaches of human existence, and reciprocally, these human depths become (to use the classical term) the *idiomata* of the Son, so that he can be said to become incarnate even in these depths.

Von Balthasar, however, has the advantage over Barth, for von Balthasar is able to recruit the believer's participation in Christ, especially in his suffering, as witness to the mysterious events of Christ's dying and presence among the dead. Here above all the christological-mystical analogies come into their own as material for elucidating the doctrine of the Incarnation.

PARTICIPATION IN CHRIST'S SUFFERING

We know that for von Balthasar the progression of self-abandon and its active form as obedience comes to term only with the ultimacy of a willingness to give over one's life itself. So when von Balthasar considers this unconditional availability in the whole range of its historical expression, he finds as its deepest common core an act of sharing in Christ's dying. Whether it has been called *apatheia, abandon*, or *indiferencia*, von Balthasar believes the phenomenon has been in large measure a participation in Jesus' own ultimate act of self-surrender. This death has thus found expression in the "'dark night' of John of the Cross, in the 'death of not being able to die' of Teresa of Jesus, in the *disponibilité* of Thérèse of the Child Jesus . . . in the love without a why of Meister Eckhart," and so on.[4]

Von Balthasar holds that no mystical itinerary of ever more complete self-transcendence is necessarily going to lead the believer into a glimpse of the beatific vision; on the other hand, if this same mystical impulse is caught up in the flame of Christ's passion, and thereby converted and stretched beyond the limits of its own ideals, then it may indeed enter into a certain experience of God, by sharing in the archetypal experience of Christ crucified.[5] It is this sharing in Christ's experience that makes the "dark night" genuinely Christian and a genuine exposure to the incomprehensible God.

Von Balthasar holds that the possibility of sharing in Christ's passion is entirely in the hands of the risen Christ, who by the power of the Spirit shares with each person the form of the passion that is most appropriate for her or him. This may be a simple experience of compunction and repentance, or it may "reach the point of an extreme powerlessness, an experience of inner darkness, abandonment and reprobation."[6] Von Balthasar allows that there is a general sharing in Christ's cross by virtue of baptism, but he suggests that the Spirit "initiates Christians throughout the centuries," sometimes "through special charisms, into the inexpressible depths of the Cross and the

Descent into Hell."[7] Indeed for von Balthasar the one true charter and justification of Christian mysticism lies in the fact that Jesus' own mission leads him beyond the bounds of self and into God.

Von Balthasar means this, as we saw in earlier chapters, in two respects. First, it is so in the sense that the Word which Jesus has to speak is beyond human utterance and so only "breaks through in the naked dying cry."[8] And second, Jesus' obedience to this same mission takes him into a fatal solidarity with alienated humanity—an existence at the mortal extremity of human life. So von Balthasar sees two corresponding strands in Christian mysticism emerging *together* from Christ's passion: an apophaticism of silence before the unutterable presence of God *and* an abandonment of spiritual desolation in the absence of God.

> All Christian mysticism of the "bright darkness," of the failure of words before the majesty of God, of falling silent after everything that can be said in Church teaching—all this mysticism of the "abyss" and the "desert of God" is seen inevitably as true mysticism of the cross, as mysticism of a sharing in the helplessness of the Word of God. Only as seen in this way can mysticism have a place in the Church.[9]

What von Balthasar wants to rule out here is a sundering of either apophaticism or desolation from its christological context. He especially wants to avoid a complete subsuming of these Christian mystical states within "a Neo-platonic schema of ascent."[10] In fact he argues that the insights of saints and mystics have not been properly valued by systematic theology (as material for a theology of the passion) partly because this mysticism of the cross "was taken captive by anthropocentric schemata of ascent and purification."[11]

Nevertheless von Balthasar is concerned to profile what he calls "an uninterrupted charismatic re-interpretation of the Cross . . . [which] runs through the centuries of the Church's life."[12] In his view this participation in the cross and death of Christ took a number of quite different but recognizably related forms.

> In the East, experiences of the Cross are closely connected with the idea of struggle against demons . . . whereas in the West, such experiences . . . are conjoined with, on the one hand, the Neo-platonic and Areopagitic comprehension of the "radiant darkness" of the unknown God, and, on the other hand, with the idea of the soul's purification through the "tests" of God-abandonment.[13]

Von Balthasar further specifies this history by arguing that the Dionysian apophaticism (which he claims "is certainly not a theology of the Passion in the proper sense")[14] has mingled with other mystical streams. Wherever this occurs, he believes, it tends to mitigate the capacity of other mystical strands to lead theology into a deeper understanding of Christ's passion and death. What bothers von Balthasar about itineraries of apophatic ascent is that, unless they are reinterpreted in terms of a christomorphic *descent*, they focus attention more immediately on the soul's progress than on the soul's participation in Christ or Christ's own experience of suffering. In terms of historical developments, von Balthasar attributes to the Rhenish mystics a full-blown "relation between the mystical experiences of God-abandonment and the cry from the Cross."[15] He places the "classic period in the theology of the Passion" in the era 1300 to 1700, with Tauler being seen as "the father of a theology of the Cross which (through Surius) spread out in a broad fan, exercising a determining influence on all the European countries as well as the great Orders."[16]

Von Balthasar, then, is convinced that in the christomorphic dark nights of certain saints and mystics one can discern vital clues and hints to the interior reality of Christ's suffering and death. Indeed it is precisely here, in this christological state which is most hidden, that the witness of mystical theology becomes especially important to von Balthasar. Yet he is equally certain that even the most profound gifts of participation in Christ's passion "are at best approaches, distant allusions to the inaccessible mystery of the Cross—so unique is the Son of God, so unique is his abandonment by the Father."[17]

Von Balthasar depicts this limitation with reference to Mark's story of Jesus' agony in Gethsemane. With the disciples removed from Jesus by distance and sleep, and even his relationship with the Father sustained now "only by way of the chalice which he would, if possible, have removed from him," Jesus enters an "aloneness" whose suffering "seems to cut off all access to its own inwardness: at the most a silent 'assisting', from a distance, is all that is possible."[18] One senses that for von Balthasar this isolation of Christ is both necessarily the case (Jesus goes on loving *alone*, for the sinful world has long since abandoned him in his fidelity to God), and at the same time a grievous loss to the world, to be so cut off from the most momentous, heartbreaking, earthshaking moments in Jesus' life. What we have left in the gospels affords "barely a glimpse of the inner drama. And yet, for Christian faith, in this inner space all the world's salvation lies enclosed. Is there no kind of access to it?"[19] For von Balthasar any such approach could only be found within a biblical and ecclesial existence, and must "safeguard that distance which protects the uniqueness of the Passion of the Redeemer from invasion."[20]

One notices here how von Balthasar balances on a knife edge with respect to Christ's relationship to believers. He clearly wants to avoid the kind of totalistic reading of Christ's suffering which he believes (in Barth's case, for example) cuts Jesus off too much from any participation by his followers, but neither does he want to trespass on that fundamental "aloneness" of Christ which he sees as being the very ground of salvation—that Christ went in fidelity where all others had gone only in bitterness.

HISTORICAL RESOURCES

We can now consider Christian apophaticism and experiences of the dark night the other way round, so to speak—not in their aspect of coming from the passion but of leading theology back into it. And so we turn to von Balthasar's consideration of these mystical states, to see how he attempts to discern in them the material for a theology of the passion.

He begins by facing one problem head-on: the major strand of the mystical tradition, which he takes to be overladen with a Platonic schemata, must be reinterpreted, reintegrated within the structure of Christ's destiny. Many of the spiritual writers of the East and Augustine in the West tended to regard the revelation given in Christ "mainly as the freely-given fulfilment of the fundamental longing placed in the soul by the Creator, and now purified from the dross of original sin."[21] This means that for them the Platonic scheme of ascent through ever less material stages to a pure "naked" vision of the superessential deity becomes a key interpretive structure for contemplation. The problem is that this approach begins to work against the humanity of Christ, the great gift to humankind of a word that humanity could at last understand and cherish. But how is this humanity, so corporeal, to be reconciled "with the Platonic conception of ascent from the corporeal"?

Von Balthasar's answer involves what we might call an ingenious recontextualizing of the Platonic impulse in Christian mysticism. His actual route to this achievement is beset by digressions and somewhat peripheral admonitions. We may, however, sketch it as follows. First, he says, one has to be willing to confess that the chief end of God's love in Christ, of "God's self-giving to the point of self-emptying (*kenosis*), is not to assist our natural religious *eros* to reach its goal." The Incarnation is not, therefore, simply a "provisional arrangement . . . something which cancels itself out and is terminated on the return of Christ to the Father."[22]

Second, therefore, the mystical itinerary, whatever its course, can never really part company with the full human reality of Jesus. Contemplation could profitably begin by dwelling upon the necessity of God's self-humbling in order to speak with humankind in a language which, given humanity's sinful turning away from God, it still hears and understands. But it would be fatal thereafter to look down on this "speech" (which is Christ's humanity) as mere condescension: "We must not turn away impatiently from the incarnate truth of the Gospel to a spiritual truth we imagine to underlie it."[23] Rather one must see that the very humility of the Word, speaking in human suffering, *is* a direct expression of the sought-after divine truth.

> The mistake of the great Alexandrians and their followers was . . . [that they] regarded sense as a prison and a disguise, *rather than a means of revealing the spiritual*. . . . Their philosophy could not rightly express the Biblical dialectic, for God's "self-emptying," his "becoming poor," is a direct image of his fulness and richness and the prodigality of his love; the spiritual is made known to us through its covering, and is brought close to us through its sensible expression.[24]

This insight—that the poverty of Christ is the revelation of the divine abundance—is the key which von Balthasar uses to unlock his christological recontextualizing of the Platonic ascent.

First one recognizes that the suffering and death of Christ are not just a condescension which in fact obscures God's nature, but rather that Christ's passion is the human historical form of the self-giving prodigality of God's love. Then it becomes possible to recognize the real aim of the Platonic ascent as finding its truest expression precisely in the *descent* of Christ into death and hell. By practicing the loving humility of Christ, the contemplative begins to learn the secret of this self-humbling, namely, that it is filled with the hidden presence of

God. And therefore by sharing in Christ's suffering and death one achieves, though with a painful hiddenness to be sure, the very intimacy with the divine that was sought for in the Platonic scheme of ascent. The purification and stripping of the senses for the contemplation of God, which had been sought in a self-transcending move away from corporeality, is really accomplished, says von Balthasar, in the night of Christ's suffering. And in the resurrection which awaits, one finds that "the ultimate, unattainable aim of Platonism is fulfilled unexpectedly and superabundantly."

> For in Christ's passion the human senses and spirit were engulfed in the night which extinguished all awareness of the divine, the night in which he was abandoned by the Father, when the human faculties were lost in the void and, deprived of their natural food, succumbed. This did not occur in the realm of philosophy but in the freedom of love taking on itself the consequences of sin. The truth of the negative theology can be seen in the cross which carried it to its furthest limit. . . . In that darkness [of hell] he [Christ] liberated the senses and the faculties subject to sin and enabled them to apprehend God in a manner befitting their redeemed state.[25]

The apprehension of God, which von Balthasar believes neo-Platonic itineraries seek in a transcendence of the bodily senses and imagination, is in fact truly achieved in a liberation of the senses and heart from sin. The apophatic ascent is given a new home by von Balthasar in mystical participation in the suffering descent of Christ.[26] Von Balthasar suggests that this has always been true of the church's greatest saints and mystics. For whenever they speak of the soul dying to all sensible forms "in order to attain the divine reality that transcends all forms, that too is to follow the Son."

> *For if the Son ceases to be a subject of contemplation, it is only to incorporate the contemplative more fully in Christ's own inward state* and allow him an active participation in Christ's death and resurrection. Indeed, the mystical night of the senses and the spirit, however solitary the person experiencing them, is always something that bears on the Church, something deeply embedded in the order of the Incarnation. Theology can demonstrate the fact, whereas the mystics, describing their experience of the night, necessarily dwell on the feeling of being alone; that is why they do not always avoid the temptation of using the categories of Platonism to describe their experiences.[27]

What seems like a leaving behind of Christ's humanity in apophatic mysticism may in fact be a participation in Christ which is so deep it disallows any awareness of him as a discrete other: Christ is not absent; he has become the embracing locus of the contemplative's existence. In the end, the neo-Platonic stream in the Christian mystical tradition, which at first von Balthasar seemed to oppose so strongly, is reinterpreted by him as one of the most powerful forms of sharing in Christ's passion.[28]

Von Balthasar takes up many of these themes in his early work on Gregory of Nyssa. He argues that one of the most important and innovative impulses in Gregory's work is his reflection on the divine infinity. Gregory had shown that for God to be without limits was not an imperfection, as a standard opinion in Hellenistic philosophy had it. Moreover, Gregory was able to translate his concept of divine being into a new understanding of the spiritual journey which, in von Balthasar's view, was crucial for the development of Christian mysticism. Most simply put, Gregory argued that if God is infinite then the goal of the spiritual life can hardly be a perfect and fixed *stasis* but rather is an ever-moving, ever-thirsting, ever-delighted but never satiated emigration into the divine infinity.

When this comes to expression in the mystical life it lends a special cast to a number of themes which are central to the tradition. Chief among these will be the dark but divine night. Von Balthasar highlights in Gregory this theme of a darkness and searching which is also the soul's light and fulfillment.

> This night is faith, in which is achieved all knowledge and which alone "re-connects and joins together the searching spirit and the ungraspable [divine] nature . . . and there is no other way to approach God" [*Contra Eunomius* 12; II, 941B]. . . . "The vision of his face *is* the journey toward him without end" [*In Cant.* 12; I, 1025D].[29]

Von Balthasar comments on Gregory: "The desire itself is the joy, and the search itself is the vision."[30] What is significant for our purposes is that von Balthasar sees here a notion of approach to God by way of suffering, of lack, of endless yearning. Already we can sense his direction: the characteristics of the apophatic journey, particularly its ascent to a transcendental vision of God, are seen in terms of a suffering of insatiable desire or thirst—with a potential for further, more cruciform darkenings—and, conversely, this same suffering darkness of the unrealizable search for God is seen to be the very joy and vision sought for in the apophatic ascent.

It is not surprising, then, when von Balthasar goes on to suggest that the knowledge of God in Gregory comes not just by way of a continual transcendence but also by a privation, a "self-negation of understanding." In order for the understanding to grasp the ungraspable it "must deny, renounce itself."[31] We are clearly moving here in the direction of that ultimate death and resurrection of the human faculties which takes place only in union with Christ. Von Balthasar remarks on Gregory's view that God is not only eternally desired by the soul but that God is that beauty which, because of its unattainability, is the despair of the soul:

> This despair is the only adequate expression of the total negation of the understanding which is at the same time its supreme act: for it is precisely in accepting this despair that the soul "receives the chosen dart of God in herself, in the mortal place of her heart" [*In Cant.* 12; I, 1037C].[32]

Again we note the transposition von Balthasar sees: the despair and the negation which must characterize the soul's night are also the supreme act and accomplishment of the soul, by which it readies itself to receive the burning arrow of the divine love. This mortal wounding of the soul is in fact its most intimate encounter with the divine presence. What von Balthasar is doing with such themes as these is to transfuse the language of mystical ascent and darkness with the even more impenetrable night of Christ's suffering and death. And in doing so he is beginning to reveal an unexpected path into the interior reality of Christ's passion. The question is already in the air for von Balthasar: on the analogy of the mystical dark night, could Christ's terrible suffering, secretly and all unknown to him, be the moment when he is engulfed in the divine love? This is one of the possibilities toward which, I believe, von Balthasar's study of the mystical tradition is carrying him. He himself concludes this section of his work on Gregory with a quotation from Fichte: "It is not death which kills, but the life which is more alive."[33] It is not just the death of sin which grips Christ in his passion, but the ever-greater life of God taking hold of creation.

Moving on to von Balthasar's sustained treatment of this theme in John of the Cross, we can see many of the same impulses now intensified. We note especially the extensive attention von Balthasar pays to the relationship between dark night and paschal mystery in John. What we saw as hints and suggestions in Gregory become for von Balthasar crucially explicit interpretations of the dark night as descent into hell and resurrection. Such material becomes his own "secret stair," by which he will grope his way through the darkness and isolation of Jesus' passion towards a new theological understanding of his suffering and death.

Von Balthasar believes that the "anthropocentric schemata of ascent and purification," which he sees as having sometimes taken mysticism of the passion "captive," is undeniably "still dominant in the doctor of the Church John of the Cross himself."[34] But with John, von Balthasar is keen to have us recognize, this schemata is not allowed to obscure the christomorphic paschal reality which is at work. The dark night is unmistakably a descent into hell for John. He realizes, says von Balthasar, that any real knowledge of God requires not so much a transcendental and ontological ascent from finite being to infinite Being as it does an experience of the broken relationship between the sinner and the holy God. "[The mystic] must enter the night of Hell, for only in the absolute distinction between the sinful creature and the absolute God in his total purity can the divine in its truth be perceived."[35] Because of the incomprehensible disparity in love between the creature and God, the more profoundly the soul experiences God the more it experiences its own death and what it can only assume is the final withdrawal of God's presence.

> Placed before the naked reality of the Absolute, which presents itself to her in the mode of privation and dispossession, the soul endures an "infinite death" in her languishing and suffering . . . "for in truth the soul experiences the sorrows of Hell, all of which reflect the feeling of God's absence, of being chastised and rejected by him" [*Night* ii, 6, 2-3].[36]

Von Balthasar highlights the soul's sense of the permanent absence of God and the consequent loss of all hope. All this must happen in order for the truth of the relationship between the creature and God to become known to the soul.

But von Balthasar is equally concerned to display the dialectical quality of John's understanding: the very reason for the extremity of the soul's night and suffering is the superabundant light of the divine presence. There is always this "double emphasis of genuine darkness for the finite subject and supereminent brightness in the infinite God-head."[37] Because God is not an object nor the divine nature in any way perceptible by the senses, humankind normally only perceives the divine presence as it "lights up" lesser beings and objects; von Balthasar notes that John at least five times employs the well-known image of the beam of light which is in itself only perceptible as it shines upon specks of dust in its way. But when the soul is present to God without any mediation whatsoever, then the soul can sense literally nothing. The divine light in effect "blinds" the soul because of its supereminent brightness. When, therefore, the human light of faith "no longer strikes against anything, and because God himself is not an object, God can be experienced by the soul only as a dark night."[38]

For von Balthasar ultimate fidelity to God, complete abandon to God, leads the human being into an extremity in which God's presence is finally experienced as a terrible void, a mortal absence in which the soul feels forsaken by God and knows itself only as an utter hollowness and extreme thirst which God alone can assuage. And here indeed are the very building blocks of von Balthasar's interpretation of the crucifixion.

He describes John's night as "privation, annihilation, crucifixion." And he also points to a profoundly paschal *transitus* hidden in this night, for though "the night is subjectively death . . . objectively it is already resurrection."[39] Out of radical deprivation emerges a humanity capable of knowing God as more than the death of its own sinfulness, and therefore a humanity capable of joy in God's presence. "All the time John stresses that God's light shines unchangingly and constantly, that it is only the unpurified state of those who approach that makes them experience it as darkness and purgatorial torment."[40] In terms of the "developmental" aspect of the Incarnation which I have been following in von Balthasar, an important theme can be noted here. I have argued that in taking account of the historical dynamic of Jesus' life, von Balthasar understands him as becoming more himself, more complete as a human being, the more he enters into the communal plight of his people.

And here in von Balthasar's treatment of John of the Cross, we see the effect this is likely to have: for while the fulfillment of Jesus' humanity takes place through his increasing solidarity with sinners, he also and necessarily enters into their very "unpurified state" which must render his experience of God increasingly dark and "purgatorial." Hence the paradox I have alluded to before, that in von Balthasar the obedience of Christ which draws from him ever more love for God and neighbor, at the same time leaves him all the more isolated and forsaken by God and neighbor. Drawing on John, von Balthasar is suggesting that the dereliction and death which Jesus suffers is actually the form which God's presence must necessarily take *in the experience of the sinner.*

Jesus surrenders himself to God and fulfills his mission—his personal existence—and thereby (because of the communal shape of the mission) he is ever more deeply implicated in humankind's sin and separation from God. But the resultant darkness and abandonment that Jesus meets with is only the transposition of his relationship with the Father into the terms of the sinner's encounter with the righteous God. From his standpoint of complete solidarity with his people, Jesus can know the perfectly loving Father only as an angry silence. Christ's relationship with the Father is reduced to a cold, implacable decree, a cup from which he would rather not drink. Von Balthasar carefully selects the following quotation from John to the same effect: "'Union with God does not consist in recreations, experiences or spiritual feelings, but in the one and only living, sensory and spiritual, exterior and interior, death of the Cross'" (*Ascent* ii, 7, 8-11).[41]

Perhaps unexpectedly, it is the much "simpler" Little Way of Thérèse (rather than the grand synthesis of John of the Cross) which seems to provide more material for von Balthasar's reflections on Jesus in hell. When her family was on a pilgrimage to Lourdes in 1890, Thérèse remarked briskly to her sister, "I have no wish to go to Lourdes to have ecstasies. I prefer the monotony of sacrifice."[42] Von Balthasar contends that Thérèse's increasing antipathy to any form of mystical experience quite distinguishes her from her great forebears John and Teresa—not, of course, in their explicit teaching (which is equally against any reliance upon "experience"), but in the actual effect of all their commentary on mystical experience:

> For whether they admit it or not, the Spaniards' whole attitude is an invitation to enter the world of mysticism, which they range over and map out with such assurance that one eventually feels as if Christian perfection is impossible without mystical experience.[43]

Thérèse specifically rejects all this; her calling is precisely to go on loving God *without* any experiential signs to confirm her progress. It is her chosen "monotony of sacrifice" that interests von Balthasar because, I believe, he senses in it a descent into a gray half-light which no longer has boundaries, even negative ones, but is only an increasingly amorphous, chaotic nothingness. Here even the stark drama of John's dark night and divine light is left behind for something less comprehensible; the salvific struggle itself seems to fade into meaninglessness where there is no longer light nor dark, nor signs of any kind.

In fact, von Balthasar calls Thérèse's version of night "something new in the history of mysticism and of tremendous significance."

> Every means of measurement is abandoned and the measure rests with God alone. Nor is this just an episode, a dark but temporary night of the senses or the spirit; it is lasting, unto the end. . . . [Thérèse] goes on striding endlessly in the darkness, below the earth, without bearings. Instead of the satisfaction of climbing higher, she puts one foot in front of the other along a road whose direction God alone knows.[44]

This humanly directionless, "subterranean" stepping into the dimness is a clue, von Balthasar feels, to the utter lostness of Christ's experience in hell.

In chapter 4 on self-surrender, we saw von Balthasar's image of the "two Thérèses": a merely provisional Thérèse who disappears more and more into the shadowy half-light by virtue of her obedience, and a fulfilled, completely actualized Thérèse who begins to emerge into the light as a result of the disappearing of the other. But von Balthasar sets this event entirely within a paschal context. Thérèse's obedience is an image of Christ's, who in all his acts and suffering "withdraws" to let the Father's mission become manifest in and through himself: "Each withdrawal takes him towards death, each manifestation to the *Parousia.*"[45] In commiting herself to this pattern, von Balthasar believes that Thérèse passes into that ultimate nonexperience which is the hiatus between Good Friday and Easter.

> For the Carmelite Cross represents that pause between suffering and resurrection during which the old, this-worldly self is dead, whilst the new self has not yet been reborn into the divine, eternal form of its subjectivity. Life in the Order—a "life of death", as Thérèse describes it—inserts itself into this pause and its deep silence, welding a great link between earthly and heavenly existence, between suffering and resurrection.[46]

The incarnational undertones are highly significant in this passage. Hell, or the "pause" between suffering and resurrection, is that state in which the old self, the self which has been given away in self-surrender and obedience, finds nothing left of the relations of love or service which used to identify the self—the aspirations, the sense of mission, the antagonism toward sin have all been surrendered and taken away. And yet the new, fulfilled existence, though it may have been tasted, has yet to be revealed. This is the ultimate moment of testing for the event of Incarnation: is Jesus' humanity lost forever in hell, or could the acts of self-surrender and obedience have "seeded" his provisional humanity with an identity and a self which might be sustained?

Von Balthasar describes this state of hell in the case of Thérèse:

> Slowly she ceases to recognize her true self; she no longer knows who she is. Is she indeed that ideal which she tries to nourish with all the strength of her mortification and sacrifice? and which still refuses to exist in reality? Or is she really the self that has been supplying the nourishment, the self that she has given away so that it no longer belongs to her? Whilst the one has passed away, the other has not come into being. Everything concerning her own self seems chaotic, cast into a world of dreams and shadows.[47]

Von Balthasar is pointing directly to the agony of the human self not knowing itself anymore, not trusting its self-understanding any longer because all the grounds for this have been taken away. We noted earlier how important this was in von Balthasar's reading of the Son of Man sayings: Jesus can only leave in the Father's hands the ultimate significance of his work. For Thérèse, this comes about through obedience to the Carmelite rule, but for Jesus it happens because obedience to his mission has led him into total identity with the increasingly nullified existence of sinners. Nothing is left to the self by which to recognize itself anymore, so cloaked has it become in the nonbeing of sin. In such a state not even a cry to the Father avails: "The Father no longer knows you. You have been eaten up by the leprosy of all creation: how should he still recognize your face?"[48]

What von Balthasar is drawing from his reading of Thérèse is a way of interpreting the hidden "events" of Holy Saturday by means of what is openly displayed on Good Friday and Easter. He has cast the Incarnation in terms of a growing reciprocal actualization in time of Jesus' humanity and of the Word: on the cross this movement seems to be shattered, for the human selfhood that has consistently given itself away has finally come to its mortal limit; and only in the resurrection does the full realization of Jesus come to term. As much as Thérèse suggests what must go on in the dreadful hiatus between these two states, she cannot mirror the depths to which the loss of self must be experienced by Christ. For Thérèse it is always the "monotony of sacrifice," i.e., she *knows* herself to be fulfilling herself through her self-abandon to God. But because of his total identification with sinners, Jesus comes to know this no longer.

> The complete night involves complete solidarity with the sinners and the damned; it means identifying oneself with their lot and sharing their fate utterly. But how could Thérèse, knowing herself to be a saint, abandon herself unconditionally to the community of sinners? It would have meant destroying her very self and her mission.[49]

Thérèse points at what must be going on in hell, this unendurable transition, but von Balthasar's reading of Christ's mission suggests that, for Jesus, such a state would mean more than Thérèse could know, a complete loss of any sense or assurance that what he is doing is of any value to God, or even recognizable to God as an act of self-giving love. Hell is that chaotic, directionless, measureless absence of light or darkness, in which knowledge of one's reality, one's identity, and one's accomplishment has apparently been lost.

DEATH AND HELL AS CHRISTOLOGICAL STATES

Von Balthasar's mystical sources for our present theme have already led us to considerable reflection on their implications for his christology. Bearing those approaches in mind, we can now turn directly to the role of Jesus' death and presence in hell in von Balthasar's treatment of the ongoing event of Incarnation.

As much as von Balthasar wants to show that the whole incarnate presence of the Word is oriented toward redemption, he also wishes to avoid a reading of Christ's life in which everything else is simply a long dress rehearsal for Golgotha. Rather powerfully, von Balthasar argues against such a view not only because it would undermine the reality of Jesus' actual ministry and teaching, but also because it would be fatally untrue to the fully human experience of God which

Jesus underwent. A truly human life would always be "a mixture of joy and suffering . . . carried by faith, love, and hope."

> The deepest experience of abandonment by God, which is to be vi-
> cariously real in the Passion, presupposes an equally deep experience
> of being united to God and of life derived from the Father—an expe-
> rience that the Son must have had, not only in Heaven, but also as a
> man, even if this does not mean that his spirit must already enjoy a
> perpetual *visio beatifica*. Only one who has known the genuine inti-
> macy of love, can be genuinely abandoned (not merely lonely).[50]

As we saw with self-surrender and obedience, von Balthasar envisions all the states of Christ's existence as primarily states of love. These take on qualities of darkness and suffering as Jesus' solidarity with sinners progresses to its ultimate depth in hell. But von Balthasar, while clearly steering away from scholastic propositions on Jesus' beatific vision, does want to ground the pain and loss of the passion precisely in Jesus' human *relationship* with the Father. It is this very "genuine intimacy of love" which, when it seems to be sundered, leaves behind the particular desolation Jesus experiences. The suffering of the cross is never simply a kind of mechanically adopted posture which Christ's redeeming work forces him to assume; for von Balthasar, the suffering is itself only the imprint of the deep love for God and neighbor which marks Jesus' soul and leaves such a painful absence when it is withdrawn. Describing this suffering of the withdrawal of love, von Balthasar writes of Christ's heart: "It is a heart like ours, a human heart, which itself thirsts for the return of love. A heart like other hearts, full of warm folly, full of imprudent hope: full of obstinacy. A heart that pines away when it is not loved."[51] This brings out well a hallmark of von Balthasar's passiology, that the re-demptive suffering of Jesus is far from being simply a penal sentence enforced on him from without; at its heart it is the deep interior pain which Christ, in his great love for his people and for God, experiences when this love is increasingly experienced as rejected.[52]

In von Balthasar's reading, Jesus does not suddenly arrive at the cross unexpectedly. There have been challenges, testings, confronta-tions during the whole course of his ministry, and these von Balthasar interprets as necessary stages of growth in that obedience which will, finally, be made perfect on the cross. The first of these is of course the temptation in the wilderness. This von Balthasar sees as the "spiritual-existential" form of that solidarity with Israel which was sacramentally marked in his baptism. This recapitulating of Israel's experience in the wilderness "is not an isolated act of Jesus, but the shouldering of a concrete situation."[53] Each act of Jesus' obedience takes him farther into the situation of the people and so, ultimately, closer to the cross.

In what is undoubtedly one of his more original achievements, von Balthasar weaves together three christological strands: Christ's solidarity with sinners, his approaching "hour," and his ever-fuller actualization of his being. Von Balthasar notes a number of different groupings of people to whom Jesus commits himself: sinners, the little ones, children, the poor, and "finally, he takes the side of those who are persecuted, cast out, belittled, those who are robbed of their good name."[54] But von Balthasar sees this solidarity as exacting a terrible cost for Jesus:

> This incarnation of God's solidarity with the poor (in every form) has, however, a catastrophic logic: if he takes this seriously, it will bring him to the cross—not most deeply for the external reason that he has appropriated to himself an authority that does not belong to him, but for an internal reason, because he now must really "be reckoned among those who have broken the law" (Lk 22.37).[55]

This theme is sometimes overlooked in criticism of von Balthasar's soteriology, as if he envisioned Jesus as suffering an artificially or forensically applied divine judgment.[56] In fact the suffering which Jesus undergoes is only the outcome of his solidarity with sinners all along. His commitment to them causes him to share, to the ultimate degree, their experience of rejection by others and the judgment of God which falls upon their sin. The substitutionary or representational force of Jesus' death derives from his desire to embrace, "voluntarily and lovingly, all that which in his brothers is opposed to God."[57] Here, then, is the linking of Jesus' solidarity and his suffering in terms of the sinful existence that Christ enters.

But von Balthasar does not see Christ placing himself among sinners solely in order to share their fate. He has taken up their cause, and would lead them. As Jesus places himself on the side of the poor "in order to lead them along an unmarked path into the kingdom of God," he realizes that this coming kingdom is tied to his own destiny. "The future of God, into which Jesus leads the poor and the sinners,

Healing Prayer at Bedtime

Jesus, through the power of the Holy Spirit, go back into my memory as I sleep. Every hurt that has ever been done to me — heal that hurt: Every hurt that I have caused to another person — heal that hurt. All the relationships that have been damaged in my whole life that I'm not aware of — heal those relationships.

But Lord, if there is anything that I need to do — if I need to go to a person because he is still suffering from my hand, bring to my awareness that person.

I choose to forgive, and I ask to be forgiven. Remove whatever bitterness may be in my heart, Lord, and fill the empty spaces with your love.

Thank you, Jesus: Amen.

Phyllis Devereux

Franciscan Mission Associates
P.O. Box 598
Mount Vernon, N.Y. 10551-0598

GRAFICHE FAVIA · BARI
PRINTED IN ITALY

LAMB OF GOD

must finally lie in himself. And what other absolute future has a man to offer than his own death."[58]

Von Balthasar is illuminating the patterns in Christ's life which point to his cross. First, there was the fact of his existence among those who are alienated, which I noted in the paragraph above. But, second, there is the fact that the future toward which he would bring his people must, since it is God's future, lie somehow beyond the limits of his own life. Von Balthasar terms this an "exorbitant demand" (*Überforderung*), a fundamental disproportion between the capacity of Jesus' human life and the divine mission he desires to fulfill. This "over-tasking" leads him to an extremity, the cross, but equally it leads him to an unanticipated prodigality of human existence and love. It calls forth from his provisional existence the fullness of a humanity which is in von Balthasar's view the very archetype of all humanity. And this calling-forth *is* in fact the drawing near and incarnation of the Word.

As Jesus carries out his mission he realizes that he is headed for some kind of hiatus, his "hour," beyond which only the Father knows what may be. This is the hour when his existence will have gone beyond its own limits in ways Jesus does attempt to know:

> [It is] the hour when he will no longer be in charge of his mission, for it will have taken charge of him at a level where human power no longer avails. He has a human horror of this hiatus but resolutely transcends it by committing himself to his Father.[59]

This "hiatus," which is Jesus' death, is a crucial and indeed constitutive state in the developing mystery of the Incarnation. Von Balthasar maintains that the universality of Christ's mission, the infinity of the Word he must speak, requires a humanity which is brought by death itself to a new development of human existence.[60] The mission and the self of Christ both come into ever-new dimensions of actualization during the course of his ministry. Yet the highest level of fulfillment comes about when Jesus hands everything over to the Father. The beyond-human-limits momentum of Jesus' mission does bring him to the "end" of human life, his death, but because Christ approaches this by entirely entrusting the meaning of his work to the Father, his self-offering is taken up into a new and unanticipated human status.

While von Balthasar certainly does emphasize that "the full universality of [Christ's] task would be unattainable without his total self-abandonment in Passion and death,"[61] as we have just noted he equally wishes to suggest that this is not a loss of Christ's humanity but its liberation into a new realm of activity.

> The Passion does not mean that the man, Christ, was more and more emptied and reduced to nothingness so as to make place, increasingly, for God. It means, primarily, that those human liabilities, which men fear, abhor, and keep silent about, are seen in their true value; that we can still achieve something when our positive and active powers fail.[62]

Von Balthasar is proposing that in the economy of God's plan the self-surrendered state, indeed even the state of dying and death, may be utilized by God in an incomprehensibly powerful way. Jesus' humanity does not have to be shuffled off the stage so that, at last, his divinity can get on with the show. Nothing could be farther from von Balthasar's view. Rather it is the suffering humanity, in its utmost extremity and its final surrendered state which, in God's hands, becomes the agent of redemption. Such a notion would certainly be familiar and appealing to von Balthasar from his reading of John of the Cross, who also emphasizes the theme.[63] Von Balthasar, like John, points to the secret and unknown work accomplished in the suffering aridity of the contemplative's surrendered soul; in a far greater and more universal way, he argues, Christ's "super-action" is accomplished in his final (and mortal) state of obedience and self-surrender.

What we have seen in von Balthasar is a reading of Christ's passion and death which brings to the fore Jesus' participation in the deepest night of human separation from God. It is a night which has imprinted upon it Christ's willing seeking after the poor, the sinners, the simple. It is a night therefore in which Jesus is, for *their* sake, led to the very last degree beyond himself. There he enters a state of human existence that is completely shrouded and hidden by sin but is nonetheless the matrix of a new stage in the unfolding of human reality. In one of his most important and programmatic statements, von Balthasar writes:

> The Incarnation takes place in the nature of the old Adam, which is to be transformed (*übergeführt*) by the entire Christ-event into what, henceforth, will be the Christ-principle operating in history. What is created is not a new human being; the same nature that belongs to the old Adam is now, through the drama of the life, death and Resurrection of Jesus, carried over (*übergeführt*) into the state of the new Adam.[64]

What is so significant here is the stress von Balthasar places on the Incarnation as humanity-creating event, a kind of process which takes place precisely "*through* the drama of the life, death and Resurrection of Jesus." As a christological state, Jesus' passion and death brings the Incarnation to an inexplicable new stage in which Jesus' mortal embrace of humankind leads to the re-creation of human nature. Speaking of the concrete historical events of Christ's life and death, von Balthasar says:

> It is only in this process that the Incarnation of the Word of God is really carried out; only thus is God's promise fulfilled. For only on the Cross will all the aspects and consequences of the old nature be resolutely adopted and suffered.[65]

In spiritual and historical terms, the Incarnation for von Balthasar is a drama, a struggle, in which the humanity of Jesus is, as it were, accomplished, not only in the day-to-day acts of self-surrender and obedience, but ultimately in that final embrace of the human situation and its handing over to God which is Christ's death. As von Balthasar suggests, only in this way can the last possible extent of human alienation from God be "adopted," "suffered," and opened up toward its re-creation. Throughout his life, says von Balthasar, Jesus

> experiences the mounting disproportion between the powers of man and the demands of God: the basic Christian experience of being asked for *more* than is possible, as he shows us in the Garden of Olives. The measure of man had been shrunk by the sinner, and the Lord had to wrench it violently open again in the extreme of suffering; in the racking of his limbs on the Cross, to which corresponds a yet deeper straining apart of all the powers of his soul.[66]

This is the drama of the Incarnation hinted at in Thérèse's dreadful hiatus between the death of the old self and the birth of the new. It is the extension of human existence beyond the sin-crippled limits that were thought to be the norm, opening the human spirit to a new possibility of loving communion and common activity with God.

There is, however, a further stage to this process, the mysterious being of Christ in hell. In an introduction to his spiritual colleague, the Swiss physician and visionary Adrienne von Speyr, von Balthasar gives a brief but potent precis of her annual Triduum experiences of Christ in hell. Of these and her mystical sharing in Christ's sufferings on the cross, he writes: "[they are] what I consider to be the greatest theologi-

cal gift she received from God and left to the Church."⁶⁷ Beginning in
1941, the year after she met von Balthasar, von Speyr began to experience a sharing or at least a witnessing of Christ's being in hell. This
usually began at about three o'clock on Good Friday afternoon and
continued into early morning on Easter Sunday. Clearly these yearly
experiences, which von Balthasar painstakingly recorded from von
Speyr's dictation and later published, were influential not only in
the structural significance von Balthasar accords to Christ's presence in
hell but also with regard to many of the material details in his interpretation.

For von Speyr, Jesus' being in hell was the fulfillment of his obedience to the Father, the last extent of his mission to be among those
who are lost. In von Speyr's experiences hell is no-where, a boundary-
less state of "sin separated from men." Christ in hell "'walks' through
sin (without leaving a trace, since, in hell and in death, there is neither
time nor direction); and traversing its formlessness he experiences the
second chaos." Hell for Jesus is "the knowledge of having lost God
forever." "It is being engulfed in the chaotic mire of the anti-divine;
the absence of faith, hope and love; the loss as well, therefore, of any
human communication. It is the metamorphosis of thought into a
meaningless prattle of lifeless logic."⁶⁸ Von Balthasar understands von
Speyr's experience as suggesting that hell is a reversion to chaos, a
return via the anti-divine work of sin to what God does *not* choose or
create. He sees in her an understanding of hell which is first and last
christological; it is not interpreted by cosmic considerations, either of
apocatastasis or of eternal judgment, rather, hell is reconceived as an
existence of total alienation from God which, however, has been en-
compassed within the obedient love of Christ.

Von Balthasar is very clear that he wishes to exclude any motifs
that modern thought might find mythological; in interpreting Christ's
being after his death he wishes to rule out any conception of an extension of some human capacities in another place, indeed any notion of
activity altogether.⁶⁹ Fundamentally for von Balthasar, Christ's being
in hell (he prefers not even to speak of a "descent") is a state of his
soul which is the final result of his obedient activity in history, his solidarity with sinners.

> When he takes on this solidarity with sinners, in their most extreme
> condition, Jesus carries the Father's saving will out to the end. It is

an absolute obedience that reaches out beyond life and stands the test precisely in the place where otherwise only coercion and servitude reign.[70]

What is so important to von Balthasar is that Jesus' (non)existence in hell is a covert interruption of hell, for in this form of existence where only "coercion and servitude reign," Christ is present *"due to his own free obedience."*[71] While Christ's soul experiences the form of death of all those whose life he had embraced, this is not the result of an active, triumphant event, but the simple impress left behind on his soul from a lifetime's obedience. It could not be obedience in any normal sense of the word because it must "take place" in a form of existence "where the last trace of God seems lost (in pure sin), together with every other communication (in pure solitariness)."[72] It would seem that von Balthasar posits a sort of momentum in Christ's soul which carries over into the nonactivity of death a sort of silent obedience, an obediential orientation.

But what is this form of solidarity which is, as it were, the "aim" of Christ's being in hell? Von Balthasar refers approvingly to Aquinas's argument: the necessity for Christ's descent into Hades "lies not in some insufficiency of the suffering endured on the Cross but in the fact that Christ has assumed all the *defectus* of sinners."[73] The argument is that in assuming the entirety of sinful human existence, Jesus also shares in the penalty of alienation from God that sin inevitably bears: "As early as the Fathers of the second century, this act of sharing constituted the term and aim of the Incarnation."[74] Von Balthasar is concerned to make clear that this ultimate solidarity has nothing to say about a "combat" or "triumphant victory"—"for precisely that would have abolished the law of solidarity. . . . among the dead there is no communication. Here solidarity means: being solitary like, and with, others."[75]

Perhaps von Balthasar's greatest dependence on Adrienne von Speyr comes here, with this concept of hell as the absence of all possibility of communication, the loss of all the media and defining structures of time, space, and direction. He argues that hell itself is a christological result, a state unknown before Christ had massed together upon himself the sin of the world and experienced it all in its "pure state"— sin in itself, "in the whole formless, chaotic momentum of its reality."[76] In this way von Balthasar attempts to bring out the christological basis for von Speyr's experience of the tracklessness of hell; its chaos is the formlessness of the sin which Christ takes to himself and so separates from all the individuals who initially commit it. Insofar as sin effects the destruction of meaning and hope, of understanding and love, this in its totality is what Christ now experiences, a virtual undoing of creation.

To the extent that Jesus wills to share and take to himself this experience of the sin of all, he secretly enters each person's solitariness and isolation; he is there as a silent, unknown companion who in that way interrupts the total alienation of sin. Jesus might even be said in von Balthasar's view to initiate a hidden reversal in the dynamic of sin: "it is *he* who sets the limits to the extension of damnation, who forms the boundary stone marking the place where the lowest pitch is reached and the reverse movement is set into operation."[77] Von Balthasar draws the conclusion from this that if Jesus "has spared others the integral experience of death . . . then he took, by substitution, that whole experience upon himself."[78] This, argues von Balthasar, is the source of the chaotic meaninglessness of hell.

In the imaginative language of *Heart of the World*, von Balthasar suggests the extremity of Jesus' state, the loss of the last vestige of his active life:

It would be too easy to suffer if one could still love. Love has been taken from you. The only thing you still feel is the burning void, the hollow which it has left behind. It would be a joy for you if, from the depths of hell, you could still, and for all eternity, love the Father who rejected you. But love has been taken away from you. You wanted to give everything away, didn't you? . . . You lived on love; you had no other thought but love; you were love. Now it has been taken away: you are smothering, starving; you are a stranger to yourself.[79]

We saw how in the christological state of his passion and death, Jesus suffers the increasing withdrawal of others' love. In hell, von Balthasar suggests, even Jesus' *own* ability to go on loving others is withdrawn—so total is his identification and assumption of the human condition. Here, then, is the full incarnational significance of Jesus' being in hell. He reaches in this lovelessness the last possible form of the human condition. This is the fulfillment of that hiatus known to Thérèse in which even the most unmistakable features of the self have been given away ("you are a stranger to yourself"), surrendered for the benefit of a new creation that is not yet revealed.

And it is precisely in this state of greatest separation from God, in this hiatus when Jesus has become "a stranger" to himself by so utterly embracing estranged human existence, that the determinative "speaking" of the eternal Word must take place. In hell, the Incarnation reaches a new stage of realization. The complete expression of the Father's love

> in the world that is not divine and is opposed to God demanded that Jesus take the path into the uttermost darkness, because otherwise there would always have been some matter that would not let itself be used for the exposition of God.[80]

Von Balthasar probes the depths of the paradox which sin forces the Incarnation to embrace: to fulfill his mission, to be drawn into the most complete form of his human selfhood, and thereby to be the most complete form of the Word possible in history, Jesus must journey not only to the limits of human existence but into what is the distorted denial of human existence—the aimless, loveless chaos of sin.

7

The States of Love, Resurrection, and Communion

Over the last three chapters we have explored von Balthasar's treatment of a series of dimensions, both spiritual and historical, of Jesus' human existence. We have sought to display the full weight that von Balthasar's understanding of the Incarnation gives to Christ's development as a historical individual. Now at last we come to that constellation of dimensions—ecstasy, rapture, resurrection, nuptiality, communion—which most simply bears the name of love. Interpreted as a state of Christ's existence, and blossoming in an unfathomable manner in his resurrection, love reveals itself as the full fruition of his mission. In fact this christological state shows itself as the secret meaning of all the others; the self-surrender which is actualized in obedience and passes beyond itself in death is finally manifested as a loving being-for-others which is both enrapturing and inclusive.

THE CHRISTIAN AROUSAL TO LOVE

Certain idiomatic features stand out in von Balthasar's discernment of the experience of love: specifically *Christian* love is always a response to the drawing near of God in Christ and is marked chiefly by a readiness for service that could as easily take the form of darkness as of illumination. In his important essay "On Defining the Place of Christian Mysticism," von Balthasar propounds the view that what sets Christian mysticism apart from mysticism more generally conceived is not simply its external forms or theoretical apprehensions—which are often shared with other religions—but its irreducible character of being a response to God's approach.

In the Bible it is not the human person who breaks into a seeking-of-God, but rather God himself who initiates, unexpectedly and spontaneously, the search for humanity. . . . Readiness of listening (*Horchens*) and obeying (*Gehorchens*) takes the place of sponta-neous [human] setting forth.[1]

The Christian is always aroused to love in correspondence with the outpoured mission of divine love in Christ. Given this, "it is not *expe-rience* of union with God which represents the measure of perfection (the highest stage of ascent), but rather *obedience*, which can be quite as tightly linked to the experience of dereliction by God as to an ex-perience of union."[2] We can see that von Balthasar very particularly specifies human *eros* for God. All the forms of human spirituality, including Platonic desire and longing, have in his view been taken up and fulfilled in Christ's own existence as "obedience in love (which be-comes obedience in mission, work, and suffering)."[3]

Von Balthasar discusses this divinely initiated christomorphic love in his study of John of the Cross. In describing John's understanding of the basis for human union with God, he writes:

> God for his part is pure, radiant love, a love that is open to the crea-ture and desires its participation in the absolute and ontological unity of the Godhead. Such participation is possible *when divine love becomes the loving action of the creature itself*.[4]

The prerequisite for mystical union with God is not just any kind of ecstatic flight into the One, but a drawing of the creature into such a sharing of the divine love that the soul begins to enact this same love in the forms of creaturely life. And of course for von Balthasar, the pattern of that divine love is marked by the cross. It would be an un-fortunate misreading of von Balthasar to think that his attention to divine glory is meant to focus our vision on anything but the glory re-vealed in the *crucified* Jesus of Nazareth.

Von Balthasar underscores John's intention to transform the vari-ous conceptions of ecstatic love which he has inherited. But at the same time it remains ultimately this enrapturing event of love which alone can draw human life into divine existence:

> In terms of being, the creature remains eternally the "other than God." But in transfiguring, nuptial love, the mutual otherness of God and man makes possible exchange and reciprocal indwelling. Thus the idea of flight, of rapture, plays a decisive role, although ec-stasy must be thoroughly purified and transformed from its present

imperfection as a bodily or physiological state of rapture into a substantial, habitual state of being borne off.[5]

This transformation of ecstatic love into a "habitual state" has significant christological weight. We have seen how von Balthasar transposes discussion of the union of the divine and human in Christ from ontological to existential terms of mission. Here in his reading of John is one of the grounds for this approach: a union at the level of being is hard to flesh out in terms of the historical pattern of Jesus' life, but a union in which the humanity of Jesus is drawn ever more fully into existence as it is drawn into the enactment of divine love is already charged with the narrative momentum of the gospels. In this conception we might think of the Incarnation as an ongoing event of *ekstasis*; Jesus is that particular historical human existence attracted into actuality by the drawing near to creation of the divine love. Von Balthasar stresses that because of the trinitarian basis of the Incarnation, that is, because God is *in se* one-with-another, the enrapturing of a human existence into union with God is never the undoing of the creature's "otherness."[6]

Whenever von Balthasar speaks of "enrapturing," he wishes to describe an ecstasy which has been transplanted into the Gospel and reconfigured by the pattern of Christ.

> "Being caught up" (*Entrückung*) must be understood in the sense of the New Testament, as man's being given a home through God's glory—through his love—so that he is no more a looker-on, but a cooperator of glory. Man is brought back from the alienation of sin, and comes in this rapture (*Entrückung*) at once to God and to himself: at once into his own depths (which he alone could never reach) and into the true fellowship of men (which can be endured only in Christ).[7]

We could only accurately interpret this passage after having already seen what shape such an enrapturing would take, namely, a life of self-surrender, obedience, and suffering—*not* because suffering is the nature of divine existence in von Balthasar's view, but because that is the only form of expression which obedient love can take in a world alienated from itself and from God. Nevertheless the true effect of ecstatic love is clear: a deeper self-realization and a deeper solidarity with others than could ever have been afforded by an apparently more self-regarding love.

This theme of ecstatic love as the realization and liberation of the self was sounded by von Balthasar in his early study of Origen. There he underlined the idea that the human person is by nature a seeking being, whose poverty and yearning is its richness because this is what draws humanity ever beyond itself. "This ecstasy of its being is at the same time a journey toward the center of itself, toward its source."[8] So for von Balthasar the ecstasy of the human person toward God is understood as a discovery and unfolding of the true depths of the human being. Not surprisingly von Balthasar also points to the divine idea of the individual as the animating and enlivening goal of the human being's search: "Every soul is by its nature itself oriented towards its Idea as the bride toward her groom."[9]

In later works von Balthasar would specify this divine idea as the divine mission intended for each individual, or rather the aspect of Christ's mission which each individual is created to share. But already he is working with a notion of the human being yearning for its true reality, drawn towards its fulfillment as it is drawn into a particular pattern of life intended for it. Commenting on Origen's nuptial imagery, he says that it is precisely this ecstatic union with the soul's "idea" (ultimately the Logos) which renders it "fruitful" (one of von Balthasar's most favored terms): it is this personal union with the "Idea-Person" which "actualizes the created spirit in fertilizing it. Without this union, it remains sterile."[10] The human being remains in only a provisional state, a kind of half-life, unless it is drawn out of itself into union with the Logos who is its archetype.

Somewhat at odds with this bridal reading of ecstatic love in von Balthasar is his deep immersion in the spirituality of Ignatius, from which such a theme is almost entirely lacking.[11] Hugo Rahner suggests that the Ignatian understanding of love is best characterized by the distinctive "more" (*magis*): a desire to love God "more and more" by ever more complete service to God, a love marked by "desiring and choosing only those things which lead more to the end for which I am created." And adds Rahner:

> The essential illimitability of the love driven on by the "more" is restricted by the ideal of service to the visible Church militant. . . . In this way, boundless love becomes for Ignatius "discreet" love. . . . Every grace must be measured by the law of the Church; every love, by the spirit of obedience; every spirit, by the Mystical Body of Christ, our Lord.[12]

We can see von Balthasar working to bring these two conceptions of ecstatic love into some kind of dialogue. He speaks of a union with the beloved precisely by way of active obedience. He comments that "the only analogy nature seems to offer to this initimacy" between the human being and God in the Spirit "is the union of the sexes."[13] But, he quickly adds, the result is the human person's fruitfulness in new dispositions and acts of love.

> This response is not "ecstasy", in the sense of violent enthusiasm or a transcending and a rejecting of one's own created reality in order to live outside oneself in God . . . . It is "ecstasy", indeed, but *the ecstasy of service not of enthusiasm.*[14]

In von Balthasar's reading, the union of the human being with God is never a pure transcending of the human reality in the sense of leaving it behind, or even rendering it simply otiose and passive in the face of the ever-greater working of the divine. Rather this Balthasarian ecstasy is a drawing of all the potential of the human being into concrete reality; it is precisely a "fecundation" of humanity, a rendering-fruitful, which the arousal to love achieves. And this fruitfulness is measured in Ignatian terms of service and obedience; this is the form which ecstatic love takes in its ever-yearning momentum.

Something of the same interpretation emerges as von Balthasar considers the final days of Elizabeth of Dijon. Earlier in her life Elizabeth had conceived of the soul's passage into infinity in rapturous terms. But as she approached her own death, she began to reconceive this itinerary as a participation in Christ's own passion. According to von Balthasar, Elizabeth believed that "the moment at which Jesus left the world and his own to enter into suffering is the moment at which he most loves her, the moment of transition into infinity."[15] For her, Jesus' passion was the moment when his love passed beyond human limits and carried him into the infinity of God, thus revealing his identity as God's limitless love incarnate. So all Christian union with God is by way of an ecstasy in the form of humble, suffering self-giving: "Because infinity is in Christ and because we know and are shaped into Christ in suffering, therefore—and not for reasons of philosophy or because we yearn for it—limitlessness is our homeland."[16] For our purposes, the important point is exactly what von Balthasar chose to highlight in Elizabeth: that the human journey into the infinity of divine love is by way of a very earthy, historical activity which requires the whole of the human being's involvement, and that the archetype of this ecstatic love is enacted in the suffering service of Christ on the cross.

ECSTATIC LOVE AS A CHRISTOLOGICAL STATE

As usual, von Balthasar's reading of the mystical writers has already initiated the discussion of the christological theme. We recall also that throughout his treatment of Christ's mission von Balthasar has carefully noted the fact that this mission, because it is divine and because it is intended universally, necessarily carries Jesus beyond the "limits" of human life. In the chapter on self-surrender we saw how von Balthasar had interpreted the Incarnation in terms of the historical self-giving of Jesus, an activity by which he is, moment-by-moment, drawn into the filial mission. In the paschal mystery this theme reaches a new consummation. The *ekstasis* of Jesus which takes him quite literally beyond his limits in the crucifixion attains its true fruitfulness in the resurrection—when Christ's loving availability to God and neighbor is transposed, in von Balthasar's view, into a definitive form of self-bestowal.

Von Balthasar keeps his eye on the developmental aspect of Christ's existence, the "dramatic dimension immanent in, and constitutive of, the person of Jesus."[17] He explains this, in human terms, as completely analogous to the situation of every human being: while each person may be unique in endowments, "he only becomes the unique person he is through the free development of these endowments in the chance medium of the world that surrounds him."[18] It has always been Jesus' encounters and relationships with others—the Father, Mary, the disciples, the poor, and so on—that have drawn him, as it were, out of himself. In Jesus' case the intensity of these relations attains the level of ecstatic love, and this becomes, I believe, von Balthasar's way of understanding the Incarnation itself: an ongoing development of the unique "endowment" (mission) of Jesus that takes place through the ever-greater love he has for God and the people.

In von Balthasar's view the ultimate threat to Jesus' humanity as well as its fulfillment lies in the nature of God's "idea" for him, the filial mission which continually enraptures him. For this mission, which is to be "God's ultimate [*end-gültig*, finally valid] Yes to the world," must take place within the confines of a mortal human life, and yet it is a mission which necessarily surpasses the capacities of any human being. Such a mission could mean the overwhelming of the one who undertakes it, unless, as von Balthasar believes is the case with Jesus, he gives himself over to it and to the ultimate interpretation of its achievement by God. The Incarnation takes place not by the crushing of Christ's humanity under the burden of an infinite mission but by Jesus' continual obedient acts of ecstatic love, which he allows to draw him into a divine "more" over which he has no power.

One can ascertain that this is in fact von Balthasar's approach to the issue by noting his dependence on the idea of ecstasy as fulfillment and liberation in the analogous mystical situation. In a crucial passage, he submits that if total availability to our divine mission seems burdensome we will find the key to freedom in the experience of Jesus:

> Let us learn from him the name of that ecstasy that can transport us out of ourselves and into the mission given us by God: the name of a love that is most free because it is most absolute. From him, we will learn that ecstasy is not a private state bestowed upon us for our own pleasure and affording us experiences that affect only ourselves. On the contrary, the ecstasy that can take us out of ourselves bears the name of that obedience by which the servant chooses to find his own ultimate pleasure only in fulfilling the will of him who sent him.[19]

Several highly significant points are worth detailing in this passage. First, von Balthasar sees Christ as "transported" by ecstatic love out of himself and into his mission.[20] Von Balthasar speaks of this love as "most free because it is most absolute," and he refers here to the inner-trinitarian love of the divine Persons; therefore Jesus is caught up by this absolute love of the Son for the Father. But in Jesus' case this is not a once-in-a-lifetime event or at best an intermittent experience. Rather, we could say that, in von Balthasar's view, *the human being Jesus of Nazareth is himself the continual event of this ecstatic love*; his humanity is drawn into ever-fuller existence precisely as he, through the course of his self-surrender, obedience, and death, is transported into the fullness of the filial mission. In this sense, then, von Balthasar might be said to interpret the Incarnation as an onging activity of love, which "depends" on the free human self-giving of Christ for its accomplishment. In terms of the dramatic theory which he uses to explicate his christology, von Balthasar can write:

> In the identity of Jesus' person and mission, we have the realization par excellence of what is meant by a dramatic "characterization":

namely, a figure who, *by carrying out his role*, either attains his true face or (in analytic drama) unveils his hidden face. In the case of Jesus Christ, we have, in the terms of real life, the truth of what is found on the stage, that is, the utter and total identification of the character as a result of his utter and total performance of his mission.[21]

It is in the enactment of this divine pattern of filial love that Jesus comes not only to his fulfillment as a human being but to an ever-deeper recognition of his own identity. For this reason von Balthasar sees the details of Jesus' daily ministry as drawing forth from him ever-new concretions of love for the Father and his people which in some, perhaps inchoate, way speak to him of that relationship to the Father which is the very definition of his Person. "It is precisely in embracing his Father's will that Jesus discovers his own, most profound identity as the eternal Son."[22]

Second, we note von Balthasar's emphasis that this ecstasy is neither an individualistic experience nor a seizure of the unwilling human heart by the divine love. Von Balthasar always strives to maintain the note of freedom; this love is liberating both because it frees from all lesser loves which could shackle the lover to what would never satisfy but only satiate, and because it is always an event of the lover's free choosing—"the servant *chooses* to find his own ultimate pleasure" in the will of the beloved. Does this mean von Balthasar thinks there is some sense in which Jesus *chooses* to be the Incarnate Word of God? We have to recall that von Balthasar's mission christology does not require Jesus, in Farrer's memorable phrase, "to know his own meta-physical status with more than Aristotelian exactitude." Jesus only needs to know *how to love* the Father with his whole heart. And in this sense von Balthasar *does* give such weight to the dramatic historical existence of Jesus that for him *the Incarnation is a kind of moment-by-moment victory of Jesus' will to love*:

> Jesus, in his mission, is plunged into a world that is estranged from God, subject to original sin and the demonic, a world that in all se-riousness offers him other ways of carrying out his mission. In each case, he reflects on his mission and rejects them as inappropriate.[23]

Jesus is always free in carrying out his mission, and von Balthasar is not shy in pointing at the testings and temptations to which he is put throughout his ministry. In each case the necessity of making the right "election" brings Jesus to an even fuller self-realization. In von Balthasar's Ignatian perspective the state of election (the equivalent of Jesus' crucial "choosings"), which the *Spiritual Exercises* are designed to facilitate, is always a state of surpassing freedom in which individuals come to a deep awareness of God's loving will for them and the fulfillment which results from their embrace of that mission. It is a case of deepening communion with the true source of one's being. And in Jesus' instance, "the more the Son unites himself with the Ground from which his person and his mission simultaneously spring forth, the better he understands both his mission and himself."[24]

Von Balthasar takes the issue of Jesus' human freedom very seriously, indeed he puts the question with starkness and gravity:

> Is the man Jesus, in his temporal dimension, only the manifestation of a divine decision that is prior to his existence (and is to that extent "alien")? That is, can he only "subsequently" ratify what has already been decided concerning him and the world? Or can his human freedom—to which Orthodox dogmatics has so resolutely held fast ever since the Monothelite controversy—exercise its rightful privilege of being able to make its own decisions?[25]

The reference to the monothelites shows the continuing influence upon von Balthasar of his great patristic source, Maximus the Confessor, that unflinching upholder of Christ's human will against the more powerful church hierarchs of his day. Like him, von Balthasar insists that it is the freely willed obedient love of the human being which needs to be recreated, and therefore any understanding of the Incarnation that would seem to mitigate the complete human will of Jesus would catastrophically undermine the fullness of redemption. Von Balthasar responds to this question about Christ's free choosing by noting first of all that it would be an unfortunate metaphysical crudeness which began to think of the relationship of eternal and temporal decisions in terms of "before" and "after"; the eternity of the Son's desire to receive and return the Father's love is as much, from the standpoint of time, a future reality as a past one.

It is not, he says, as if the eternal Son made one decision as God, in eternity, and a second as human being, in time: "The Son's eternal decision includes his temporal one, and his temporal decision holds fast to his eternal decision as the only one that comes into question."[26] The point is that there is one continual act of choosing to do the Father's will, eternally expressed by the procession of the Son and historically expressed by the obediential love of Jesus. The eternal Son cannot be conceived of as ever giving his free love to the Father without eternally knowing and accepting that he also does this as the human being Jesus of Nazareth.

In order to give some account of the *freedom* with which Jesus is "enraptured" by his eternal mission, von Balthasar draws on the analogy of artistic inspiration. First he quite vigorously rejects the "false theory that the Holy Spirit used prophets or hagiographers like passive musical instruments." Rather, he says, consider how

> the artist is never more free than when, no longer hesitating between artistic possibilities, he is, as it were, "possessed" by the true "idea" that presents itself to him in finite form and follows its sovereign commands. And, if the inspiration is genuine, the work will bear the utterly personal stamp of the artist in absolute clarity. . . . Sublime inspiration awakens in the person inspired a deeper freedom than that involved in arbitrary choice.[27]

The freedom von Balthasar is pointing us to is of course the perfect freedom of Augustine and Bernard; it is not a freedom of utterly indifferent and infinite choices but a total freedom to choose the good. Christ may be said to choose his mission freely in this sense; he is so *attracted* by the one course in life which is his own meaning and fulfillment that he is free to give himself to it at every moment. Von Balthasar conveys the sense of discovery and joy which comes on such occasions, when the human being recognizes, "Yes! This is truly the deepest desire of my heart, this is what I was created for!"

Furthermore von Balthasar understands this process of enrapturing or inspiration as freshly and historically unfolding: "This mission was not waiting for [the human being] ready-made, in some preexistence: it was slumbering within him like a child in its mother's womb, pressing to be delivered—out of the womb of his most personal freedom."[28] If we draw out the analogy, von Balthasar seems to suggest here that Jesus' experience of yearning to enact his mission might be compared to the urgency of equally mingled hope, fear, and love which an expectant mother feels in the days before delivery. Neither she nor Jesus can know the full reality of what is coming to birth, only that they long, not without anxiety, for it to appear. Von Balthasar picks up this theme when he says of Jesus:

> Nor is it his sense that [his mission] lies ready, prefabricated, so that he only needs to assemble it. No; he must fashion it out of himself in

utter freedom and responsibility; indeed, in a sense, he even has to invent it. This is particularly the case when "the Spirit drives him" into the wilderness (Lk 4:1) or back to Galilee (4:14).[29]

It is particularly in these times of testing and challenge that Jesus is forced to search his own heart, his relationship with the Father, in order to bring to birth a new and more complete stage of his existence-in-mission. And so it is in this sense that we can understand the Incarnation, in von Balthasar's thinking, as an ongoing event of love that takes Jesus beyond himself and into his own truth at the same time.

BEING AS COMMUNION

We have seen how von Balthasar sets the Platonic *eros* within an Ignatian framework of service and obedience. He also understands the gift of love as inherently social in orientation. Christian love for von Balthasar is always being-for-other, existence as expropriation, being as communion.

Drawing broadly on the New Testament witness, von Balthasar elucidates the trinitarian basis of existence-as-expropriation. The Spirit who draws close to the believer and pours the love of God into the heart reveals

> the Father who from the beginning has made the gift of himself to his Son, and who has carried on this handing over of himself (*Selbstübereignung*) up to the place and condition that are ours: to the point of becoming human and of being lost. It is therefore not possible to take God to oneself through the act of appropriating (*aneignet*) him, because God is personified handing-over (*die Übereignung*), and one "knows" him and "possesses" him only when one is oneself expropriated (*enteignet*) and handed over (*übereignet*).[30]

This is in von Balthasar's view the other side of his reading of ecstatic love as obediential service; one "possesses" God only as one is drawn into God's own *Selbstübereignung* and is therefore handed over oneself. Again we note that for von Balthasar this is never an absorption of the human being into indistinction with the One. Because the trinitarian handing over is itself always the *constitution* of the other (e.g., the Father constitutes himself precisely in giving his entire existence to the Son), there is a place within the triune love for the continuing otherness of the creature.

Von Balthasar holds that when this eternal self-bestowing life en-counters humanity, it effects a shift in the human center of gravity. Self-expropriating life has penetrated into the ego of sinners in which they "privatize" themselves "and has robbed this space of its private character." This opening of the "dungeon of the self" is the "liberation that brings us into freedom."[31] He elaborates this theme in interpreting Elizabeth of Dijon: grace draws the solitary self out of itself. "Each person is mysteriously socialized into the Church by the indwelling of God's grace, without ceasing to be a person."[32] Von Balthasar envi-sions the drawing near of God as exciting a reciprocal drawing out of the self, beyond the confines of the ego and into the commmunion, exchange, and mutual sharing which is the life of the saints in God: "Something of the relational character of the Divine Persons has penetrated the creaturely person through 'participation in the divine nature,' rousing the creature to adventures in love that cannot be imag-ined by natural means."[33] We note again the theme of the creature being "set in motion" (*Bewegung*) by love toward the acts of love which will free the self from the constraints of what it has come to *think* (falsely) are the real limits of its nature. "Nothing is so free as love. . . . Anyone who begins to love feels himself breaking out of his own private world."[34]

In commenting on the final "Contemplation to Attain Love" of the *Spiritual Exercises* (nos. 234–37), von Balthasar articulates the di-mensions of love as self-bestowal in correlation with the different perspectives in this section of the *Exercises*. In the first, he says, the exercitant comes to appreciate the presence of God in all things "as companionship, kind providence, merciful guardianship and consider-ate unwillingness to impose itself."[35] Knowing Christ, the believer recognizes the divine condescension in this "letting be" of creation and God's desire to hand over the divine self-giving love to the believer. "In doing so, [God] demands that anyone who receives the gifts of being freed into existence and of being accompanied by God will in turn place his own creaturely space at God's disposal."[36] So this is the pre-liminary stage in which the divine relationality begins to work its own loving life of self-expropriation in the believer.

Moreover, one can discern Christ's indwelling in creatures by noting "the images of this inner divine self-giving existence that be-comes more explicit as [the believer] discovers them in the structure and craving and yearning of everything created."[37] The real meaning of being is now recognized as always a "being-for."

In becoming aware of the extent of the divine self-giving, the individual who meditates is catapulted out of his would-be closed personal being, not into a destruction of his personhood but into its fulfillment: the creature's attainable approximation to the unalloyed being-for-others within the divine, trinitarian mystery.[38]

In all of this von Balthasar will find fruitful analogies with which to deepen his understanding of the Incarnation. The ongoing reality of the Incarnation might, in other words, be thought of as a kind of continual setting in motion of Jesus' humanity towards ever greater "adventures in love." In the Incarnation human nature is freed from the false privatized limits of sin and expropriated to share in the divine self-bestowal.

RESURRECTION AND COMMUNION
AS CHRISTOLOGICAL STATES

As an ongoing, reciprocal ecstasy of divine and human love, the Incarnation would not be complete in von Balthasar's mind apart from the resurrection of Christ. We have seen that the eternal significance of the Word that Jesus speaks in his life has gathered momentum throughout his ministry. Von Balthasar conceives of the Incarnation in terms of an ever deepening self-surrender in which the ecstatic force of his mission attracts Jesus farther and farther into solidarity with his people. But von Balthasar also argues that God's Word to creation is a universal word which extends beyond the limits of human life. "What Jesus was able to say and do as an earthly and mortal being was not the entirety of the Word of God."[39] Therefore as Jesus is drawn into the self-bestowing life of this Word he is necessarily drawn beyond the limits of human life (in his death) *and* into the most perfect form of human life (in his resurrection). The full Word can only be spoken, and therefore the Incarnation can only be fully accomplished, insofar as Jesus passes by way of his availability, obedience, and death into a new and perfect state of self-bestowing love:

> The self-utterances of the earthly Jesus, in word, deed and Passion, are only a part of his own totality as the Word of God; and this part can only attain its totality, and hence its full expressive power, when it has undergone a particular transposition, a transposition that also involves that human, finite horizon that is indispensable if a man is to speak and act.[40]

What exactly is the transposition that von Balthasar believes the resurrection brings about? In simplest terms it is the establishment of Jesus' human availability to God and neighbor in a permanent form, a perfect state of "handed-overness" which now enlarges to become universally participable.

As ever, this could never for von Balthasar mean any leaving behind of Jesus' full humanity in the resurrection. Speaking of Jesus' wounds, von Balthasar comments:

> The stigmata are more than an external sign, a kind of honorable distinction for having suffered; they are, beyond the gulf between death and Resurrection which reaches to the bottom of hell, the identity of the subject in the identity of consciousness. It is always this man who suffered this life, this cross, this death.[41]

What sustains the identity of Jesus, including his own consciousness, is the very pattern of loving self-giving by which he has progressively come to the full stature of created existence as envisioned by God.

So it is this identical Jesus who by his self-abandonment puts himself at the disposal of the Father's completing act, the resurrection. And in this state of resurrection the Incarnation reaches its definitive form of availability. For in von Balthasar's view the most complete state of abandonment is not the crucifixion but the resurrection. He argues that the resurrection achieves a veritable "liquefaction" (*Verflüssigung*) of Christ's existence, confirming him in a state of eternal self-bestowal to the world.[42] Only in his resurrection do Jesus' mission and therefore his personal existence reach consummation. In von Balthasar's view this final *handing over* of Christ in the resurrection gifts of eucharist and scripture is in no sense a passive or depersonalizing event for Jesus. It is truly his own act by which he attains his own form "on the far side of himself," beyond the limits of individualized mortal life. Christ is finally and totally himself in this state of inclusivity, of corporate life and communion. By his utter self-abandonment to God, his own human capacities are released into the divine freedom, and in this state he is able "by the power of this handing over" in resurrection life (sacrament and word) to "become what he should be for God and humankind."

Thus it would be true to say that for von Balthasar the resurrection is by no means purely a "manifestation" of what is already sufficiently accomplished on the cross. The "more" which constitutes the christological state of resurrection is in fact the opening of the Incarnation to include all people. If we conceive of the Incarnation in Balthasarian terms as a continual event of reciprocal ecstatic love (of God for humanity and humanity for God), then *the resurrection is the incarnational state in which Jesus, by a new act of self-bestowal, effects the ecstasy of those to whom he draws near, arousing them to a love and awe which attracts them out of themselves and into his expropriated being-as-communion.*

To a certain extent, von Balthasar believes that this enrapturing quality is intrinsic to the Incarnation in all its states or moments.

> That the absolute Being of God should have decided to present itself in a human life, and should be able to carry out his will should be a perpetual source of wonder to anyone contemplating the life of Jesus, should seem a thing impossible and utterly bewildering. [The believer] ought to feel his mind reeling at the idea, feel as if the ground were giving away under his feet, and experience the same "ecstasy" of incomprehension which seized Christ's contemporaries.[43]

In the same passage von Balthasar goes on to list some of the many references in the gospels to the astonishment, fear, joy, and awe which Jesus is reported to have evoked. In von Balthasar's reading, the shocking coincidence of opposites which is the Incarnation is perfectly expressed in the outward activity of Jesus, his total authority on the one side and his total humility and poverty on the other.[44] To be sure it is not so much the metaphysical wonder of the Incarnation to which von Balthasar would draw attention as to its heart-stopping historical enactment in Jesus' living, dying, and rising; but it is fair to say that the effect he believes this must have upon the believer is "ecstatic." As Christ draws near to people, they are drawn out of themselves, expropriated, and so "go beyond" by participating in his obediential love.

This is supremely the case with respect to Jesus in his resurrection state. Indeed the resurrection presence of Christ—enrapturing yet vanishing, intimate yet withdrawing—is, as it were, designed to have just this effect on Christ's people. The disciples, says von Balthasar, "had to be transformed and raised up" from a carnal love of Christ purely according to his humanity to a spiritual love of him in his divinity. This classic pattern of mystical progression is accomplished insofar as the disciples are "carried, entranced, into the sphere of the Spirit."[45]

And in von Balthasar's view, "the Resurrection appearances are themselves a training in just such a transformation."[46] The aim is by no means that Jesus' humanity should somehow be discarded in this enrapturing of the disciples, but rather that just as Jesus' own humanity is fulfilled as it is drawn increasingly into the sphere of his divine mission, so the disciples make the great *ekstasis* from themselves into the divine idea of their reality precisely as they are caught up in the reciprocal love of the divine and human in Christ. It is a question of their being drawn into the depths of Christ's identity and mission, and therefore freed for their own full participation in that mission.

Hence the Incarnation in the state of resurrection attains a new level of impact on those around Jesus. Every encounter now begins to effect conversion, transformation, a new and deeper inclusion of the disciples in Christ's existence. In meeting the risen Jesus

> the disciples know themselves to be not only recognised but also seen through; and more, in their very own reality (which exists in him) he knows and understands them—so they now realize—much better than they know and understand themselves. Hence the broken-hearted confession of, for example, the disciples on the Emmaus road.[47]

The risen Jesus arouses in the disciples a mixture of fear, sorrow, and pure joy which in von Balthasar's mind is the prerequisite for their liberation from self; it is their act of confession before him, the sacramental reality of which "continues Jesus' activity of revealing and convincing during his days on earth." Even Jesus' most severe words of judgment are "always words of salvation and healing, as the story of Thomas shows."[48] The resurrection state of Christ is a state that effects a transition, not just in Jesus' own existence, but precisely as he comes to be the "home" for his people, the new basis of their own life: Jesus' heart must go on beating in the disciples.[49]

In a similar way the story of Mary searching for the absent Jesus at the tomb displays, in von Balthasar's view, the church's experience of Christ withdrawing himself for the express purpose of drawing the believing community with him into his expropriated life. The "excess" of that love brought Mary out from the limits of her own life, is deepened in her experience of Jesus' dying, and reaches a consummate level in his withdrawing from her and his sending her to the others at his resurrection.[50] Christ's dispossession of the disciples is for the very purpose of uniting them with his own *ex-cessus* into the ultimate freedom of being-as-communion. Von Balthasar emphasizes what he takes to be the profound desire of the risen Christ to ensure the freedom of the disciples in their encounters with him and to bring them more fully into the work of redemption. He describes Mary's meeting with the risen Jesus as an event in which Mary's own will is drawn into the whole momentum of Christ's existence; in John's narrative she meets him before his ascent, and "to this *resurrectio in fieri*, she must give her consent by not holding back the Risen One (John 20,17), but letting him go free."[51]

In the same way, says von Balthasar, Christ's mother had to consent to the Spirit for Jesus' conception, and Mary of Bethany, in her "burial" anointing of Jesus, gave her consent to his death. Von Balthasar sees these three women depicting the church's experience of having been brought profoundly into Jesus' mission, consenting to his birth, his death, and his resurrection. "For the three chief articulations of the redemption *in fieri*, the 'Yes' of the three Marys is required. Beyond all contestation they symbolise here the believing and loving Church."[52] In this way he seeks to portray the resurrection not solely as a past historical moment but as a continuing state of the Incarnation, a state which progresses by the inclusion of an ever-widening circle of human consent and action in the divine mission of Christ.

If we understand the Incarnation as reaching a new level of fullness as Christ draws others into his existence, then we could say that for von Balthasar the Incarnation is a communal event with an individual center, Jesus of Nazareth. This is not to say that he simply elides the distinction between Christ and Church, but he does want to underscore the identity-in-distinction of historical Christ and mystical Body. Certainly his early study of Origen continued to have great significance for him in this regard. In this work von Balthasar unfolds Origen's concept of the three Incarnations of the Word: as Scripture (which signifies the revelatory property of the Word), in the Flesh of Jesus (which indicates the personal nature of God), and as the Church (which points to the infinite nature of God).[53] As can be seen already, the ecclesial form of the Incarnation is precisely that which points to what is beyond all limits, and in that respect it may be said to correspond rather well to the theme that has been important to von Balthasar all along, that Jesus comes to himself and fulfills his mission as he is drawn beyond the scope of what one individual mortal can accomplish. In this sense "communion" is the ultimate state of the Incarnation, just as self-giving availability has been its necessary presupposition.

Von Balthasar summarizes his interpretation of Origen on this communal aspect of Christ's existence:

> The historical life of the Savior, so precious in itself, is however only the prelude, the example, the symbol of a life of Christ which is much more vast, that of his mystical body across the history of the world. . . . The historical life of the historical Christ and the historical life of the mystical Christ are thus not two distinct lives, but only one life under two aspects.[54]

As von Balthasar develops his own christology, he moderates this Origenian perspective to alleviate any sense that the historical life of Jesus is *only* a symbol for the real thing, the corporate ecclesial life.[55] Rather von Balthasar will stress the primacy and centrality of the historical human individual, Jesus of Nazareth, but he argues that the very historical unfolding of Jesus' mission leads to the increasing inclusion of others in his *mission*, which is after all, in von Balthasar's scheme, the actual basis of his personal identity.

Perhaps his clearest presentation on this score is his "dramatic" analogy, in which the details of Jesus' concrete daily existence open a new realm of personal freedom (*Freiheitsraum*) within which particular individuals "are given their ultimate human face, their mission or 'role'; it is left up to them to play their part well or ill."[56] Jesus, in von Balthasar's reading, becomes a stage for the drama of human existence; the new shape and dynamic which he gives to humankind's relationship with God becomes the free space that each human being needs to enact her or his particular mission and so come to personal fulfillment. Human beings come not only into a full personal existence but to redemption expressly by taking up their particular share in Christ's mission.

Two points are especially vital in von Balthasar's dramatic analogy. The first has to do with our suggestion that in von Balthasar the Incarnation comes to be seen in almost developmental terms, as an ongoing historical event. Von Balthasar believes that Jesus' consciousness of his mission and his consciousness of his self are identical, but since Jesus' mission is universal in scope, it may take "a whole lifetime, or even the entire world time, to carry it out."

> Once this identity [of mission-consciousness and self-consciousness] has been firmly established, it follows that, in the acting area opened

up as the mission proceeds, the "I" of the mission-bearer himself is rendered present; it too becomes an "area" wherein are found those who have been touched, transformed and resettled in it.[57]

Clearly for von Balthasar, Jesus' self-understanding, his fullness as a human being (in an existential and spiritual sense), is neither a static form imprinted upon him once-for-all from above at the moment of conception, nor an inner play of subjective states of consciousness. Jesus develops as a human being through the interactions he has with others, through the ever-onward yearning he feels for his mission, and through the sharing and communion he comes to have with those who participate in his mission. In the course of this history Jesus' full "I" is realized (*vergegenwärtigt*) not in a solipsistic fashion that would isolate him from others permanently, but rather his "I" becomes an "area" in which his people can also live and discover the reality of the human nature they were created to enjoy.[58]

Second, von Balthasar is concerned to reflect the very real involvement of others in Christ's mission and so in the unfolding of the full extent of his "I". As men and women are drawn into the acting "area" of Christ's existence "they are rendered 'persons' in the theological sense; that is, they are not only negatively 'redeemed' but positively enrolled with missions ('charisms') that make them persons of profile and quality within the prototypical mission of Jesus."[59] We see again here how forcefully von Balthasar has managed to reintegrate the theological categories of Christ's person and work, for in this reading Jesus' "person" in fact comes to full realization through the very "work" of his mission. Moreover his "work" is not only a suffering or obedience *in the place of* others, but the creation within his own self, i.e., his relationship with God and neighbor, of an acting area in which a new kind of selfhood on the part of the redeemed can be realized:

> We can also see that Christ's mission on our behalf is more than a work and a suffering on his part to spare others the punishment they have justly deserved . . . it involves his coworking and cosuffering with those who are estranged from God. In this way, the Second Adam opens up an area of Christian mission in which [others], *en Christoi*, can be given a share in his salvific work and suffering for the world.[60]

In a very real sense for von Balthasar, the Incarnation reaches its full extent not only through the historical unfolding of Jesus' mortal life and his death but through the ongoing inclusion of all the members in their head, through the expropriation of human beings from their self-centeredness into the free obedience of Christ. For that very reason the event of the Incarnation could not be, in any final sense, complete only with Christ's atoning death.

For von Balthasar it is the work of the Holy Spirit, beginning with the "Forty Days" of the resurrection appearances, to accomplish the continuing enfleshment of the Word in a universal fashion. It is the Spirit who transposes Christ's historical existence into a form that becomes the "immediate and inward norm of every life." In this way the Holy Spirit creates "the missions of the Church and individuals as applications of the life of Christ to every Christian life and the whole life of the Church."

> [During the Forty Days] the Lord's earthly life is not, as far as he himself is concerned, "past" (though it must necessarily appear so to the disciples); the whole of it is transformed into his Resurrection, taken up into it, eternalized, and thus made a living possession that he can share, the thing of which he is going to build his Church.[61]

All the events and turning points that together constitute Jesus' earthly ministry become, through the Holy Spirit, the dynamic framework within which every human life can come to fulfillment. It is not that the historical shape of the Incarnation is lost, in von Balthasar's view, by its ongoing inclusion of the redeemed, but rather the shape it attains through Jesus' historical ministry is the very pattern into which Christ's people come to participate. We might say that this brings to fruition the state of self-surrender with which we began, for in the christological state of resurrection and communion, the self-surrender and obedience of Jesus have passed through the limits of mortal selfhood in his death and reached their definitive form of self-bestowal. Jesus' giving away of himself to God and neighbor has been prodigal, but it has proved to lead, in von Balthasar's reading, not finally to the squandering and loss of his human existence but to its full stature as that form of existence which is generative of full personhood and life for all human beings.

8

THE HUMANITY OF CHRIST

It is as if the still transcendence of God in his aseity suddenly became vibrant with the energy, the strain, the joy, the grief, the triumph and the failure of the ministry of Jesus.

Donald MacKinnon

At the intersection of spirituality and theology we have discovered the details of von Balthasar's treatment of the Incarnation. We have seen him develop what I have called a christology from within, an account of the historical existence and accomplishment of Jesus which is neither simply a gingerly teasing out of what might be said of Jesus from a historical-critical standpoint, nor a co-opting of Jesus' historical life to fit a predetermined understanding of the Logos; rather von Balthasar has discovered in the saints and mystics a witness both to the human struggle of Jesus and the divine force which animates that struggle.

My suggestion all along has been that by interpreting the Incarnation in this way, von Balthasar is able to produce a christology that is very classical (in assuming that the personal subject of Jesus is the eternal Son), and that also gives full weight to the historical humanity of Christ. By what criterion might we judge the success of such a christology? Perhaps no one has put such an attempt to the test more trenchantly than Wolfhart Pannenberg:

> A Christology that takes the divinity of the Logos as its point of departure and finds its problems only in the union of God and man in Jesus recognizes only with difficulty the determinative significance inherent in the distinctive features of the real, historical man, Jesus of Nazareth. . . . Only the participation of the Logos in everything that belongs to general human nature is important, since our human participation in divinity through Jesus depends upon that. But no

determinative significance can accrue to the historical particularity of Jesus, unless it be to his death as a payment that atones for sins.[1]

Now it would be unfortunate if the features of Pannenberg's description which do apply to von Balthasar were to give the mistaken impression that the negative shortcomings necessarily apply as well. For undeniably von Balthasar does desire to understand more fully the union of God and humanity in Christ—particularly the reality of the human freedom thereby established; and he is concerned that no aspect of human existence whatsoever be excluded from the Incarnation, but not only for the classical reason that whatever has not been assumed cannot be healed. For in von Balthasar's view what the divine mission of the Son brings into historical existence *is* precisely this particular perfect human being, Jesus of Nazareth. In other words, the very characteristics which Pannenberg notes as tell-tale marks of a christology "from above" become in von Balthasar's approach, I suggest, the basis for a new and deeper understanding of the determinative significance of Jesus exactly as a historical human being.

The evidence for this interpretation of von Balthasar's achievement has necessarily been produced as we have gone along, emerging through our reading of his four christological states. Three common themes have come to light from these four different perspectives of abandon, obedience, death, and love. First, von Balthasar characteristically sees Christ developing humanly as he commits himself to his divine mission; each act of his loving obedience, each encounter with God and others, brings the hidden possibilities of his human nature forth into historical existence. And this does not happen as though it were simply a foregone conclusion; each development in Jesus' life comes about as he struggles to discern the particular shape that his love for God and neighbor must take in every moment.

Second, as Jesus comes to human fulfillment—drawn ever forward into his mission—he is by these same acts drawn ever more deeply into the concrete historical predicament of the people; it is not a typological or universal "human condition" which Jesus increasingly shares but the very particular historical nexus of his place and time. He is in von Balthasar's view drawn profoundly and fully into a historical setting, and only because of that can he be said to share the equally time-bound existence of every human being. This means that Jesus is carried into the darkness of alienation from God, including an evaporation of any certitude he may have once felt regarding God's saving will for him personally.

Third, von Balthasar conceives of the Incarnation as an ongoing historical event: Jesus Christ as the Incarnate Word is constituted through reciprocal acts of self-giving love, the kenotic love of the eternal Son which comes to historical existence precisely as the self-abandoning love of the historical human being Jesus of Nazareth. It is expressly the historical activity of Jesus in carrying out his mission that brings him to fulfillment both as a human being and as the Word spoken into time. And because this mission, in von Balthasar's view, is intended to embrace all persons, the Incarnation reaches its ultimate goal only as all people come to find their own true identity within the "acting area" of Jesus' relationship to the Father in the Spirit.

In terms of Pannenberg's test, then, von Balthasar's undoubtedly strong assumption of Jesus' full divinity seems *not* to have undermined for him the determinative significance of Jesus' historical humanity; indeed in his explication the Incarnation depends entirely for its full reality on the active historical willing, loving, hoping, and fearing of Jesus and his encounters with others. It would seem, to refer to the epigraph for this chapter, that von Balthasar has taken the historical human life of Jesus so seriously that he believes our very conception of God must be entirely infused with the energy, strain, joy, grief, failure, and triumph of Christ's human ministry.

Having seen how von Balthasar conceives the Incarnation as coming about, we want to offer as a final test of his approach a consideration of the *role* of the human Jesus. Is he merely "there" by definition? What role does he have, not just as a necessary metaphysical presupposition (i.e., for the Incarnation to be complete, Jesus must be fully human, therefore he is so, etc.), but as an identifiable partner in God's work?

KENOSIS AND EXALTATION

The question one must put to von Balthasar is whether his emphasis on Christ's participation in the eternal filial mission might tend to convert Jesus into too much of an archetypal human being, removed from the limits and lacks of historical life. Von Balthasar is himself very aware of this as a problem in some christologies; as we have seen, he specifically criticizes Karl Barth on this score (which shows how serious a fault it is for him, since Barth is more often than not a spring-board for von Balthasar). Von Balthasar feels that Barth's aim is laudable, i.e., that by describing Jesus as the one who exists "*for* others," he is showing in historical terms "that the human nature of Christ is totally monopolized by the redeeming action of God and must be understood in terms of it." With this von Balthasar agrees, but he believes Barth has settled on a way of expressing it which in-evitably tends to elevate Jesus too much "above" his people: "This does involve the danger of looking upon the oneness of Christ and mankind as merely analogical. It would lead on to the conclusion that the 'brethren' cannot, as is envisaged in Catholic teaching, participate in God's action in Christ."[2] We have seen that von Balthasar himself draws close to this theme of Christ being completely "for" others, at their disposal. But he does so by emphasizing the particular acts and spiritual stances (readiness, obedience, suffering, loving) which most completely integrate Jesus with the struggles of anyone who would join him in his mission. Moreover he also undergirds this with a notion of Christ's historical relationship with the Father, rendered into its definitive form in the resurrection, as an inclusive and participatory "acting area" in which men and women themselves come to the full personhood their humanity is created to enjoy.

So when von Balthasar speaks of Jesus' human personality coming to fulfillment as he enacts the mission of the Son he intends neither

the removal of an individual from the sphere of his fellow human-kind (Elias being snatched from among men in the fiery chariot, as it were): nor the translation of a normal human nature to a higher level of being; this would be something which the very fact of cre-ation makes impossible.[3]

What von Balthasar intends is a discovery within the very parameters of a human lifetime (with all its attendant ambiguities) of the true possibilities of human relationship to God. It is not into a quasi-divine life which Jesus' mission takes him, but into the depths and heights of human nature itself, heretofore obscured, poisoned, or barricaded in human awareness by the contrary limiting momentum of sin. These re-created possibilities of human existence are not handed over ready-made to Jesus, but he comes in von Balthasar's view to discover them as he is drawn into utterly unexpected "adventures of love."

In all of this von Balthasar remains convinced by the teaching of Maximus on the true relationship of human and divine existence in

Christ. Commenting on Maximus, he writes that the historical humanity of Jesus is

> not a pure negative of God, therefore not itself by an unbalanced mystical dissolution in God; but rather his [human] nature can become redeemed by elevation to participate in God, by dying to this world, yet only through intentional testing and perfecting.[4]

We can see how von Balthasar has specified here the manner of human participation in God or exaltation: the assumption of human nature in the Incarnation does not mean its simple dissolution (as though human nature and divine nature were somehow competing for existence), but an engagement in an intentional, willed process of discernment, testing, and perfecting. In other words, Jesus' humanity comes to full relationship with his divine mission through the temporal unfolding of his life. Indeed von Balthasar goes on to say that this participation of Christ's human nature in divine grace means its "confirmation and perfection" (*bekräftigt und vollendet*) *as* human nature.[5]

But for von Balthasar the full human participation of Jesus' humanity in God "calls for the yet deeper descent of God himself, his humbling, his kenosis."[6] And it is this unvarying emphasis on kenosis which might be said to be even more problematic than any questions about Jesus' divinization. For one might ask, does von Balthasar not see a risk that the kenotic momentum of the eternal Son, when incarnate in human existence, might threaten to lead Jesus' humanity to an oppressive and ultimately *in*human state? At first sight the evidence would seem to weigh heavily in this direction: the talk of self-surrender and abandonment, obedience, and a pure readiness to suffer, all suggests a pattern of human existence which can easily be infected by human domination or self-disparagement, and so become just the opposite of the liberating and empowering form of human life which Jesus as savior might be expected to model.

For this reason I have situated these kenotic themes within their proper context in von Balthasar, namely, his interpretation of the spiritual life. It has been my aim to demonstrate that, seen in this light, the self-surrendering obedience of Jesus is not only *intended* to lead him into the fullness of human experience but actually does bring him, as von Balthasar sketches out the gospel narratives, to a realistically developing sense of self, of authority in the face of human evil and poverty in the face of human indifference.

It can scarcely be overstated that von Balthasar's great emphasis on self-emptying and receptivity does not derive from some fixed presupposition regarding the divine nature which is then imposed on Jesus' humanity. The theme of kenosis always arises for von Balthasar from his reading of the very concrete historical frustrations and failures which are the lot of Jesus' entirely human condition. It is because of the historical realities of Jesus' life that von Balthasar, trying to conceive the trinitarian conditions for the possibility of this real life, comes to underscore the eternal self-giving love of the Trinity. Commenting on this theme in *Mysterium Paschale*, Donald MacKinnon remarks with great insight:

> This very dense monograph dares to treat the unity of the Triune God, the very consistency of God with Himself, as something needing affirmation in relation to creation. It is as if that unity were not an eternal self-sufficiency, a transcendent and formally complete wholeness, but something which because its eternal realization is in and through the perpetual mutuality of the processions of the Three comprising it, may find itself at risk by the predicament of its creation, and by the cost exacted for that creation's fulfillment by reason of that predicament. It is as if the theology of the Triune God, *understood as a completion of the theology of Christ's kenosis* and the complex simplicity of his redeeming mission, provided the context within which traditional debates concerning the alleged divine passibility, or impassibility are transformed.[7]

MacKinnon confirms the idea that it is exactly because von Balthasar takes the human and historical predicament of Jesus so seriously that he is willing to risk a radical reconsideration of what form the divine triune love may take. If Jesus' humanly tragic failure is truly an event of the Son's mission, it must speak of an unutterably powerful humility in God, which can accomplish the purpose of its love even through the path of human alienation from God. The haunting finality of Jesus' self-giving is, for all the "weight" of its trinitarian background, never portrayed by von Balthasar as self-diminishing or enfeebling. His "receptivity never rots away into a passive acceptance."[8] Indeed it is the very mark of his stature and his endurance. So while von Balthasar undeniably stresses the self-abandoning stance of Christ, he is thereby attempting to sketch painfully but realistically the honest cost of Jesus' full share in historical existence, of his struggle to love God and neighbor in a setting fraught with antagonism and lack of understanding and sheer human frailty.

Von Balthasar speaks quite soberly of the determinative significance that Jesus' historical existence has for our understanding of the Trinity:

> The event of the Incarnation of the second divine Person does not leave the inter-relationship of those divine Persons unaffected. Human thought and human language break down in the presence of this mystery: namely that the eternal relations of Father and Son are focussed, during the "time" of Christ's earthly wanderings, and in a sense which must be taken with full seriousness, in the relations between the man Jesus and his heavenly Father, and that the Holy Spirit lives as their go-between who, inasmuch as he proceeds from the Son, must also be affected by the Son's humanity.[9]

What von Balthasar extrapolates from Jesus' living, dying, and rising is an eternal trinitarian self-emptying; "this does not mean, however, that God's essence becomes itself (univocally) 'kenotic,'" but rather that each of the divine Persons is constituted expressly by self-giving to the Others, and therefore the eternal might or power of God lies solely in this eternal triune event of self-bestowing love. "God is not, in the first place, 'absolute power,' but 'absolute love,' and his sovereignty manifests itself not in holding on to what is its own but in its abandonment."[10]

And, for von Balthasar, just as the reality of Jesus' historical human life "must be taken with full seriousness" in reconceiving the Trinity, so also a reciprocal effect is possible: the trinitarian background sheds light on the hidden meaning of Christ's experience. In this context Jesus' very human self-abandon and self-giving is interpreted not as self-despairing weakness or repression but as the hidden manner in which he comes to be most fully who he is in the very act of giving to others their own true life. As the human Word of God, Jesus' life is the very image and pattern of the Father's own existence, which for von Balthasar is truly "constituted" in the act of giving himself to be the life of the Son and the Spirit.[11] The human kenosis of Christ is not the reduction of his humanity to a nullity; it is the activity through which he comes to the fulfillment of human loving, verified for von Balthasar by the fact that this same pattern becomes, for those who share Christ's life, not an oppressive or self-destructive burden but an empowerment to grow beyond sin's crippling infringements upon human life.

CHRIST THE HUMANLY REVEALING WORD OF GOD

Certainly von Balthasar thinks of Christ's humanity as far more than a metaphysically necessary temporal place-holder for a divine life which, allegedly, cannot by definition exist in human terms; nor is Jesus a kind of human puppet who obligingly dances to the behind-the-scenes motions of the eternal Son. It is above all von Balthasar's great aim to show that the eternal mission of the Son comes to historical realization in the free, considered, compassionate, and prodigally life-giving acts of the human being Jesus of Nazareth—this *is* the event of the Incarnation in von Balthasar's estimation.

In this light it comes as no surprise that von Balthasar understands the historical event of revelation in Christ as requiring the whole of Jesus' humanity, not just as a necessary mouthpiece, a condescending lisp adopted merely in order to sound agreeably upon the infant ears of humankind, but as in fact revelatory of the whole divine Word through the entirety of Jesus' most mundane acts. Moreover the revelatory event occurs not simply by virtue of Jesus happening to be a human being, so that it might as well happen through the life of any human person or indeed through the accumulated human wisdom of the ages; rather for von Balthasar, God's Word is spoken in and through the very particular choices which Jesus makes, through his characteristic form of companionship and anger, sorrow and exultation, in short, through his unsubstitutable identity and presence.

We begin by noting von Balthasar's insistence that while in some sense the divinity of Christ is concealed by his humanity, it is far more true that the divinity is revealed by the humanity, which is "never, in all eternity, to be discarded or disparaged."

> All that is human in Christ is a revelation of God and speaks to us of him. There is nothing whatever in his life, acts, passion and resurrection that is not an expression and manifestation of God in the language of a created being.[12]

What is brought home in this passage is the importance of Jesus *beyond* the sheer fact of his being human. We have seen how much weight von Balthasar gives to Jesus' acts of self-giving and obedience, for it is through the very idiomatic shape of his activity that the Son's mission comes to be fulfilled. In the same sense, what Jesus historically undertakes, and says, and fails to accomplish, is the utterance of God's Word in time.

Furthermore there is no sense in von Balthasar that this must be only a partial or preliminary revelation.

> God's word is no longer an abstract law, it is this man. Everything God had to say or give to the world has found a place in him. The whole objective spirit of religion, of law, of ritual is identical with the subjective spirit of this particular man, a man like us.[13]

It is noteworthy how von Balthasar avoids an exclusive view of revelation. He is not saying that God does not reveal divine reality in all human religion, law, or ritual, but that whatsoever is truly revelatory in these things is expressed indelibly, concretely, and concisely in the life of Jesus, indeed in his "subjective spirit." It is not only Christ's individual acts which are revelatory of God but his whole being, including his spiritual dispositions, his yearnings. And this revelation is unfolded as humankind comes to share in Christ's pattern of life and interior dispositions. In the spiritual explorations of the mystics, in the "adventures in love" of the saints, the church represents to the world the eternal richness of revelation that is known by participating in Christ.

Yet the significance of Christ's humanity is even greater than this. In von Balthasar's view, Jesus Christ himself is the veritable speaking of God; Christ's historical existence is drawn developmentally into being as the Father speaks the Word. Simply because the divine Word is the subject of Christ's activity does *not* mean that Jesus' life is any less the free activity of a historical human being. In fact it is just this factor which is most important if God is to be revealed accurately as the self-giving love which always brings the *other* into free existence. If Jesus' humanity were fundamentally insignificant in the work of revelation, that would reveal a different kind of god, not the divine being who expresses self through the self-moving freedom of creation, but a false or quasi-divine being which can only manifest itself in competition with lesser beings by means of their manipulation and subjection.

Explicating Maximus on these themes, von Balthasar argues that Christ's acts are always both divine and human simultaneously, and that the embrace and liberation of Jesus' human activity into the eternal trinitarian activity in no way abolishes the authentic humanity of Jesus or his acts. Indeed, "the divinity of his activity has its ultimate guarantee in the uncurtailed and uninjured authenticity of his humanity."

> Precisely [Jesus'] speech, breathing, walking, his hunger, eating, thirst, drinking, sleeping, crying, anguish is the particularized place

of appearing of what is divine. . . . Insofar as that which is characteristically human is lived out, in that much God appears.[14]

It is the very humanity of Jesus which assures us that it is really *God* who is revealed. Nor is it at all the case that the humanity of Jesus only reveals God's humility and condescension. We could say that for von Balthasar, it is the Father's ability to speak his Word precisely as that which is fundamentally other than God which demonstrates the true power and divinity of God. And this especially means not a generic otherness, or creation in general or even humanity taken as a whole; in von Balthasar's view it is God's speaking as this particular human being which reveals the true uniqueness and personal reality of God. The divine love which shows itself to humankind in Jesus

> far from being a universally pervading medium in which everything dissolves in a vague emotionalism, is shown in a clearly delineated figure, occupying a definite place in history (in no other way can the personality of the Father appear in the world), taking visible form in distinct words, acts, sufferings and miracles. Consequently every beginning of love that reaches out from the world towards God must let itself be transformed and integrated into the drama of this unique, distinct person.[15]

The determinative significance which von Balthasar accords to Jesus' historically concrete human life is shown by his counsel that whoever would love God shall find the way to that love in "the drama of this unique, distinct person." We return again to the importance of Jesus' own most characteristic features as themselves the revelation of God.

It is worth reminding ourselves here that beside von Balthasar's theological arguments in this regard, there is also in the background the Ignatian concept of spiritual attunement. In the *Exercises* this is the idea of asking "for an interior knowledge of Our Lord, who became human for me, that I may love him more intensely and follow him more closely" (*Sp.Exs.* no.104). De Guibert notes that one of the most prominent features of the *Exercises*

> is the place given to the humanity of Christ, to the events of His life on earth, to the imitation of the examples which He gave and which are the sovereign norm of our service to God, and to the identifica-

tion between the service to Jesus, Leader of all men, and the service to the Father.[16]

Once again we see the integrity of spirituality and constructive theology in von Balthasar; the theological warrants for the significance of Jesus' humanity in revelation have a firm basis also in the insights von Balthasar draws from Ignatian spirituality: because of the determinate personal existence of God as love, it is only through commitment to the very determinate features of the particular human being Jesus—through fidelity, comradeship, and service to him—that one can truly come to know and serve God.

This leads us to what is perhaps most notable in von Balthasar's effort in this regard, his sustained attempt to hold up actual historical features of Jesus' existence as crucial for revelation. We can see this most broadly from the standpoint of Jesus' self-surrender. For von Balthasar holds that Christ's readiness to express the divine Word comes about through a living, ongoing commitment which Jesus has to make continually. Divine speech in a human life is not, to von Balthasar's mind, simply a given. It is only possible insofar as Jesus chooses, not automatically or unconsciously but freely and with mounting awareness of the costs, "to place his entire existence in the flesh, mortal and futile, at the disposal of the divine Word."[17] It is not simply in virtue of being *a* human being that Jesus is the Word but in virtue of the actual life he lives.

Rather movingly, von Balthasar captures the mysterious sense in which Jesus, giving himself so totally to the work of being the Word, may even be said to contribute humanly to the divine meaning.

> It is not a pale image of heavenly truth that is acted out on earth; it is the heavenly reality itself, translated into earthly language. When the Servant here below falls to the ground tired and spent from the burden of his day's labor, when his head touches the earth to adore his God, this poor gesture captures in itself all of the uncreated Son's homage before his Father's throne. And the gesture forever adds to this eternal perfection the laborious, painful, inconspicuous, lusterless perfection of a human being's humility.[18]

Again the developmental quality of the Incarnation is in evidence here, for the eternal Word is spoken not more or less in spite of or aloof from the poor human Jesus who bears the Word's meaning into the world's unhearing sinfulness. In von Balthasar's view the Word is yet more complete, more fully spoken, in the hidden but perfect love of Jesus' laborious human existence.

THE HUMAN ROLE OF JESUS IN REDEMPTION

Much of what would need to be said under this heading has already been adumbrated in the previous sections: von Balthasar's rendering of the kenosis theme in terms of the actual constraints which Jesus must historically face; the fact that, in his view, it is the particular traits of Jesus' humanity (his humility, his authority, his poverty, his compassion) which are significant, and not just the fact that he is a human being; and above all the degree to which the Incarnation is an ongoing historical act, so that for Christ to *be* the Word of God is not an automatic process but requires a continual historical involvement of all his human faculties and strength—to give himself, to be obedient, to die, to love in such a way that these acts may be entirely the property of God as well as his own acts. All this is equally applicable when we come to Jesus' role in redemption.

What is perhaps the most significant additional point is von Balthasar's notion of redemption itself. For while themes of atonement and the reconciliation of God and humankind are undoubtedly central in his thinking, he reinterprets them within the framework of the reharmonization of creation with God. Whereas for Maximus this is achieved through a cosmic ontological synthesis in Christ, von Balthasar works with a parallel scheme but in obediential terms: Christ as the structuring center of created existence, through whom and for whom all things were made, accomplishes a new relationship to God through his perfect adoration and obedience. It is precisely the fact that Jesus accomplishes this as a human being which is central to the redemptive work of God, not only because the free and loving obedience of humanity is the missing piece in God's plan, but also because Christ carries out his obedience by drawing humankind into the drama of his own pattern of life.[19]

We could in very rough terms sketch von Balthasar's theory of redemption under three headings: first, Christ's role as keystone of the cosmos and center of the relationship between God and humanity; second, the redeeming work of obediential love that he accomplishes in his pivotal position in the cosmos; and third, the inclusivity of this redeeming work which is from the beginning intended to take effect by drawing humankind into participation. In each of the three points, the humanity of Christ is essential to redemption.

Under the first point, von Balthasar draws heavily on the themes of Christ's cosmic role which he finds in Colossians and Ephesians as these have been developed in patristic thought, especially in Maximus. Von Balthasar argues that Jesus himself is the perfect fufillment of God's eternal idea for the world (*Weltidee*).

> He is this idea, not in some unspecified place outside the real world and its history, but by his very coming into that world and its history "to reestablish all things" (Eph 1:10) from within himself as head. . . . It is pointless to object that he came into the world only in the fullness of time, for the process of creating the world would never have been begun if this moment in the fullness of time had not been foreseen. Indeed, *this realization of the idea of the world in the Incarnation* was possible only because it already existed as a concept among the free possibilities of the eternal reality of trinitarian life.[20]

Throughout his works von Balthasar operates with this concept of creation having been ordered to the Incarnation as its fulfillment. But he does not conceive of this simply as a piecing together of the crucial central bits in some metaphysical puzzle. It is precisely what Jesus does, what he accomplishes between God and humankind, that is vital to the reharmonization of the cosmos. Von Balthasar emphasizes that from his pivotal point in creation Christ "is no God in disguise simply coming to give us an example of how to live, like a teacher writing on the blackboard the solution to a problem which presents no difficulty to him."[21] The world and humankind attain fulfillment in Jesus through his inward and outward struggle to love; it is, in other words, a fulfillment which is won and accomplished in Jesus' life-act, his steadfastness in the filial mission. It is in this sense that "Christ is the summit of the world which strives upwards to the Father, and [that] he clears the way by becoming the spear-head of all its endeavours."[22]

Which brings us to the second point in elucidating von Balthasar on redemption: what exactly is it which Christ performs, which makes his divine-humanity the "spear-head" of all the world's striving towards the Father? It is not simply Jesus' final self-oblation on the cross that is of determinative significance, but his whole life of praise, reverence, and service to the Father. In fact von Balthasar gives considerable attention to the *whole* of Jesus' life as a work of redemption. As we have seen, the whole process of Incarnation comes about through his continuing acts of self-renouncing love. It is not simply the great public acts which are significant for salvation, but equally

> his hidden acts, his prayer to the Father, his obedience, his love for the Father unto death. It is precisely this inner aspect that is most essential, definitive, in the whole economy of redemption. For it is not true that the acts and states of the Redeemer, *by which he makes for redeemed humanity a new spiritual and heavenly home,* are only partially human acts (that is to say, a subordinate part therefore), while those where the human nature as such falls short of the divine call for the intervention of the higher nature, that of the God-man. That would be pure Arianism. The acts and states by which Christ redeems us are genuine human acts, from the lowest to the highest; though they are never solely human they are always human.[23]

We can see how utterly important it is in von Balthasar's view that the redeeming work of Christ is not something done solely by the divine nature, with Jesus as human being simply acting as a kind of visible temporal sign of what is being accomplished hiddenly by the eternal Son.

Nothing could be farther from von Balthasar's intention or from the structure of his own explication. For the work of redemption described by von Balthasar is entirely achieved in, through, and for the stuff of human existence: the suffering of the cross is not seen as some superhuman event, far removed from normal existence, but is rather integrated as the final stage of a very human spiritual journey of adoring and obedient love, the same path we have already traced in the preceding chapters.

What Jesus accomplishes in both his outward deeds and his inward spiritual states is, of course, the eternal filial pattern of life; and it is the opening of that mode of existence, that particular form of relationship with God, to the whole of humankind, which is the work of redemption in the fullest sense (the third aspect of redemption in von Balthasar). As we saw in the last chapter, Christ opens within himself a new stage for humanity's encounter with God, a framework or "climate" of trusting availability and liberating service in which all persons can come to know the full reality of their human identity. Jesus' human activity of redemption is in fact generative of true human existence.[24]

Jesus' created striving for God is an activity entirely open and inclusive of all human beings—not, again, in a kind of automatic, ontological sense, but in terms of their actual life according to the pattern of Jesus' reverential love. "It would not conform to the authentic human solidarity of Jesus were he to carry through his work of salvation in an exclusive fashion, shutting out all others."[25]

This theme of the participation of humankind in the work of redemption underscores the determinative significance of Jesus as a particular historical human being. For it is not merely the fact that men and women undertake these kinds of acts and not others which gives them a share in redemption; rather what matters is that in their personal fidelity and spiritual intimacy with Christ their acts are caught up and given a place in the new relationship with the Father which he has won for them. And that kind of personal discipleship requires, in von Balthasar's view, a real, concretely particularized, human Christ who in the most mundane ways possible affords "authentic human solidarity": "[Christ] desires nearness; he would like to live in you and commingle his breath with your breathing. . . . He seeks trust, intimacy (*Vertrauen, Vertraulichkeit*); he is a beggar for your love."[26] In his doctrine of the Incarnation von Balthasar has sought to show us something of what the saints and mystics have encountered in their intimacy with Christ, above all an awareness of the real struggle of his very human life and the intensity of his openness to others.

Do the kenosis and the exaltation of Jesus undermine, or rather do they make more concrete, the full reality of his historical humanity? Does Jesus as a particular historical human being have a determinatively significant role to play in the divine work of revelation and redemption? These are the questions I have asked in this chapter in order to draw together and test many of the cardinal lines of my argument. I have sought to verify that the same Jesus who has emerged in my analysis of von Balthasar on the Incarnation also provides a positive answer to the questions just stated. In each case we have seen that von Balthasar's conception of Jesus Christ brings the full stature of his humanity to light.

It could never be said that Hans Urs von Balthasar is an easy writer or that he does not, by his forcefulness, sometimes leave himself open to misimpressions. Yet he is an imaginatively commited thinker and a consistent one. His interpretation of the Incarnation is seeded through nearly all the pages of his voluminous work, but everywhere there springs up a characteristic sensibility, a curiously familiar line of thought. And at the heart of this christological exposition there lies the persuasion that the eternal Word of God has become incarnate in the compassionate and adoring self-giving of Jesus, in his steadfast obedience, his fateful passage beyond the limits of human life, and his enrapturing communal existence beyond the grave.

We have been able to notice and interpret this scheme because we have taken into account the analogies which von Balthasar has seen between Christ's own experiences and those of the women and men whom he has drawn into his life. In them von Balthasar senses that "living contemporaneity" with the Gospel which he believes can re-open and set flowing the living sources of theology. He has, I think, attempted to see Jesus through the eyes of those who have most given themselves to his mission. And there he has discerned a historical spiritual journey in which the developing and unfolding human life of Christ and the eternal Word of God are one.

NOTES

1. FINDING ONE'S WAY IN VON BALTHAZAR

1. "In Retrospect," trans. Kenneth Batinovich in *The Analogy of Beauty: The Theology of Hans Urs von Balthasar*, ed. John Riches (Edinburgh: T. & T. Clark, 1986), 196. And consider his own important pre-Vatican II work, *Schleifung der Bastionen* (Razing the Bastions, published 1952), "which blew the last, impatient trumpet blast calling for a Church no longer barricaded against the world, a trumpet blast that did not die away unheard, but which has subsequently forced the trumpeter himself to pause and reflect" (Von Balthasar, "In Retrospect," 196).

2. "Integralism is the debilitating, mechanical attempt to hold together a disparate collection of individual truths and traditions; integration, in contrast, is the spontaneous art of aiming always at the Whole through the fragments of truth discussed and lived. The Whole, then, is always greater than us and our powers of expression, but precisely as greater it animates our Christian life" (Von Balthasar, "Another Ten Years—1975," trans. John Saward, in *The Analogy of Beauty*, 231).

3. Rowan Williams, *The Wound of Knowledge*, 2d ed. (Boston: Cowley Publications, 1991), 1.

4. For two fine sketches of von Balthasar's life and thought, see Medard Kehl, "Hans Urs von Balthasar: A Portrait," in *The Von Balthasar Reader*, ed. Medard Kehl and Werner Löser, trans. Robert J. Daly and Fred Lawrence (New York: Crossroad, 1982), 3–54; and Peter Henrici, "Hans Urs von Balthasar: A Sketch of His Life," in *Hans Urs von Balthasar: His Life and Work*, ed. David L. Schindler (San Francisco: Ignatius Press, 1991), 7–43.

5. "Another Ten Years—1975," 223.

6. "The fact that von Balthasar understands himself primarily as a pastor and only secondarily as an academic theologian is of significance. He invests time and effort in presenting actual correlations in which human longing finds its fulfillment in faith because such correlations may help to strengthen the faith of believers. He is less concerned to work out a formal theory of this correlation in the precision which modern academic discussion demands" (Hilary A. Mooney, *The Liberation of Con-*

sciousness: Bernard Lonergan's Theological Foundations in Dialogue with the Theological Aesthetics of Hans Urs von Balthasar [Frankfurt: Verlag Josef Knecht, 1992], 251).

7. The respective proponents of these views (which von Balthasar holds together) were actually in opposing camps during the postconciliar interpretive battles over Chalcedon's meaning. The theological dispute of the post-Chalcedonian period is clearly described by John Meyendorff, *Christ in Eastern Christian Thought*, 2d ed. (St. Vladimir's Seminary Press, 1975), esp. 29–89.

8. See Juan-Miguel Garrigues, O.P., "La Personne composée du Christ d'après S. Maxime," *Revue Thomiste* 74 (April 1974): 181–204.

9. "For how can divine and human be thus brought together under any single conception, as if they could both be more exact determinations, coordinated to each other, of one and the same universal? Indeed, even divine spirit and human spirit could not without confusion be brought together in this way" (F. Schleiermacher, *The Christian Faith*, 2d ed. [Edinburgh: T. & T. Clark, 1986], para. 96, p. 392).

10. Karl Barth, *Church Dogmatics* IV/2 (Edinburgh: T. & T. Clark, 1958), 106.

11. Austin Farrer, "Incarnation," sermon in *The Brink of Mystery*, ed. Charles C. Conti (London: SPCK, 1976), 20, preached in Keble College chapel, 1961. Or consider Newman, preaching in the same city 130 years before Farrer: "We speak of [Christ] in a vague way as God, which is true, but not the whole truth; and, in consequence when we proceed to consider His humiliation, we are unable to carry on the notion of His personality from heaven to earth. He who was but now spoken of as God, without mention of the Father from whom He is, is next described as if a creature; but how do these distinct notions of Him hold together in our minds? We are able indeed to continue the idea of a Son into that of a servant, though the descent be infinite, and, to our reason, incomprehensible; but when we merely speak first of God, then of man, we seem to change the Nature without preserving the Person. In truth His Divine Sonship is that portion of sacred doctrine on which the mind is providentially intended to rest throughout, and so to preserve for itself His identity unbroken" (John Henry Newman, "The Humiliation of the Eternal Son," in *Parochial and Plain Sermons*, vol. 3 [1836] (San Francisco: Ignatius Press, 1987), 586–87).

12. The whole of von Balthasar's *Theologie der drei Tage* (Einsiedeln: Benzinger, 1969) is a sustained articulation of this theme. (Eng. ed, *Mysterium Paschale*, trans. Aidan Nichols, O.P. [Edinburgh: T. & T. Clark, 1990].)

13. For an introductory assessment of the role of Jesuit spirituality in von Balthasar, see Werner Löser, S.J., "The Ignatian *Exercises* in the Work

of Hans Urs von Balthasar," in *Hans Urs von Balthasar*, ed. David L. Schindler (San Francisco: Ignatius Press, 1991), 103–20.

14. For useful analyses of von Balthasar's complex interpretation of the immanent and the economic distinction in trinitarian life, see John J. O'Donnell, S.J., "God and World in Trinitarian Perspective," chap. 10 in *The Mystery of the Triune God* (New York: Paulist Press, 1989), 159–72; and also Gerald F. O'Hanlon, S.J., "Is the Trinitarian God Immutable?" chap. 4 in *The Immutability of God in the Theology of Hans Urs von Balthasar* (Cambridge: Cambridge University Press, 1990).

15. Von Balthasar says that "we can be happy to describe, with Karl Barth, the identity of existence and mission," so that Jesus might almost be said to become who he is as he enacts the particular pattern of his mission: "One can give this the rather unlovely name of functional Christology, but it is at any rate the interpretation of the existence of Jesus as the substantial mission of the Father, something that, on the one hand, opens access to the Trinity in the process of revelation (Eberhard Jüngel is correct to draw attention to this anew) and, on the other hand, gives the correct guiding-line for exegesis . . . which however *also expresses precisely the central concern of the Ignatian Christology of obedience*" ("Two Modes of Faith," in *Explorations in Theology* III: *Creator Spirit*, trans. Brian McNeil [San Francisco: Ignatius Press, 1993], 100–101).

16. To refer again to Austin Farrer: "How can a person who knows his unique metaphysical status with more than Aristotelian exactitude be a largely self-taught Galilean village boy whose store of ideas derived from the Synagogue? . . . On the other hand he *knows how* to be Son of God in the several situations of his gradually unfolding destiny, and in the way appropriate to each. He is tempted to depart from that knowledge, but he resists the temptation. And that suffices for the incarnation to be real. For 'being the Son of God' is the exercise of a sort of life; and in order to exercise it he must know how to exercise that life: it is a question of practical knowledge" ("Very God and Very Man," in *Interpretation and Belief*, ed. Charles C. Conti [London: SPCK, 1976], 135).

17. Peter Eicher, *Offenbarung. Prinzip neuzeitlicher Theologie* (Munich: Kösel-Verlag, 1977). See also Hans-Peter Heinz, *Der Gott des Je-mehr: der christologische Ansatz Hans Urs von Balthasar* (Bern: Herbert Lang, 1979), 95.

18. *Herrlichkeit, Theodramatik, Theologik*; fifteen volumes in all, published between 1961 and 1987.

19. Eicher, 340–41.

20. *Karl Rahner in Dialogue: Conversations and Interviews, 1965–1982*, ed. Paul Imhof and Hubert Biallowons (New York: Cross-road, 1986), 124–25.

21. Ibid., 126–27.

22. Von Balthasar is painfully aware of the gnostic temptation for Christianity. In his treatment of Irenaeus's confrontation with the Gnostics, he remarks with an interesting ambivalence that "Gnosis, which, largely with the tools and materials of the Bible, had erected a totally un-Christian structure of the highest intellectual and religious quality and won over many Christians, *Gnosis was the opponent Christian thought needed in order fully to find itself*" (*The Glory of the Lord* II, trans. Andrew Louth et al. [Edinburgh: T. & T. Clark, 1984], 32. My emphasis).

23. For comprehensive bibliographies of all von Balthasar's writings, see *Hans Urs von Balthasar. Bibliographie 1925–1990*, ed. Cornelia Capol (Einsiedeln: Johannes Verlag, 1990).

24. *Parole et mystère chez Origène* (Paris: Ed. du Cerf, 1957), originally published serially in *Recherches de Science Religieuse* in 1936–37; *Présence et pensée. Essai sur la philosophie religieuse de Grégoire de Nysse* (Paris: Beauchesne, 1942); *Kosmische Liturgie: Höhe und Krise des griechischen Weltbilds Maximus Confessor* (Freiburg: Herder, 1941), 2d expanded ed., 1961.

25. Originally published in 1950 and 1952, respectively, both works are subtitled "history of a mission," and a second edition published them together as *Schwestern im Geist* (Einsiedeln: Johannes Verlag, 1970).

26. *Das Herz der Welt* (Zürich: Arche, 1945).

27. *Das betrachtende Gebet*, (Einsiedeln: Johannes Verlag, 1955). (Eng. tr., *Prayer*, trans. A. V. Littledale [New York: Paulist Press, 1967].)

28. *Christlicher Stand* (Einsiedeln: Johannes Verlag, 1977).

29. Von Balthasar, "Another Ten Years," *Analogy of Beauty*, 226.

30. Ibid.

2. A MYSTICAL CHRISTOLOGY

1. The following are given over entirely to the problem: "Theologie und Heiligkeit," *Wort und Wahrheit* 3 (1948): 881–96; "Theologie und Heiligheit," in Verbum Caro: *Skizzen zur Theologie* I (Einsiedeln: Johannes Verlag, 1960); "Theologie und Spiritualität," *Gregorianum* 50 (1969): 571–87; "Theology and Holiness," *Communio* 14 (Winter 1987): 341–50.

2. "In the whole history of Catholic theology there is hardly anything that is less noticed, yet more deserving of notice, than the fact that, since the great period of Scholasticism, there have been few theologians who were saints. . . . If we consider the history of theology up to the time of the great Scholastics, we are struck by the fact that the great saints,

those who not only achieved an exemplary purity of life, but who also had received from God a definite mission in the Church, were, mostly, great theologians. They were 'pillars of the Church,' by vocation channels of her life: their own lives reproduced the fullness of the Church's life" (von Balthasar, "Theology and Sanctity," in *The Word Made Flesh: Explorations in Theology* I [Eng. ed. of "Theologie und Heiligkeit, in *Verbum Caro,* 1960], trans. A. V. Littledale, 2d ed. [San Francisco: Ignatius Press, 1989], 181).

3. "einen Dualismus entstehen zwischen einer polemischen Theologie, die sich in begriffliche Subtilitäten (die doch nicht vermeidbar sind) zu verlieren droht, und einer innerkirchlichen, unangefochtenen Theologie, die sich aus der Fülle des Bundesgedankens heraus entfaltet" ("Theologie und Spiritualität," *Gregorianum* 50 [1960]: 577). I will generally quote from available translations. When none is noted, as is the case here, the translation is my own.

4. Von Balthasar will say of even one of his least favorite patristic figures, Evagrius, that his theology, though it "might have led to a spirituality independent of dogmatic theology . . . was more steeped in dogma than its counterparts among the spiritual writers of the *grand siècle*" ("Theology and Sanctity," 190).

5. *Présence et pensée. Essai sur la philosophie religieuse de Grégoire de Nysse* (Paris: Beauchesne, 1942), 141: "Loin de s'opposer, théologie dogmatique et mystique sont inséparable, elles sont même, si l'on conçoit la théologie comme une realisation dynamique, identique. C'est ainsi que la comprenaient tous les Pères, et très particulièrament Origène et les Cappadociens."

6. "Theology and Sanctity," 190.

7. "Spiritualität," in *Verbum Caro,* 1960; Eng. ed. "Spirituality," in *The Word Made Flesh* (San Francisco: Ignatius Press), 211.

8. "Theologie und Spiritualität." 580.

9. "Theology and Sanctity," 186.

10. *The Glory of the Lord* V: *The Realm of Metaphysics in the Modern Age,* trans. Oliver Davies et al. (Edinburgh: T. & T. Clark, 1991), 26–27.

11. "Theology and Sanctity," 208. The remarkable work of Michael J. Buckley would seem to confirm von Balthasar's reading to a large extent. Buckley notes how scientific theology (already divorced from spirituality), for the sake of strengthening its position in the argument with atheism, chose completely to avoid all recourse to spirituality and the christological framework of theology which alone could have afforded the real evidence which Christian theology does have to offer. "The theists and the putative atheists had to find a common ground, and that ground was neither the

person of Jesus nor the individual or communal experiences of religion. . . . [so] it is not remarkable that neither Lessius nor Mersenne appealed to participative religious experience. This had already been relegated to the practices of piety, to the private progress of contemplative development, and to the tractates in spirituality that abounded in the Netherlands and in France. . . . But the discipline and study of religious experience presumably had nothing to say to the rising sense of atheism. 'Natural theology' and 'mystical theology' never intersected except in a genius such as Blaise Pascal, even though a theologian like Lessius could write insightfully in both fields. These fields were kept abstracted one from another. . . . It is not without a sense of wonder that one records that the theologians bracketed religion in order to defend religion" (*At the Origins of Modern Atheism* [New Haven: Yale University Press, 1987], 345).

12. "Theology and Sanctity," 192.

13. Ibid., 191. Or again: "The mere fact that Bremond could write such a comprehensive *Histore littéraire du sentiment religieux* without even having to mention the contemporary state of theology as the science of doctrine is one of the more alarming facts of recent Church history" ("Theology and Sanctity," 187). Nine years later he adds caustically: "Henri Bremond could draw together the whole sublime and yet latently tragic history of this era under the dreadful [*schrecklichem*] and basically Schleiermacherish [*schleiermacherischen*] title of a '*Histoire du sentiment religieux en France*'" ("Theologie und Spiritualität," 581).

14. *Glory* V, 115. For most texts quoted from published English translations, I will give the original German in brackets immediately following the citation of the English text. ["Die fromme Vernunft ist sich ihrer selbst bewußt und nimmt sich paradoxerweise in ihrer von sich wegstrebenden Transzendenz zum Gegenstand. . . . Der unbedachte Zug zur Selbstbespiegelung . . . legt sich wie Mehltau (oder soll man sagen: wie Puder?) über die berühmte Spiritualität des Grand Siècle" (*Herrlichkeit: Eine theologische Ästhetik* [Einsiedeln: Johannes Verlag, 1965], vol. III/1, *Im Raum der Metaphysik: Neuzeit*, 467–68).]

15. "There is no question of turning back the wheel of history, and proposing a renascence of patristic theology at the expense of Scholasticism" ("Theology and Sanctity," 208).

16. Ibid., 193.

17. "Spirituality," *The Word Made Flesh*, 214.

18. *Mysterium Paschale,* trans. Aidan Nichols, O.P. (Edinburgh: T. & T. Clark, 1990), 38.

19. "Theology and Sanctity," 205.

20. Ibid.

21. *The Spiritual Exercises of Saint Ignatius,* no. 104, trans. George E. Ganss, S.J. (Chicago: Loyola University Press, 1992), 56. "I translated the

Exercises into German and had the opportunity of conducting them some hundred times: here if anywhere is Christian joy" (Von Balthasar, "In Retrospect," 196).

22. *Mysterium Paschale,* 40.

23. "Theology and Sanctity," 203.

24. "In saying that their constant aim is to steep themselves in the stream of life ever issuing from the mouth of the eternal Word, we have tacitly indicated the form of theology. Their one desire is to be receptive, men of prayer in other words. Their theology is essentially an act of adoration and prayer" (ibid., 206).

25. Von Balthasar, *Prayer,* trans. A. V. Littledale (New York: Paulist Press, 1967), 86.

26. Von Balthasar, *Thérèse of Lisieux: The Story of a Mission,* trans. Donald Nicholl (New York: Sheed and Ward, 1954), xvi–xvii.

27. *Glory of the Lord* I, 408.

28. Ibid., 411.

29. Ibid., 414.

30. Von Balthasar, "Zur Ortsbestimmung Christlicher Mystik," in *Grundfragen der Mystik,* with Werner Beierwaltes and Alois M. Haas (Einsiedeln: Johannes Verlag, 1974), 59: "die entscheidende Maxime, daß nicht die *Erfahrung* einer Einigung mit Gott den Maßtab der Vollkommenheit (der höchsten Aifstiegsetappe) darstellt, sondern der *Gehorsam,* der auch in der Erfahrung der Gottverlassenheit mit Gott genauso eng verbunden sein kann wie in der erfahrenen Einigung."

31. Maximilian Greiner, "The Community of St. John: A Conversation with Cornelia Capol and Martha Gisi," in *Hans Urs von Balthasar: His Life and Work,* 87–101, here 94. On the theme of obedience, M. Gisi comments: "I believe what the Herr Doktor's and Adrienne's reflections had in common with the view of St. Ignatius lies in the idea of obedience as following the obedient Christ. This is really the central idea. And when one speaks in this context about our community one can understand obedience only in the light of this theology: obedience as following the crucified Lord. This is what was alive in him [von Balthasar] and in Adrienne as something coming from Ignatius, and it is here that one can see the true core of their Ignatian thinking and faith" (ibid).

32. Ibid., 95.

33. "Theologie und Spiritualität," 581: "wesentlich um das Fortkommen des frommen gottseligen Ich, die «Philothea», geht."

34. "Spirituality," 221. And further on this: "One certain means for the discernment of spirits is to test the presence, open or latent, of a certain ill-feeling toward other states of life or forms of spirituality" (ibid., 222).

35. Von Balthasar, "Zur Ortsbestimmung Christlicher Mystik," 66: "Der Maßtab, an dem der Christ (der Mensch überhaupt) in Gottes Ge-

richt gemessen wird, ist seine Gottes- und Nächstenliebe und nicht der Grad seiner religiösen Erfahrung."

36. Bernard McGinn, "Resurrection and Ascension in the Christology of the Early Cistercians," *Cîteaux: Commentarii Cistercienses* 30 (1979), 10.

37. "Theology and Sanctity," 196. This is not the place to decide what role such a theology could have in modern theology or even academic theology, but it might at least be argued that if a "formational" theology succeeds in making elements in the divine-human encounter perspicuous which might otherwise go unremarked, and moreover does so in a manner which communicates something of this encounter's startling and passionate gratuity, then such a theology has an important role in any attempt to understand and interpret the depths of Christian religious existence.

38. Von Balthasar, *A Theology of History*, 2d ed. (New York: Sheed and Ward, 1963), 79–80. See also "Theology and Sanctity," 204: "Though objective revelation was concluded with the death of the last apostle, it does not follow that, in the Church of the saints, nothing further happens that touches on revelation. After all, the miracles of absolution and consecration are continually repeated, and they bring about again and again a new presence of the events of Good Friday and Easter within the Church. Why should it not be the same with the constant repetition of the theological existence of the Lord in the life of his faithful and saints?" We note here that von Balthasar mentions this re-presencing of Christ in connection with the faithful generally, and not only with the saints.

39. "Theology and Sanctity," 204; emphasis mine.

40. *Theology of History*, 66.

41. *Prayer*, 49. Von Balthasar goes on to say, as we might well expect him to do, that for all this Christ always remains one who confronts the believer in a "manner wholly free," always "something fundamentally other than the 'depths of my soul'" (ibid., 51–52).

42. *Spiritual Exercises*, 56, no. 104. Or, as Hugo Rahner put it: "For Ignatius the life of Christ was more than just an edifying example in the sense understood by the *devotio moderna*—it was the fundamental theological principal behind Christian spiritual life, which is ultimately nothing more nor less than the conforming of one's whole being through grace with the crucified and risen Lord of glory" (*Ignatius the Theologian*, trans. Michael Barry [San Francisco: Ignatius Press, 1990], 99).

43. "A situation in the life of Jesus must not be regarded as a closed finite thing, delimited by other historical situations, previous, contemporaneous or subsequent. Since it is the manifestation in this world of the eternal life of God, it always has a dimension open to that which is above. Its meaning, the numbers of its possible applications, is, even at its own

historical level, something limitless. . . . That is why Christians have found in each of these situations objects of contemplation which can never be used up" *(Theology of History*, 67).

44. *Thérèse of Lisieux*, 16–17.

45. *Glory of the Lord* V, 122. ["Mit Eckhart unterstreicht er zunächst das Je-Jetzt der menschwerdenden Liebe Gottes, die im ewigen Je-Jetzt des trinitarischen Prozesses gründet. In diesem Je-Jetzt ist im Gottmenschen 'der actuelle Geschmack, die lebhafe Geneigtheit, womit Jesus ein Geheimnis [seines Erdenlebens] gewirkt hat, immerfort wach, aktuell und gegenwärtig fur ihn'" (474).] The quotation from Bérulle is from the 1856 Migne edition, pp.1052f.

46. "One can see here how Bérulle gives a metaphysical foundation to the Pauline concept of the indwelling in Christ by faith and thus surpasses and removes the poison from the Platonism of Eckhart and Ruysbroeck, the Platonism which taught that the creature lives more in its divine idea than in its own existence outside of God. Existence in Christ, integrated by the integration of his human states in his fundamental state as the God-Man, is an existence which explains our spiritual capacity (*capacité* in the sense of the possibility of existing spiritually in another, the world or God) in terms of Christ's capacity for us" (ibid., 123). ["Man sieht, wie Bérulle den paulinischen Gedanken der Einwohnung in Christus durch den Glauben metaphysisch begründet und damit den Platonismus von Eckhart und Ruisbroeck überholt und entgiftet, der die Kreatur mehr in ihrer göttlichen Idee als in ihrem Außer-Gott-in-sich-Sein zu leben anwies. Existenz in Christo, mitintegriert bei der Integration seiner menschlichen Zustände in seine grundlegende gottmenschliche Zuständlichkeit, ist Existenz, die unsere geistige Fassungskraft (capacité als Möglichkeit, geistig in Fremdem, Welt oder Gott zu sein) aufgehen läßt in sein Fassungskraft für uns" (475).]

47. *Mysterium Paschale*, 133.

48. Ibid., 41.

49. "Theology and Sanctity," 199.

50. Ibid., 199–200.

51. Von Balthasar, *La foi du Christ: Cinq approches christologiques* (Paris: Aubier, 1968), 108.

52. *Parole et Mystère chez Origène* (Paris: Les Editions du Cerf, 1957), n. 31, p. 123: "Si, au contraire, la vérité réside surtout dans l'assimilation d'un être a son Idée, qu'elle soit par conséquent une vie, une tension, une chose secrète, l'être devra se livrer pour être saisi."

53. *Prayer*, 117–18. Von Balthasar is particularly critical of Evagrius in this regard, seeing in him a fatal tendency to evaporate every distinctive historical feature in favor of the unitary divine essence. While acclaiming Evagrius's ascetical theology, he also complains: "He knows the Incarna-

tion of Christ, but only as a transitory episode of the cosmic development that is in no wise definitive. Rather he holds that one must strive to pass beyond the corporeal Christ, who is only a penultimate form of the Logos. To be sure, Evagrius knows the mystery of suffering: the cross, burial, resurrection; but these are only the symbol for the interior, two-fold process of *gnosis*" ("The Metaphysics and Mystical Theology of Evagrius," in *Monastic Studies* 3 [1965]: 183–95, 193).

54. *Mysterium Paschale*, 56.

55. Ibid., 60.

56. Cf., von Balthasar, *Love Alone: The Way of Revelation* (London: Sheed and Ward, 1968), 47: "This form [of divine love] is so majestic that, without expressly demanding it, its perception exacts from the beholder the attitude of adoration."

57. "[One] cannot proceed beyond this pre-understanding to a recognition of the sign without a radical conversion; conversion not only of heart—and with it the admission that in the light of this love one has never loved—but also of the mind with the realization that one must start from the beginning to re-learn what love really is" (*Love Alone*, 51).

58. See here the helpful readings of Mooney, *The Liberation of Consciousness*, esp. 183–84, 249–50, and Treitler, "True Foundations of Authentic Theology," in *Hans Urs von Balthasar: His Life and Work*, 169–82.

59. Brian McNeil, C.R.V., "The Exegete as Iconographer: Balthasar and the Gospels," in *The Analogy of Beauty*, 134–46, here 143.

60. "The exegete may be justified in the view that he, *qua* exegete, is not qualified to pronounce on questions of dogmatic theological interest: the importance of Balthasar's work lies in its stringent reminder to the exegete that he is *not* justified in dismissing dogmatic questions as irrelevant to his own researches" (ibid., 146).

61. *The Glory of the Lord* VII, trans. Brian McNeil (Edinburgh: T. & T. Clark, 1989), 321ff. [*Herrlichkeit* (Einsiedeln: Johannes Verlag, 1969), vol. III/2, *Theologie: Neuer Bund*, 299ff.]

62. "La conscience de Jésus et sa mission," in *Nouveaux Points de Repère* (Paris: Librairie Arthème Fayard, 1980), 167–74, here 163.

63. Ibid., 164–65.

64. Ibid., 166.

65. *Theo-Drama* III, trans. Graham Harrison (San Francisco: Ignatius Press, 1992), 109. ["Wer diesen 'Überhang' an Dogmatik im Neuen Testament als 'Überbau' über eine schlicht-menschliche . . . Existenz Jesu interpretiert . . . der muß zusehen, ob er nach Wegschaffung der Zutaten noch ein plausibles Bild des historischen Jesus vorweisen kann" (*Theo-dramatik* [Einsiedeln: Johannes Verlag, 1978], vol. II/2, *Die Personen des Spiels: Die Personen in Christus*, 99).]

66. *Theo-Drama* III, 110f. [99f.]

67. Von Balthasar, "The Word, Scripture and Tradition," in *The Word Made Flesh*, 11–26, here 20–21.

68. *Prayer*, 162.

69. Von Balthasar, *Christian Meditation*, trans. Sr. Mary Theresilde Skerry (San Francisco: Ignatius Press, 1989), 23.

70. *Glory of the Lord* VII, 154–55. [142–43.]

71. Ibid., 154. ["Der Gehorsam an den Geist erfordert, daß im Interesse der Identität der Person (des historischen Jesus und des in der Kirche gegenwärtigen geschichtlichen Christus) da und dort eine unerläßliche Transposition erfolgt" (142).]

72. *Theo-Drama* III, 114.

73. "Those who are ashamed of me and of my words in this adulterous and sinful generation, of them the Son of Man will also be ashamed when he comes in the glory of his Father with the holy angels."

74. "And I tell you, everyone who acknowledges me before others, the Son of Man also will acknowledge before the angels of God."

75. *Theo-Drama* III, 115.

76. Ibid., 116–17. [Wenn er [Jesus] trotzdem statt «Ich» «Menschensohn» gesagt haben sollte, dann würde dies zeigen, wie übermäßig und unanschaulich für ihn das Verhältnis zwischen ihm als dem irdisch mit einer bestimmten menschlich bewältigbaren Sendung Lebenden und ihm als dem in die eschatologisch durch die Erfahrung der «Stunde» (Passion-Auferstehung) überdehnte, einstweilen unabsehbare Sendung Eingesetzten bleiben mußte (106).]

77. *Glory of the Lord* VII, 338.

78. *Mysterium Paschale*, 68.

79. Ibid., 69.

80. See especially here his comments on the Petrine, Pauline, Johannine, and Marian traditions in the church: *Glory of the Lord* I, 352–64.

81. "The Absence of Jesus," in *New Elucidations*, trans. Sr. Mary Theresilde Skerry (San Francisco: Ignatius Press, 1986), 55–56.

82. Ibid., 56. My emphasis.

83. Ibid., 57.

84. In other words, the claim here is not so much on the level of direct biblical exegesis, for if it were, on that level von Balthasar would indeed seem to know more about the interior life of Christ than contemporary biblical critics generally allow is possible for us, given the biblical writings per se. No, the issue is joined at the level of the living enactment of and participation in the biblical narratives by the followers of Jesus. It is from this experience, interpreted within the framework of the gospels, that von Balthasar develops certain aspects of his exegesis. That is, he wishes to complement the historical and literary exegesis of the biblical critic with

the participative and lived exegesis of the saint. Whether this latter form of exegesis is acceptable to modern theology as a basis for theological claims remains another issue, one which returns us again to an awareness that the biblical critic's methods are no more theologically neutral than the saint's.

3. THE STRUCTURE OF BALTHASARIAN CHRISTOLOGY

1. Von Balthasar, *Kosmische Liturgie: Das Weltbild Maximus des Bekenners*, 2d ed. (Einsiedeln: Johannes Verlag, 1961), 55–56. (The 1st ed. appeared in 1941.)

2. Ibid., 207–8.

3. Ibid., 209: "Die Einheit von Gott und Welt in Christus war durch eine reine 'Wesens'-Philosophie nicht auszudrücken. Würde sie als 'physich' und 'ontisch' betont . . . so war die Folge eine Mischung der beiden geeinten Pole zu einer neuen 'Wesenheit' . . . wollte man aber diese Mischung vermeiden, so gelang anscheinend nur eine akzidentelle, äußerliche, 'moralische' Einheit durch 'geistige Beziehung' . . . zwischen beiden Naturen."

4. The passage continues: "Everything that is human is found anew in this new way, though it is nevermore "purely human" (*philos anthrōpos*) or "simply human" (*haplōs anthrōpos*). Rather it appears mysteriously inhabited by an Other (*tō enoikein*). This inhabitation seems at once the most interior and intimate one could imagine . . . and the most gently concerned to safeguard everything human and natural." (Ibid., 212: "Ladet uns nicht ein gleichsam phänomenoligischer Blick auf die Erscheinung Christi dazu ein, die uns ein Wesen zeigt, dessen ganzes Gebaren bis in letzte Work, in die kleinste Geste hinein eine menschliche Natur verrat, aber eine menschliche Natur, die als ganze auf einen andern Modus des Daseins übersetzt ist? Alles, was zum Menschen gehört, findet sich im dieser neuen Weise wieder, und doch ist nichts mehr davon ein 'rein Menschliches,' ein 'Nur-Menschliches,' sondern erscheint wie geheimnisvoll 'durch-wohnt' von einem Andern. Diese Durchwohnung gibt sich zugleich als die innerlichste und intimste, die denkbar ist, und die am zartesten besorgte, alles Menschliche un Natürliche zu wahren und in sie hineinzuretten.")

5. Ibid., 244: "Was den Logos vom Vater unterscheidet, unterscheidet sich in der Einigung nicht mehr von dem, was den Menschengewordenen von den übrigen Menschen unterscheidet. Mit dieser Formel erreicht die formale Christologie ihren Höhepunkt."

6. Ibid., 243. The whole passage reads: "Während im Menschen die Fähigkeiten der Seele und des Leibes aufeinander zugeordnet sind und

sich antworten, ist jede derartige Entsprechung zwischen den Naturen Christi ausgeschlossen. Gerade diese Nicht-Entsprechung aber ist das einzigartige Mittel, die Menschheit zu vergöttlichen. Denn so vermag die menschliche Natur ohne Einbuße ihrer Natürlichkeit an der göttlichen Hypostase teilzuhaben; ihre Hypostase kann der Logos selbst sein . . . weil umgekehrt diese vergöttlichende Hypostase sie in ihrem wesentlichen Menschsein befestigt und bewahrt."

7. *Thérèse of Lisieux*, 225–26; a second German edition was published in *Schwestern im Geist: Therese von Lisieux und Elisabeth von Dijon* (Einsiedeln: Johannes Verlag, 1970), 292–93: "Die patristische und noch die mittelalterliche Spiritualität setzte . . . das Ziel der Menschen vorwiegend in die Anschauung Gottes oder in die ewige Glückseligkeit; die übernatürliche Finalität der menschlichen Natur konnte darum, unter dem erhebenden Antrieb der Gnade, in jedem Augenblick als Kompaß auf dem geistlichen Wege dienen. Der Mensch brauchte zum Beispiel nur auf sein «unruhiges Herz» zu lauschen, um zu wissen, welchen Weg er einschlagen sollte zum «ewigen Ruhen in Dir». Der Akzent verschiebt sich in dem Augenblick, da Ignatius in seinem «Prinzip und Fundament» das Ziel des Menschen als «Lob, Ehrfurcht und Dienst Gottes»bestimmt und dieser Bestimmung alles, auch die Anschauung Gottes und die eigene Seligkeit, hintansetzt. Nunmehr kann der Kompaß nicht mehr in einer auch übernatürlich erhobenen Physis des Menschen liegen, die Letztentscheidung über das Wie des lobenden und ehrfürchtigen Dienstes liegt bei Gott selbst, in der Offenbarung seines Willens. Ignatius baut folgerichtig seine ganze Spiritualität auf den Begriff der Wahl hin: der Wahl Gottes nämlich, die, in ewiger Freiheit vollzogen, dem Menschen zur Mit- und Nachwahl geoffenbart und angeboten wird. Um aber die Einheit des göttlichen und des geschöpflichen Willens im Wahlakt zu ermöglichen— jener neuen «Identität» und «Verschmelzung», die von jetzt an immer deutlicher das antike Ideal einer mystischen Wesensidentifizierung oder «Vergottung» ersetzt—, muß des Menschen höchste Anstrengung dahin gehen, alle Störungen und Hindernisse von seiner Seite aus dem Wege zu räumen, sich in «geistlichen Übungen» auf die reine «Disposition» zum Empfang des Willens Gottes vorzubereiten."

8. Cf. Von Balthasar, "Zwei Glaubensweisen," in *Spiritus Creator* (Einsiedeln: Johannes Verlag, 1967), 90: "In their life-of-Jesus meditations, the *Spiritual Exercises* emphasize in late medieval fashion a strongly pictorial illustration of scenes. However, they do so only in order to allow the person who prays to reach in each scene the full personal concreteness of the call to follow."

9. Von Balthasar, *Prayer*, 47–48.

10. Harvey Egan, S.J., *Ignatius Loyola the Mystic* (Wilmington, Delaware: Michael Glazier, 1987), 124.

11. "If he is the personal unity of a divine and a human nature, must we attribute to him a single being or a twofold being? The first seems impossible, since the *analogia entis* that prevails between God and the creature, albeit in a fundamental and ultimate "greater dissimilarity" (DS 806), goes right through the incarnate Son of God. The second [that Christ exists in twofold being] seems to threaten his personal unity and make him into a mythical chimera" (*Theo-Drama* III, 202–203). ["Ist er die personale Einheit einer göttlichen und einer menschlichen Natur, muß man ihm dann ein einziges oder ein doppeltes Sein zusprechen? Das erste scheint unmöglich, weil die *Analogia Entis* zwischen God und Geschöpf—in der unübersteigbar «größere Unähnlichkeit» herrscht (DS 806)—mitten durch den menschgewordenen Sohn Gottes hindurchgeht. Das zweite scheint seine personale Einheint zu gefährden und ihn zu einem mythologischen Doppelwesen zu machen" (186).]

12. Ibid., 223–24. ["Was im Seinsaspekt (der abstrakter ist) sich einigermaßen glaubhaft machen läßt, wird im Bewußtseins-Aspekt akut schwierig: Wie kann sich die Identität des Bewußtseins einer (göttlichen) Person in der angenommenen Menschheit mit dem angestammten göttlichen durchhalten, zumal dann, wenn die angenommene Natur im Modus der Entfremdung von Gott existiert?" (205).]

13. Ibid., 224. ["Jesus lebt sein menschliches Bewußtsein vollkommen als Sendung" (206).]

14. *Theo-Drama* III, 59–63. [53–56.]

15. Ibid., 63–80. [57–73.]

16. Ibid., 86. ["Wie seinen Auftrag innerhalb des ihm gewährten Lebensraumes verstand. War er nur der «Zeuge des Glaubens», oder wußte er sich als mehr?" (78).]

17. Ibid., 110–11. ["Sollte das Auftragsbewußtsein Jesu nicht darin gelegen haben, daß er die Entfremdung der Welt von Gott im ganzen—also bis an ihr Ende—aufzuheben hatte, oder, paulinisch und johanneisch gesprochen, mit der Sünde der Welt im ganzen fertig werden mußte? Wäre dem so, dann stünde dem Irdischen der entscheidende, aber menschlich unmeßbare Teil seiner Sendung noch bevor. . . . es kann . . . keine Rede davon sein, daß sein irdisches Wirken, Beten, Sichmühen nicht integrierender Teil seiner Gesamtaufgabe war, daß sich also die erlösende Tat einzig im Kommenden, im Kreuz, konzentriert. . . . Aber das Bewußtsein, auf eine «Taufe» hinzuleben, auf jenen «Kelch» hin, den er wird trinken müssen (und der, wenn die Stunde kommt, sich als das menschlich Unerträgliche, gänzlich Überfordernde erweist, Mk 14, 34.36), auf die Stunde der Vollmacht der Finsternis (Lk 22, 53), läßt dieses Leben nicht in einem weisheitlichen Rhythmus verlaufen, sondern in einem apokalyptischen: vorlaufend auf eine *Akmē*, die er als Mensch nur so wird bestehen können, daß er über sein Handeln nicht mehr (gemäß dem Vaterwillen)

verfügt, sondern als Ganzer von diesem Willen verfügt wird (Lk 22,42 par). . . . Wenn das Apokalyptische zentral als die Naherwartung des Endgerichts Gottes über die alte Welt und damit der äonischen Wende zu einer neuen Welt definiert werden kann, dann ist dieses Apokalyptische— falls Jesus in diesem Erwartungshorizont lebt—durchaus in ihm. . . . er mit seinem menschlichen Handeln nicht ans Ende seines Auftrags gelangen kann, sondern . . . *sich selbst* dafür dem Handeln des Vaters ausliefern muß" (100–101).]

18. Ibid., 113. ["Sein Leiden und Sterben ist keine bloße Passion, son- dern eine Super-Aktion, die er freilich nicht wie seine früheren Taten aus seinem aktiven Geistzentrum vollzieht, in der vielmehr sein Jawort zu Gott über alle endlichen Ausmaße" (102–3).]

19. *Theodramatik* II/2, 109.

20. *Theodrama* III, 166. ["Daß dem individuellen menschlichen Bewußtsein Jesu ein Moment innewohnt, das den rein menschlichen Be- wußtseinshorizont eindeutig und zwar grundsätzlich immer schon über- steig . . . . «Ich bin der, dem dieser Auftrag obliegt», ist ausgewortet die Urintuition Jesu von seiner Identität. «Ich bin der, durch den das Reich Gottes kommen muß und kommen wird»" (152).]

21. Ibid., 169. ["Man würde alles mißverstehen, wenn man darin Het- eronomie sähe; solche ist durch die anfangs gesetzte Identität von Person und Sendung ausgeschlossen" (155).]

22. Ibid., 172. ["Der Auftrag des Vaters, Gottes Vaterschaft durch sein ganzes Sein, sein Leben und Sterben in der Welt und für sie auszudrücken, füllt und beschäftigt dieses Bewußtsein bis zum Rand, es versteht sich gesamthaft als das, was «vom Vater her» zu den Menschen kommt, so sehr als «Auslegung des Vaters», «Wort des Vaters», daß kein Raum und keine Zeit bleibt für eine von der Sendung abgehobene Reflexion auf ein «Wer bin ich?»" (157).]

23. Ibid., 179. [164.]

24. Ibid., 178: "In principle, the entire temporal and eternal destiny of any and every other person comes to lodge within *his own* sphere." ["so daß prinzipiell das ganze zeitliche und ewige Geschick eines (schließ- liche beliebigen) andern in seinen eigenen Bereich zu liegen kommt" (163).]

25. Ibid., 181. [166.]

26. Ibid., 188. ["Den väterlichen Willen in der Gestalt einer unbe- dingten, im Leiden sogar unerbittlichen *Regel* vorzustellen" (173).]

27. Ibid., 197. ["Läßt sich von der ebenso großen Variabilität der christlichen mystischen Gotteserfahrung her—zwischen leuchtenden Au- genblicken und verengender Trockenheit und Verlassenheit—etwas von der möglichen Vielfalt der Wissensformen des irdischen Jesus erahnen" (180).]

28. Ibid., 202. ["Wie kann einer, der ganz und abstrichlos Mensch ist, der «uns in allem gleich ward außer der Sünde», nun doch, wenn er Ich sagt, nicht als eine menschliche, sondern als eine göttliche Person sprechen? Oder, falls er zugleich als ein menschliches Ich spricht: Wie bestehen dann in ihm nicht zwei wenn auch noch so innig vereinte Personen?" (185).]

29. Ibid., 149–50. ["Wer so fragt, geht aus von einer «Christologie von unten»; er fragt nicht unmittelbar z.B. nach dem Inhalt des Wissens Christi, gar nach der Verfaßtheit seiner Person, sondern nach den Bedingungen der Möglichkeit dessen, was sich in ihm empirisch offenbart. . . . kann der sie überbringende Bote jemals mehr sein als ein partiell, fragmentarisch Beauftragter? Kann er so sehr Gesendeter sein, daß seine Sendung zusammenfällt mit seiner Person, und daß beides in Einheit die erschöpfende Selbstmitteilung Gottes wäre?" (137).]

30. Ibid., 207, my emphasis. ["Dort, wo Gott einem Geistsubjeckt zusagt, wer es für ihn, den ewig bleibenden und wahrhaftigen Gott ist, wo er ihm im gleichen Zuge sagt, wozu es existiert—ihm also seine von Gott her beglaubigte Sendung verleiht—dort kann von einem Geistsubjekt gesagt werden, daß es Person sei. Das aber ist einmanl, archetypisch, bei Jesus Christus geschehen, dem seine ewige «Definition» verliehen ward— «Du bist mein geliebter Sohn»" (190).]

31. Von Balthasar, *A Theology of History* (New York: Sheed and Ward, 1963), 26.

32. Ibid., 27.

33. *Theo-Drama* III, 207–8. ["Daß in dieser Vertiefung oder Erhöhung keine Selbstentfremdung des Geistsubjekts, sondern ein innerstes Zusichkommen liegt" (191).]

34. Ibid., 51. ["Gewinnt jeder einen personalen Auftrag, in dem er zugleich mit etwas Einmaligen betraut und damit zum Handeln freigelassen wird . . . . Dieses Personale und Personalisierende . . ." (47).]

See also von Balthasar, *The Christian State of Life*, trans. Sr. Mary Frances McCarthy (San Francisco: Ignatius Press, 1983), 74: "Grace gives man a task, opens up for him a field of activity, bestows upon him the joy of accomplishment, so that he can identify himself with his mission and discover in it the true meaning of his existence. . . . For man's mission in life is not something general and impersonal like a ready-made coat; it has been designed specifically for him and given into his possession as the most personal of all gifts. *By it he becomes, in the fullest sense of the word, a person*" (my emphasis).

35. *Thérèse of Lisieux*, xii–xiii. ["Daß diese Idee, die einmalig und persönlich ist und die dem Einzelnen zugedachte Heiligkeit verkörpert, fur irgend jemand nicht hoch, nicht weit genug wäre. . . . Die «Erfüllung des Willens Gottes» ist weder die Befolgung eines allgemeinen, anonymen

Gesetzes, das für alle gleich wäre, noch die sklavische Nachzeichnung einer individuellen Vorlage . . . sie ist die Verwirklichung in Freiheit eines Liebesplans Gottes, der mit Freiheit rechnet und, mehr noch, Freiheit schenkt: Niemand wird so sehr er selbst wie der Heilige, der sich dem Plan Gottes einfügt und sein ganzes Sein, Leib, Seele und Geist, seinem Plan bereitstellt" (*Schwestern im Geist*, 16–17).]

See also *Theodramatik* II/2, 207: "It is like the artist or scholar who is so possessed by his vocation that he only feels free, only feels totally himself, when he is able to pursue the task that is so much his own" (*Theo-Drama* III, 225). One senses that von Balthasar may be speaking personally here!

36. Ibid., 203. ["Die Beziehung der göttlichen Person des Logos zur Gesamtheit der Menschennatur, die er, sofern er nicht in unserer beschränkten Weise individuiert zu sein scheint, irgendwie als ganze angenommen haben muß, so daß es auch glaubhaft wird, daß sein Sühnewerk sie als ganze betroffen hat." (186).]

37. *Glory of the Lord* VII, 82. [73–34.]

38. Ibid., 84. [76.]

39. Ibid.

40. Von Balthasar, "Experience God?" in *New Elucidations*, trans. Sr. Mary Theresilde Skerry (San Francisco: Igantius Press, 1986), 38.

41. Von Balthasar, *Christian Meditation*, trans. Sr. Mary Theresilde Skerry (San Francisco: Ignatius Press, 1989), 48.

42. *Glory of the Lord* V, 102–3.

4. THE STATE OF SELF-SURRENDER

1. *Christian Meditation*, 19.

2. *Heart of the World*, trans. Erasmo S. Leiva (San Francisco: Ignatius Press, 1979), 94. ["Man fragt nach mir, man möchte mich haben, scheint mich sogar zu brauchen. Irgendwo gibt es ein lichtes Bild von mir, von dem, was ich hätte sein können, was ich—aber wie?—noch immer zu werden vermöchte" (*Das Herz der Welt* [Zürich: Peter Schifferli, Verlags AG, 1945], 3d ed., 67).]

3. Von Balthasar, *Prayer*, 21.

4. Von Balthasar, *Glory of the Lord* V, 93–94 (my emphasis). [". . . darf nicht die Vermutung wecken, es handle sich um ein platonisch-augustinisches desiderium als ontologische Kreaturliebe zum absoluten Gott: nicht um Erlangen und Besitzen Gottes dem Bedürfen und Erwarten Gottes zu entsprechen" (448).]

5. *Thérèse of Lisieux*, 239–40. ["Damit eine solche Haltung nicht abstrakt und unmenschlich werde, müssen innerhalb der Klammer der

Indifferenz alle menschlichen Regungen und Wünsche lebendig bleiben. . . . Wie wenig Therese daran denkt, ihren geschöpflichen Willen
in einer Art mystischen Quietismus einfach im Willen Gottes untergehen
zu lassen, wie sehr vielmehr das Geheimnis der Indifferenz ein Geheimnis persönlicher Liebe und Willensaustausches ist, ein Geheimnis . . .
nur trinitarisch erklärt werden kann" (309).]

6. *Prayer*, 21.

7. It will be useful here just to note very broadly what exactly von
Balthasar means by "sin." In its most fundamental form this is in his eyes
always the "terrible possibility and reality—finite freedom rejecting infinite love" (*Does Jesus Know Us—Do We Know Him?* trans. Graham
Harrison [San Francisco: Ignatius Press, 1980], 33). So when von Balthasar speaks of human separation from God he is including a general human
experience of alienation but only as that is concretely instanced in particular human refusals to love. Sin is described by actual human choices
against the offer of God's love and companionship, and for this reason, as
we shall see, von Balthasar reckons the gravity of sin to reach a new mortal
intensity with the presence of Christ: as the presence of God's offer of love,
Jesus is the event of judgment for everyone who rejects him and fidelity to
him and his mission, but he is this precisely in embracing and immersing
himself in this rejection, "taking it upon himself."

8. Von Balthasar, *The Moment of Christian Witness*, trans. Richard
Beckley (New York: Newman Press, 1968), 17.

9. *Heart of the World*, 91–92, 94. ["Leise, fast unhörbar und doch
ganz unüberhörbar kommt es heran: ein Strahl aus Licht, ein Angebot
von Kraft, ein Befehl, der mehr und weniger als ein Befehl: ein Wunsch,
eine Bitte, eine Ladung, eine Lockung: so kurz wie ein Augenblick, so einfach zu begreifen, wie der Blick zweier Augen. Ein Verheißen darin: Liebe,
Lust und Ausblick in eine unabsehbare, schwindelerregende Ferne. Be-
freiung aus dem unerträglichen Verließ meines Ich. Das Abenteuer, das ich
von jeher ersehnte. Das vollkommene Wagnis, in dem ich sicher wäre,
alles verlierend, alles erst zu gewinnen. Die Quelle des Lebens, uner-
schöpflich erschlossen mir, der ich Durstes sterbe. Der Blick is ganz ruhig,
er hat nichts von magischer Kraft, von hypnotischen Zwang; er ist fra-
gend, er läßt mir die Freiheit. Auf seinem Grund wechseln die Schatten
der Kümmernis und der Hoffnung. Ich senke die Augen; ich blicke zur
Seite. Ich will es jenen Augen nicht antun, ihnen ins Angesicht Nein zu
sagen. Ich lasse ihnen die Zeit, sich abzuwenden. . . . Seltener stets wurden
diese Geisterstunden, und die Schalen des Alltags wachsen und wuchern
immer dichter um mich . . . die Abdichtung gegen Gott zu meiner
Gewohnheit, meiner zweiten Natur. Vielleicht ist es die Gewohnheit der
Sünde, die schlechte Gewohnheit" (65, 67).]

10. *Thérèse*, 234–35. ["Zur rechten Zeit erinnert sie sich ihres kleinen Weges, dessen Wesen ja darin liegt, alles Eigene abzubauen, am Gott allein verfügen zu lassen. Sie liebt die Opfer, die der Herr von ihr varlangt" (303).]

11. *Glory of the Lord* V, 21–22.

12. "Transcendence as a going beyond the self clearly becomes [in Christianity] the yielding of the self . . . to the unfathomability of divine love. The technique of *apatheia* in antiquity for self-salvation from the world becomes, in the Christian age, the ascetic expansion of the heart and its preparation in order that it should flow into an unlimited readiness to love, and ultimately into God's greater glory of love in the Cross" (ibid., 22).

13. Ibid., 23. This concern of von Balthasar's was already very apparent in his early review, critically favorable, of Rahner's *Geist im Welt*, when he asked whether the experience of intersubjectivity was perhaps lost in favor of a too-negatively abstractive and selftranscending agent intellect. See Rowan Williams, "Balthasar and Rahner," in *The Analogy of Beauty*, ed. John Riches (Edinburgh: T. & T. Clark, 1986), 11–34, esp. 19–23.

14. Ibid., 36.

15. Ibid., 37.

16. Ibid., 38.

17. Ibid., 51. ["In der Nacht, darin Gott sich verbarg, lag die Finsternis einer äußersten Liebe, die auch in der Nichtsicht und im nackten Glauben der Indifferenz noch bejaht werden konnte" (409).]

18. Von Balthasar, *Elizabeth of Dijon*, 117. ["Gnade ist Teilgabe an einer Gesinnung Gottes, an der inwendigen Selbstlosigkeit seiner dreifachen Verströmung. Und ewige Seligkeit kann nichts anderes sein als das Eingehen in die Endgültigkeit dieser Demut, in die Seligkeit des Nichts-für-sich-seins" (459).]

19. *Thérèse*, 17–18. ["Die andere erfüllt sich, im genauen Maß als die erste abnimmt, immer mehr, blüht auf, erwacht zu einem himmlischen Selbstbewußtsein" (53).]

20. Hugo Rahner, S.J., *The Spirituality of St. Ignatius of Loyola: An Account of Its Historical Development*, trans. Francis John Smith, S.J. (Chicago: Loyola University Press, 1980, reprint ed.), 56–58.

21. A very helpful elucidation of this idea is found in the contemporary British Carmelite Ruth Burrows: "In true love for our neighbour lies all the asceticism we need. Here is the way we die to self. What are the disciplines, artificial practices of penance and humility compared with this relentless pursuit of love. Perfect love of the neighbour means complete death to the self and the triumph of the life of Jesus in us" (*Before*

the Living God [London: Sheed and Ward, 1975], 75). I remain happily indebted to Gabriel Everitt, O.S.B., for bringing this work to my attention.

22. Joseph de Guibert, S.J., *The Jesuits: Their Spiritual Doctrine and Practice*, trans. William J. Young, S.J. (Chicago: The Institute of Jesuit Sources, 1964), 59.

23. *Glory of the Lord* V, 104–5. ["Christliche Gelassenheit impliziert, auch wo sie abstrichlos gedacht und gelebt wird, nicht die antike hyle-morphistische Schematik von Form (Gott) und Materie (Geschöpf). So braucht Indifferenz nicht in Richtung auf Vernichtung des Eigenseins und Eigenwillens der Kreatur hin geübt zu werden. . . . Das wahre Mysterium der christlichen Offenbarung ist vielmehr, daß die Vollendung des Gottesreiches . . . als das Allwirken Gottes im aktiven Mit-Wirken des Geschöpfs—in Gelassenheit, Hingabe, Dienst—gesucht werden darf" (457).]

24. Ibid., 106. ["Ohne deswegen aufzuhören, ein spontanes und freies menschliches Subjekt zu sein" (459).]

25. Ibid. ["Er bleibt Person, aber diese wird als ganze durchsichtig auf die sendende Person." (459).]

26. *Glory of the Lord* VII, 115–42.

27. "If the divine and eternal word wished to give itself adequate expression in mortal flesh—however mysterious the manner of this might be—this could not happen through man himself, unless he were to place his entire existence in the flesh, mortal and futile, at the disposal of the divine Word in such a self-exposition, by *handing himself over* like an alphabet or a keyboard, for the act of formulation in words, handing himself over as a whole; birth and death, speaking and silence, waking and sleeping, success and failure, and everything else that belongs to the substance of human existence" (ibid., 143). ["Sollte sich aber göttliches, ewiges Wort in sterblichem Fleisch—auf wie geheimnisvolle Art auch immer—adäquat ausdrücken wollen, so könnte dies nicht durch den Menschen selbst geschehen, es sei denn so, daß er sein ganzes, fleischliches, sterblich-vergebliches Dasein zu einer solchen Selbstauslegung göttlichen Wortes zur Verfügung stellte, indem er sich als Ganzer mit Geburt und Tod, mit Reden und Schweigen, Wachen und Schlafen, Erfolg und Vergeblichkeit und was sonst noch zum Wesen menschlichen Daseins gehört, wie ein Alphabet oder eine Klaviatur zur Auswortung *überließe*" (131–32).]

28. Von Balthasar, *Theo-Drama* III, 186. ["Dieses Sich-Überlassen ist, wie wir oft betont haben, keine bloße Passivität, sondern eine Form des Handelns, die—menschlich gesprochen—vom Subjekt mehr Selbstbesitzt und Einsatz fordert als die Ausführung selbstgefaßter Vorsäte und Verfolgung selbstentworfener Ziele" (170–71).]

29. *The Christian State of Life*, 194–96. [154–155.]

30. *Glory of the Lord* VII, 146. [134.]

31. Ibid., 147. [135–36.]

32. *Theologik* II (Einsiedeln: Johannes Verlag, 1985), 257–59, esp. 258: "'When the Logos becomes human,' says Karl Rahner very rightly, 'then this humanity is not priorly existing; but rather is that which is constituted in essence and existence when and insofar as the Logos empties himself.'" (Von Balthasar goes on to quote at length from Rahner, "Zur Theologie der Menschwerdung," *Schriften* IV, 147–49.)

33. *The Christian State of Life*, 38. [28.]

34. *Mysterium Paschale*, 104.

35. Ibid., 105.

36. Ibid., 117.

37. Maximus the Confessor, *Liber Ambiguorum 7*, *Patrologia Graeca* 91, 1084CD.

38. *Glory of the Lord* VII, 145. ["So zeigt doch gerade diese . . . Steigerung kein entsprechendes Ansichreißen der Führung, sondern das Gegenteil: ein steigendes Sich-überlassen an die Führung Dessen, der allein aus dem ganzen gelebten Dasein jenes endgültige Wort herausheben kann, das Gott zum Abschluß seines Neuen und ewigen Bundes braucht" (133).]

39. Von Balthasar, *Love Alone: The Way of Revelation* (London: Sheed and Ward, 1968), 101–2.

40. Ibid., 102.

41. *The Christian State of Life*, 198. ["Der Vater ist es, der ihn gleichsam aus der Welt an sich zieht, aus der Welt nicht nur seiner Familie, seiner Sippe und seiner Vaterstadt (Mk 6,4), sondern aus der Welt seiner menschlichen Natur und ihrer Gesetze, aus der Welt seines Gedächtnisses, seines Verstandes und Willens, da er alle diese innern, natürlichen Reichtümer, die der Sohn ihm freiwillig anbietet, in der Erlösungsnacht der Passion ihm auch entzieht. . . . Im Kreuz ist die volle Ekstase des Sohnes in den Vater hinein vollendet" (158).]

42. Ibid., 199. ["Indem er so den Weltplan des dreieinigen Gottes erfüllt, geht er nicht (weltflüchtig) aus der Welt zu Gott, sondern in den Grund der Welt hinein oder erweist sich vielmehr selbst als der Welt innersten Grund" (159).]

43. *Mysterium Paschale*, 34, 94.

44. Von Balthasar, *Au coeur du mystère Rédempteur* (Paris: Editions C.L.D., 1980), 39–40: Et il me semble que cette proposition du Fils atteint le coeur du Père—humainement parlant—plus profondément que même le péché du monde ne pourra l'atteindre, qu'elle ouvre en Dieu une blessure d'amour . . . blessure identitique à la procession et à la circumin-

cession de la personnes divines dans leur béatitude parfaite. . . . Je ne pense pas que cette interpretation, que Moltmann et moi-même avons proposée quasi simultanément, soit gnostique ou autrement téméraire, mais je pense qu'elle seule parvient à interpréter les faits évangéliques sans altérer le poids: *ut non evacuatur crux Christi* (1 Cor. 1.17).

45. *Mysterium Paschale*, 215.

46. *Christian Meditation*, 61.

47. *Glory of the Lord* VII, 213ff. III/2 [198ff.].

5. THE STATE OF OBEDIENCE

1. *Glory of the Lord* V, 104–5. ["Sofern dieses Mit-Wirken nich mehr bei der Indifferenz als *bloßem* Geschehenlassen stehenbleiben kann, vielmehr der besondere Wille Gottes, der aktiv gesucht werden muß" (457–58).]

2. Ibid. [458.]

3. Von Balthasar, "Experience God?" in *New Elucidations*, trans. Sr. Mary Theresilde Skerry (San Francisco: Ignatius Press, 1986), 26.

4. Ibid., 36.

5. Ibid.

6. *The Christian State of Life*, 72–73. ["Schon der allgemeine Stand des Menschen ist Begnadung durch Gott, nicht nur ein Geschenk, wenn auch ein unerhörtes, das der Mensch passiv in Empfang nimmt, sondern Belehnung mit einer auszuführenden Aufgabe, Machtübergabe des Urbildes an das Abbild, Auftrag, den dieses in der Selbständigkeit seines Abstands vom Urbild durchführen sollte und zu dem es mit den nötigen Vollmachten und Mitteln ausgestattet wurde. Diese aktive Seite seiner Bestimmung enthebt den Menschen des Gefühls, immer nur der Beschenkte zu sein, und berechtigt ihn erst zu einem entsprechenden Standesbewußtsein" (56).]

7. See also von Balthasar's clarification regarding Thérèse's active work of self-surrender: "The result is something far removed from passivity which slackly waits on the turn of events, or resignation which bows its head in advance to whatever is to come. Her attitude remains intensely active; she is ready to plunge into the fray. . . . Surrender, *abandon*, is a human act, the highest of human acts since it passes over into the omnipotence of God" (*Thérèse of Lisieux*, 242 [311]).

8. Von Balthasar, *Prayer*, 84.

9. *Christian State*, 30. [21.]

10. Ibid., 38–39. ["Liebe kann sich nie damit begnügen, nur für den gegenwärtigen Augenblick eine Tat der Liebe zu setzen. . . . Sie will

ihre Freizügigkeit ein für allemal beim Geliebten hinterlegen, um ihm ein Pfand der Liebe zu lassen. . . .Jede wahre Liebe hat deshalb *die innere Form des Gelöbnisses*: sie bindet sich an das Geliebte und zwar aus Motiven und im Geist der Liebe" (28).]

11. E.g., "In virtue of the Spirit's anointing, it is possible for *one who obeys* to compare ecclesial authority's allusion to the evangelical norm with the norm itself, and possible to ascertain such a divergence between them that his ecclesial conscience compels him to prefer the gospel norm that seems judicious to him rather than the concrete directive of the authorities. This would certainly be the case if the command prescribed something culpably deviating from the norm" ("Obedience in the Light of the Gospel," in *New Elucidations*, 243).

12. William Temple makes a similar point with characteristic lucidity when he writes: "The action of God is through our wills, and does not override them. He draws us by his love; and men are never so free as when they act from the love in their hearts which love shown to them has called forth" (*Readings in St. John's Gospel* [Wilton, Connecticut: Morehouse Barlow, 1985], 246).

13. *Prayer*, 21–22.

14. Ibid., 49.

15. Ibid.

16. *Thérèse of Lisieux*, 95–96. ["Was Therese braucht, ist jene radikale Entpersönlichung, die die ganze Person in etwas Höheres einspannt, dafür anfordert und gefangennimmt. . . . Durch die neue Standesform wird Therese in die Möglichkeit versetzt, über ihre persönlichen Grenzen hinauszuwachsen und die Dimensionen anzunehmen, die in ihrer nur von Gott her verständlichen, von ihm geschenkten und der Kirche zugedachten Sendung liegen" (139).]

17. Ibid., 97. ["Verschwinden bis zum Tod, Erscheinen bis zur Parusie" (140).]

18. Ibid. [140.]

19. E.g., "The Spirit takes over the function of presenting the obedient Son with the Father's will in the form of a *rule* that is unconditional and, in the case of the Son's suffering, even appears rigid and pitiless" (*Theo-Drama* III, 188). See also "The Holy Spirit as Love": "The Spirit of the Father who is present in Jesus is the absolute and inflexible rule for him, which demands absolute obedience (as the Garden of Olives will show); but precisely in this way, the Spirit is for Jesus the power in which he trusts in all his weakness, in order to win the victory over the apparently infinitely superior opposite power" (*Explorations in Theology* III: *Creator Spirit*, 120).

20. *Theo-Drama* III, 154–59. [141–46.]

21. Ibid., 155. ["In der Linie dieser Identifikation steht abschließend und sie überbietend auch die Zusage der Sendung durch den Sendenden an Jesus im Ereignis seiner Taufe" (142).]

22. Ibid., 157. ["Weil aber eine Sendung nur im Ablauf einer Zeit erfüllt werden kann und weil gerade in der Sendung Jesu die Schlußphase, die «Stunde» in der Erledigung der Sendung das größte Gewicht hat, so besteht in seiner Sendungsexistenz eine paradoxe Einheit von (Immer-schon-) Sein und von Werden. «Gott sandte seinen Sohn» (Röm 8,3; Gal 4,4) gesamthaft und endgültig schon bei der Menschewerdung . . . aber mit einem Auftrag, der, obwohl täglich und stündlich befolgt, doch erst am Kreuz «vollbracht» sein konnte (Joh 19,30). Sofern das Subjekt, in dem Person und Sendung identisch sind, nur göttlich sein kann, ist wirklich «Gottes Sein im Werden» (E. Jüngel), hat der, welcher als der Sohn Gottes geboren wird, eine «Wesensgeschichte»" (143–44).]

In an important footnote at this point, von Balthasar credits the work of the New Testament scholar H. Schlier for elucidating this theme in the gospels of a *"Wesensgeschichte"* by isolating texts which display how Christ's personal "nature emerges in and through the history of that nature" Or reciprocally understood, "This history is recapitulated and unveiled in the Person who manifests the nature" (Schlier, "Die Anfänge des christologischen Credo" in "Zur Frühgeschichte der Christologie," *QD* 51 [Herder, 1970], 47, quoted by von Balthasar in *Theodramatik* II/2, 144, n. 14; Eng. trans. pp. 157–58).

23. Ibid., 159. [". . . eines ewigen Seins sind, das, wenn auch nicht Werden, so doch strömendes ewiges Leben und (Über-) Ereignis ist. Die Dramatik, die in die Bestimmung der Person Jesu mithineingehört, fällt nicht einfach als ganze auf die weltliche Seite seines Seins, sondern hat ihre letzten Voraussetzung im göttlichen Leben selbst" (145).]

24. *Mysterium Paschale*, 89.

25. Ibid., 90.

26. Ibid., 90–91. See also his description of the "rule" of the Spirit in Christ's earthly life as effecting the translation of the eternal Son's "correspondence" (*Entsprechung*) with the Father into its historical form as "obedience" (*Gehorsam*) (*Theodramatik* II/2, 175; Eng. trans., *Theo-Drama* III, p. 191).

27. Von Balthasar, *Christian State of Life*, 78–79. Further on this, he writes: "The mystery of this mutual deference of Father and Son in the Holy Spirit is explainable only in terms of love; it has nothing to do with the neo-Platonic theory of the assimilation of the contingent and finite will to the unchangeable decree of 'absolute being'. . . . Much of this philosophical concept of man's relation to God has been incorporated, though certainly not intentionally, into the history of Christian spiritu-

ality. Nor will it be exorcised until we have come to realize, through the trinitarian mission of the Son, that the essential unity of the divine will is not incompatible with the autonomy of the Persons who possess it" (*Christian State of Life*, 402 [326–27]).

28. Cf. ibid., 400: "In the renunciation of every desire to realize the possibility of human freedom as an autonomous freedom independent of God and in the perfect binding of oneself, in obedience, to God's call, his grace and his mission, Ignatius sees man's highest opportunity of sharing the absolute freedom that is in God" [325].

29. Ibid., 400. ["So besteht auch die Freiheit Christi darin, daß er durch seinen Gehorsam teilnimmt an der Allmacht und Freiheit des Vaters" (325).]

30. Ibid., 401. ["Hier gerade wird sichtbar, daß die Übergabe der menschlichen Wahl in den göttlichen Ruf keineswegs die Auslöschung der geschöpflichen Funktion zugunsten der göttlichen ist. Der Akt des Gehorsams ist kein quietistischer Verzicht auf das Eigensein des Geschöpfs, und der Akt der Liebe Gottes ist keine Erdrückung der Selbständigkeit seines Geliebten. . . . Nichts macht den Menschen selbständiger als die göttliche Sendund, die er in freiem Gehorsam verantwortungsvoll übernimmt" (326).]

31. Von Balthasar, *Glory of the Lord* VII, 55. [49.]

32. Ibid., 56. [50.]

33. "Le conscience de Jésus et sa mission," in *Nouveaux points de repère* (Paris: Librairie Arthème Fayard, 1980), 161–74, here 170–71: "Avec le mot d''obéissance', nous touchons à coup sûr à la disposition la plus intime de Jésus, et il est sans doute plus importante et plus salutaire à l'obéissance parfaite de ne pas vouloir connaître à l'avance l'avenir, pour accueiller, veiller de la main de Dieu avec une parfaite fraîcheur quand il arrive."

34. For a helpful summary and interpretation of Maximus on christological obedience, see the very fine work of Alain Riou, *Le monde et l'église selon Maxime le Confesseur* (Paris: Beauchesne, 1973), esp. 80–88.

35. Karl Barth, *Church Dogmatics* I/2 (Edinburgh: T. & T. Clark, 1956), 156.

36. Von Balthasar, *La foi du Christ: Cinq approches christologiques* (Paris: Aubier, 1968), 97–98: "L'opposition absolu entre la grâce et le péché ne devait surgir que dans la disponibilité totale de l'obeissance inconditionée. Cette obeissance se révèle maintenant comme la donnée fondamentale de la christologie: elle rend possible aussi bien l'événement de l'Incarnation et l'existence humaine du Christ que son oeuvre décisive."

6. PASSION, DEATH, AND HELL AS CHRISTOLOGICAL STATES

1. Von Balthasar's emphasis on Christ's death is rather double-edged in respect of our running question about the significance of Jesus' human-ity for salvation in von Balthasar. On the one hand, this very emphasis is what immediately sets von Balthasar apart from all docetic views of the Incarnation in which a purely spiritual Christ only *seems* to suffer and die. On the other hand, the very detail with which, as we shall see, von Balthasar describes Jesus' death and presence in hell tends to arouse ques-tions: is he really talking about the actual historical human being Jesus or a kind of mystical-theological construct?

2. Herbert McCabe, O.P., *God Matters* (London: Geoffrey Chap-man, 1987), 93: "The mission of Jesus from the Father is not the mission to be crucified; what the Father wished is that Jesus should be human. . . . and this is what Jesus sees as a *command* laid on him by his Father in heaven; the obedience of Jesus to his Father is to be totally, completely human. This is his obedience, an expression of his love for the Father; the fact that to be human means to be crucified is not something that the Father has directly planned but what we have arranged. We have made a world in which there is no way of being human that does not involve suf-fering."

3. *Church Dogmatics* IV/2 (Edinburgh: T. & T. Clark, 1958), 292–93.

4. Von Balthasar, *La foi du Christ: cinq approches christologiques* (Paris: Aubier, 1968), 92–93.

5. See especially "Zur Ortsbestimmung Christlicher Mystik," 60: here von Balthasar argues that no form of mystical union with God is promised the Christian but only the gift of following the entire destiny of Christ.

6. Von Balthasar, *Prayer*, 235.

7. *Mysterium Paschale*, 76.

8. *A Theological Anthropology*, 282.

9. Ibid.

10. See *Mysterium Paschale*, 125: the experiences of God-abandon-ment in Scripture "are not at all, in the first place, tests of a pedagogic kind, or (certainly not!) stages in a neo-Platonic schema of ascent, but must be interpreted, rather, in christological fashion."

11. Ibid., 39–40.

12. Ibid., 76.

13. Ibid., 77.

14. Ibid., 38.

15. Ibid., 143–44, n. 70.

16. Ibid., 39.

17. Ibid., 79.

18. Ibid., 72.

19. Ibid.

20. Ibid.

21. *Prayer*, 206.

22. Ibid., 208.

23. Ibid., 213.

24. Ibid. My emphasis.

25. Ibid., 214.

26. So von Balthasar adds: "'No man cometh to the Father but by me.' This was of course known to Origen, Denis the Areopagite, Eckhart and St. John of the Cross. Being touched by God, they strove for the veiled vision of the divine being. But, whatever the process of thought, whatever the theoretical arguments they used in their endeavour, they always acted as believers, disciples of the Son whom they followed, and, in their 'vision' of the Father in the Holy Spirit, they knew themselves to be on the way of Christ and within the framework of the laws of his discipleship. It is not in by-passing or soaring above him that Christian contemplation strives to reach the *speculatio majestatis*" (*Prayer*, 215–16).

27. Ibid., 216. My emphasis.

28. Whether von Balthasar's reinterpretation is more successful as historical analysis or as a feat of theological prestidigitation is perhaps somewhat of an open question. For my purpose, the point is that von Balthasar himself believes that this is how best to interpret matters and therefore it explains how he can choose to avail himself of dark-night analogies in his christology.

29. Von Balthasar, *Présence et pensée: Essai sur la philosophie religieuse de Gregoire de Nysse* (Paris: Gabriel Beauchesne et ses Fils, 1942), 75: "Cette nuit, c'est la foi, dans laquelle s'achève toute connaissance et qui seule «rattache et joint ensemble l'esprit chercheur et la nature insaisissable . . . et il n'y a d'autre voie pour s'approcher de Dieu.» . . . «La vue de sa face, c'est la marche vers Lui sans repos.»"

30. Ibid.

31. Ibid., 76.

32. Ibid., 78: "Ce déséspoir n'est que l'expression adéquate de la négation totale de l'intelligence, qui est en même temps son acte suprême: c'est précisément en acceptant ce déséspoir que l'âme «reçoit la flèche élue de Dieu en elle-même à l'endroit mortel du coeur.»"

33. Ibid., 79.

34. *Mysterium Paschale*, 40.

35. *Glory of the Lord* III, 110. ["Er muß . . . in die Nacht der Hölle, denn nur aus der absoluten Unterscheidung der sündigen Kreatur vom

absoluten und reinsten Gott kann das Göttliche in seiner Wahrheit an-
sichtig werden" (470).]

36. Ibid. [470.]

37. Ibid., 134. ["Wiederum mit dem Doppelakzent echter Finsternis
für das endliche Subjekt und übergroßer Helligkeit im unendlichen Gott"
(494).]

38. Ibid. [". . . auf nichts mehr auftrifft, und Gott selber kein Gegenstand ist, kann er von der Seele nur als finstere Nacht erfahren werden. Im
liebenden und hoffenden Glauben schaut sie ins Offene, ja ist selber zum
Offenen gewordenen, zum geöffneten Mund, den nur Gott füllen kann"
(494).]

39. Ibid., 136. [496.]

40. Ibid., 137. ["Juan betont durchgehend, daß Gottes Licht ewig un-
verändert und gleichmäßig scheint, daß nur der ungereinigte Zustand der
sich Nähernden es zuerst als Finsternis und Fegfeuerqual erleben läßt"
(496).]

41. Ibid., 162. [521.]

42. Thérèse of Lisieux, *Collected Letters*, ed. Abbé Combes (New
York: Sheed & Ward, 1949), 128; quoted in von Balthasar, *Thérèse of
Lisieux*, 256.

43. Von Balthasar, *Thérèse*, 253.

44. Ibid., 203.

45. Ibid., 97.

46. Ibid., 97–98. [". . . und zwar eines Kreuzes . . . in jener großen
Pause zwischen Leiden und Auferstehung, wo das alte Ich mit seinen
Menschlichkeiten gestorben, das neue Ich mit seiner göttlichen und jen-
seitigen Subjektivität noch nicht auferstanden ist. In diesem der Welt so
verborgenen Zwischen, das—wie Therese sagt—ein «Leben des Todes»
ist, ist das Ordensleben beheimatet und bildet die große verbindende Klammer zwischen Leiden und Auferstehung, zwischen weltlicher und himmlischer Existenz" (141).]

47. Ibid., 126. ["Und sie kennt dieses wahre Ich allmählich gar nicht
mehr. Sie weiß nicht mehr, wer sie ist: ist sie dieses Ideal, das sie mit allen
Kräften ihres entsagenden, absterbenden Ich ernährt und das doch keine
existentiale Realität annehmen will? Oder ist sie dieses ernährende Ich,
das in den letzten Zügen liegt, das sie weggegeben hat und das sie nichts
mehr angeht? Während dieses vergeht, ist jenes noch nicht geworden.
Alles ist wie entrückt, wir traum- und schattenhaft, was ihr eigenes Ich
betrifft" (175).]

48. *Heart of the World*, 110.

49. *Thérèse*, 259. ["Volle Nacht ist volle Gemeinschaft mit den
Sündern und Verlorenen, ist Identifizierung mit ihrem Los bis zur vollen

stellvertretenden Übernahme ihres Schiksals. Aber wie soll Therese, die von sich selber weiß, daß sie eine Heilige ist, sich in eine letzte, beding- ungslose Gemeinschaft mit den Sündern begeben können? Sie müßte ihre ganze Wahrheit aufgeben. Sie müßte den Sinn ihrer theologischen Existenz preisgeben. Eine solche Gemeinschaft wäre für sie die Selbstver- nichtung ihres Daseins und, in ihren Augen, die Preisgabe ihrer Heilig- keitssendung" (331).]

50. *Glory of the Lord* VII, 216. ["Die tiefste Erfahrung der Gottver- lassenheit, die stellvertretend in der Passion real werden soll, setzt eine tiefste Erfahrung der Gottverbundenheit und des Lebens aus dem Vater voraus, eine Erfahrung, die der Sohn nicht nur im Himmel gemacht, son- dern auch als Mensch erlebt haben muß, selbst wenn sein Geist nicht des- halb schon in einer immerwährenden visio beatifica zu weilen braucht. Wirklich verlassen (nicht bloß einsam) kann nur sein, wer wirkliche Intimität der Liebe gekannt hat" (200–201).]

51. *Heart of the World*, 66. ["Es ist ein Herz wie unsers, ein Mensch- enherz, das selbst nach Gegenliebe dürstet. Wie eben Herzen sind, voll warmer Torheit, unverständiger Hoffnung. Voll Eigensinn. Ein Herz, das hinsiecht, wenn es nicht geliebt wird" (45).]

52. In this respect Gerald O'Collins is perhaps not so accurate when he paints von Balthasar's soteriology as a stereotype of penal substition- ary atonement, and objects vociferously against von Balthasar when the latter refers to Jesus as taking on the condition of a sinner and suffer- ing the dereliction of God and humankind (*Interpreting Jesus* [London: Geoffrey Chapman, 1983], 151). O'Collins apparently fails to see that for von Balthasar, Jesus' substitutionary suffering is in no sense a crush- ing subjection to some implacable decree of a wrathful God, but the very enactment of the Father's love in the world, seeking total solidarity with those who had alienated themselves from God, and therefore embracing their suffering distance from God within the yet greater "distance" of the trinitarian love itself.

53. *Glory of the Lord* VII, 70–71. [63.]

54. Ibid., 137.

55. Ibid., 138.

56. See n. 52 above.

57. "At the center of the event of the cross is situated without doubt the experience of dereliction by God. This experience is that of sin deliv- ered into the hands of divine justice, to the fire of the holiness of God. . . . In order for Christ to know this rejection, it was necessary for him to identify in some way with the sin of others. The Christ no longer wants to distinguish between himself, the innocent, and his guilty brothers. He does not even want God to distinguish" (Von Balthasar, *Au coeur*

du mystère Rédempteur [Paris: Editions C.L.D., 1980], 35–36): "Au centre de l'événement de la Croix se situe sans aucune doute l'expérience du délaissement par Dieu. Cette expérience est celle du péché livré aux mains de la justice divine, au feu de la sainteté de Dieu. . . . Pour qui le Christ puisse connaître cette répulsion, il a dû en quelque sort s'identifier avec le péché des autres. Le Christ ne veut plus distinguer entre lui-même, l'innocent, et ses frères coupables. Il ne veut même pas que Dieu distingue."

58. Ibid., 139.

59. Von Balthasar, *Theo-Drama* III, 226. ["Der «Stunde» . . . weil dann nicht mehr er über die Sendung, sondern die Sendung über ihn (jenseits alles menschlichen Könnens) verfügen wird. Es ist wie ein menschliches Grauen vor diesem Hiatus und dann ein entschlossener Überstieg durch Überlassung an der Vater" (207).]

See also *The Heart of the World*, 108–10: "Is fear finally coming over you—a fear men know nothing about? . . . The fear which is the core of sin. . . . The fear of never again seeing the face of the Father for all eternity. . . .'Father,' you cry out, 'if it is possible . . .' But now it is not even possible. . . . The Father has heard nothing. You have sunk too low into the depths. . . . Are you sure he still really exists? Is there a God? If a God existed he would be love itself; he certainly could not be sheer hardness, more unrelenting than a wall of bronze. . . . But instead of gazing into the pupil of God's eye, you stare into the void of a black eye-socket."

60. "If this mission could only be fulfilled by stepping beyond what could be achieved within a mortal life (that is, by purely "letting go," surrendering himself to God in death), a huge chasm opens up in the historical fulfillment of Jesus' mission—and hence in the "development" of his "self"—namely, the very chasm that, right from the start, had been addressed by the two-*status*-doctrine. Gregory of Nyssa expounded it with particular clarity, assuming that human nature could "progress toward perfection," specifically as a result of the great change from the first state (the humiliation) to the second (the exaltation)" (*Theo-Drama* III, 159–60; the published English translation makes an egregious blunder here, which I have corrected in the English above, of translating "Zwei status-Lehre" as "the doctrine of the two natures," which most erroneously suggests that von Balthasar thinks Christ's humanity does indeed disappear into the hiatus only to be transmuted and vanish into the divinity!) ["Wenn seine Sendung eine das Weltheil im ganzen betreffende, universale war, und wenn diese Sendung nur in einem Überschritt über das innerhalb eines sterblichen Lebens Leistbare erfüllbar war (also in einem reinen «Geschehenlassen» in der Selbstübergabe an Gott im Tod), dann klafft in der geschichtlichen Erfüllen der Sendung Jesu (und darin in

seinem «Selbst-Werden») jener Abgrund auf, der durch die Zwei-*status*-Lehre von jeher theologisch beachtet wurde. Gregor von Nyssa hat sie besonders klar dargelegt, indem er von der menschlichen Natur einen «Fortschritt auf die Vollendung hin» annimmt, und das gerade durch die große Veränderung vom ersten Stand (der Erniedrigung) zum zweiten (der Erhöhung)" (146).]

61. Ibid., 170. ["Ohne die totale Selbstüberlassung in Passion und Tod wäre die volle Universalität des Auftrags nicht zu erreichen" (155–56).]

62. Von Balthasar, *Prayer*, 140.

63. "At the moment of his death [Christ] was certainly annihilated in his soul, without any consolation or relief, since the Father had left him that way in innermost aridity in the lower part. . . . This was the most extreme abandonment, sensitively, that he had suffered in his life. And *by it he accomplished the most marvelous work of his whole life* surpassing all the works and deeds and miracles that he had ever performed on earth or in heaven. That is, he brought about the reconciliation and union of the human race with God through grace. The Lord achieved this, as I say, at the moment in which he was most annihilated in all things" (John of the Cross, *The Ascent of Mount Carmel* [II, vii, 11], trans. Kieran Kavanaugh, O.C.D. [New York: Paulist Press, 1987], 97. My emphasis).

64. *Theo-Drama* III, 37. [34.]

65. Ibid. My emphasis. [". . . erst am Kreuz werden alle Aspekte und Folgen der alten Natur unerbittlich angeeignet und durchlitten." (34).]

66. Von Balthasar, *A Theology of History*, 64. See also *Heart of the World*, 64: "[Jesus] must first fashion eyes which can see him; he must implant in [the people] nonexistent ears, that they may hear; an unknown sense of touch, that they may feel God, new senses of smell and taste that they may smell God's fragrance and savor his fare. He must make their whole spirit new, new from its very foundations. But the price for this will be an exorbitant one: he will have to take their dead, dull senses upon himself and lose his Father and the whole heavenly world. In death, in hell, his pregnant heart will have to dissolve and—now as a wholly ruined heart which has melted into a shapeless sea—he will give himself to them as their drink: the love potion which will at last bewitch their all-too-sober hearts."

67. Von Balthasar, *First Glance at Adrienne von Speyr*, trans. Antje Lawry and Sr. Sergia Englund, O.C.D. (San Francisco: Ignatius Press, 1981), 64.

68. Ibid., 66–67.

69. *Mysterium Paschale*, 150–52. In attempting to dramatize the social and soteriological impact of Christ's presence among the dead, von Balthasar suggests, Western mystery plays and Eastern iconography have obscured the silent corpse-obedience with which Christ "accomplishes"

the liberation of the souls in prison: "The dramatic portrait of the experience of triumph, of a joyful encounter between Jesus and the prisoners, and in particular between the new Adam and the old, is not prohibited as a form of pious contemplation, but it does go beyond what theology can affirm" (*Mysterium Paschale*, 180–81).

70. *Glory of the Lord* VII, 230. ["In diesem Solidarischwerden mit den Sündern in ihrem äußersten Zustand vollzieht aber Jesus bis ans Ende den Heilswillen des Vaters. Es ist absoluter Gehorsam, der über das Leben hinausreicht und sich gerade noch bewährt, wo sonst nur noch Zwang und Unfreiheit herrscht" (213–14).]

71. Ibid., 231. My emphasis. ["In die Ohnmacht gebunden zwar, aber aus freiem Gehorsam" (214).]

72. Ibid., 233. ["Wo die letzte Spur von Gott (in der reinen Sünde) und von jeder sonstigen Kommunikation (in der reinen Einsamkeit) verloren erscheint" (216).]

73. Von Balthasar, *Mysterium Paschale*, 164, referring to *In Libros Sententiarum* III. d. 22, q. 2, a. I, qla. 3.

74. Ibid.

75. Ibid., 165.

76. *Glory of the Lord* VII, 233. ["Die vom Menschen getrennte Sünde in ihrem «Reinzustand», die «Sünde an sich» in der ganzen formlosen, chaotischen Wucht ihrer Realität" (216).]

77. *Mysterium Paschale*, 167.

78. Ibid., 168.

79. *Heart of the World*, 115–16. ["Es wäre zu leicht, zu leiden, wenn man noch lieben könnte. Die Liebe ist dir genommen. Das einzige, was du noch fühlst, ist die brennende Leere, der Hohlraum, den sie zurückließ. Es wäre deine Freude, wenn du aus der Tiefe der Hölle den Vater, der dich verstieß, noch lieben dürftest, eine Ewigkeit lang. Aber die Liebe is dir genommen. Du wolltest ja alles hingeben, nicht wahr? . . . Du lebtest von der Liebe, du hattest keinen andern Gedanken als die Liebe, du warst die Liebe. Nun ist sie dir entzogen: du erstickst, du verhungerst, du bist dir entfremdet" (83).]

80. Von Balthasar, "The Holy Spirit as Love," in *Explorations in Theology* III, trans. Brian McNeil, C.R.V. (San Francisco: Ignatius Press, 1993), 117–34, here 122.

7. THE STATES OF LOVE, RESURRECTION, AND COMMUNION

1. Von Balthasar, "Zur Ortsbestimmung Christlicher Mystik," in *Grundfragen der Mystik*, ed. Werner Beierwaltes, H.U. von Balthasar,

Alois M. Haas (Einsiedeln: Johannes Verlag, 1974), 37–71, here 57–58: "In der Bibel ist es nicht der Mensch, der zur Gottsuche aufbricht, sondern Gott, der sich unerwartet, spontan auf die Suche nach dem Menschen aufmacht. . . . An die Stelle spontanen Aufbrechens tritt die Bereitschaft des Horchens und Ge-horchens."

2. Ibid., 59: "Nicht die *Erfahrung* einer Einigung mit Gott den Maß-tab der Volkommenheit (der höchsten Aufstiegsetappe) darstellt, son-dern der *Gehorsam*, der auch in der Erfahrung der Gottesverlassenheit mit Gott genauso eng verbunden sein kann wie in der erfahrenen Eini-gung."

3. Von Balthasar, "The Gospel as Norm and Test of All Spirituality in the Church," *Concilium* 9 (1965): 7–23, 17.

4. *Glory of the Lord* III, 108. My emphasis.

5. Ibid., 129. ["Im Sein bleibt das Geschöpf ewig das Andere als Gott; aber das gegenseitige Anders-sein wird in der verwandelnden ehe-lichen Liebe die Ermöglichung des Austausches und der reziproken Ein-wohnung. So spielt die Idee des Fluges, der Entrückung eine entscheidende Rolle, auch wenn das Ekstatische sich von den noch Unvollkommenheit anzeigenden körperlich-physiologischen Entrückungszuständen durch-läutern muß zu einem substantiallen, zuständlichen Hingenommensein" (489).]

6. See, e.g., *Glory* VII, 396: "It is only within the New Testament's trinitarian revelation that it is possible to conceive of such a process pre-cisely as *not* leading to the identification of the giver and the one who receives the gift."

7. Ibid., 29 [26.]

8. *Parole et mystère chez Origène* (Paris: Ed. du Cerf, 1957; orig. pub. 1936), 23: "Cette extase de son être est en même temps une marche vers le centre de lui-même, vers sa source."

9. Ibid., 27.

10. Ibid.

11. See for example, Harvey Egan, S.J.: "Never does it [Ignatius' mys-ticism] depict the triune persons or Christ as the love or spouse of the soul united in mystical marriage. Reading Ignatius' works, one is struck by the complete absence of the nuptial aspect that predominates in other mystical classics" *(Ignatius Loyola the Mystic* [Wilmington, Delaware: Michael Glazier, 1987], 122).

12. Hugo Rahner, S.J., *The Spirituality of St. Ignatius Loyola: An Account of Its Historical Development*, trans. Francis John Smith, S.J. (Newman Press, 1953; reprint ed., Chicago: Loyola University Press, 1980), xii–xiii.

13. *Prayer*, 64. My emphasis.

14. Ibid.

15. *Elizabeth of the Trinity* in *Two Sisters in the Spirit: Thérèse of Lisieux and Elizabeth of the Trinity*, trans. Dennis Martin (San Francisco: Ignatius Press, 1992), 434.

Cf. also von Balthasar's description of Elizabeth's understanding of the nature of ecstatic love: the emphasis is precisely *not* as an experience of the last and expected stage of ascent but that which surpasses one's own longings by taking them beyond even their hopes in a way which is yet possible for the soul to bear: "The loving one does not enter the kingdom of eternal love exulting in having found the crown of all yearnings (*Sehnsucht*), rather, she enters humbly, dumbstruck, because love has unimaginably surpassed all her expectations and even herself. One can endure the unbearable: the presence of love. To describe the Unbearable as bliss, as the ecstasy of love, is miserably inadequate!" (ibid., 439. [417]).

16. Ibid., 436.

17. Von Balthasar, *Theo-Drama* III, 16. [15.]

18. Ibid. [15.]

19. Von Balthasar, *The Christian State of Life*, 77–78. ["Dort wird er lernen, welchen Namen diese Ekstase aus sich in die Sendung Gottes hinein trägt: den Namen der freiesten, weil absolutesten Liebe. Dort wird er darum auch verstehen lernen, daß Ekstase kein privater, um der eigenen Lust willen verliehener Zustand ist, worin der Ekstatiker Erlebnisse hat, die niemand berühren als ihn selbst, sondern daß dieser Herausstand aus sich den Namen Gehorsam trägt, worin der Dienende seine endgültige Lust in nichts anderem will als in der Erfüllung des Willens dessen der ihn gesandt hat" (60).]

20. Cf., ibid., 81: "By reason of the original ecstasy (*ursprünglich Ekstase*) by which [the human being] is transported into the mission decreed by God, he comes to share in that movement that opens the very depths of his being to God."

21. Von Balthasar, *Theo-Drama* III, 201 (emphasis mine). ["In der Identität der Person Jesus mit seiner Sendung die überschwengliche Erfüllung dessen, was eine dramatische «Person» ist: eine Gestalt, die in der Durchführung ihrer Rolle entweder zu ihrem wahren Gesicht gelangt oder (im analytischen Drama) ihr verborgenes Gesicht enthüllt. Die dem Bühnenvorgang entsprechende Wahrheit im wirklichen Leben, die restlos gelingende Identifizierung der Person aufgrund ihrer rest-los durchgeführten Sendung wird im Fall Jesu Christi erreicht" (184).]

22. Ibid., 199–200. ["Gerade in diesem Ergreifen findet Jesus seine eigene tiefste Identität als des Sohnes von jeher" (183).]

23. Ibid., 168. ["Jesus ist mit seiner Sendung hineingehalten in die gottferne, erbsünde und dämonische Welt, die ihm allen Ernstes andere Wege zur Durchführung seiner Sendung anbietet, Wege, die er jeweils im Rückblick auf seine Sendung als unangemessen ablehnt" (154).]

24. Ibid., 169. ["Aber der Sohn erfaßt seine Sendung, sich selbst, um so besser, je mehr er sich dem Grund verbindet, aus dem beides gleichzeitig entquillt" (155).]

25. Ibid., 197. ["Hier entscheidet sich endgültig, ob der Mensch Jesus in seiner Zeitlichkeit nur die Erscheinung einer seiner ganzen Existenz voraus-liegenden göttlichen (und damit «fremden») Entscheidung ist, er somit nur «nachträglich» ratifizieren kann, was über ihn und die Welt beschlossen worden ist, oder ob seine menschliche Freiheit—an der die orthodoxe Dogmatik seit dem Monotheletenstreit so unbedingt festhält—ihr angestammtes Privileg eigener Entscheidung zur Geltung bringen kann" (181).]

26. Ibid., 199. The published translation has as the concluding phrase the very misleading ". . . the only one which matters," which suggests that von Balthasar has undermined his position if indeed he wants to argue, as he does, for the determinative significance of Jesus' human power of choosing. In the original: *Theodramatik* II/2, 182–3: "Die ewige Entscheidung des Sohnes schließt seine zeitliche in sich ein, und die zeitliche ergreift seine ewige als die einzige, die in Frage kommt."

27. Ibid., 197–98. ["Nie ist ein Künstler freier, als wenn er nicht (mehr) zögernd zwischen Möglichkeiten der Gestaltung auswählen muß, sondern von der endlich sich darbietenden wahren Idee (wie) «bessen» ist und ihrer gebieterischen Weisung folgt; nie wird auch, wenn seine Inspiration echt ist, das Werk mehr sein persönlichstes Gepräge tragen" (181).]

28. Ibid. ["Dabei liegt diese [Sendung] nicht in irgendeine Präexistenz wartend für ihn bereit, sondern sie schlummerte in ihn selbst wie ein Kind im Mutterschoß und drängte zur Geburt—aus dem Schoß seiner eigensten Freiheit" (181).]

29. Ibid. ["Und zwar so die seine, daß sie nicht wie vorfabriziert bereitliegt und von ihm nur mechanisch zusammengesetzt werden müßte, sondern so, daß er sie mit seiner ganzen freien Verantwortung aus sich selbst heraus gestalten, ja in einer wahren Hinsicht sogar erfinden muß. Dies gerade auch dann, wenn «der Geist ihn treibt»: in die Wüste (Lk 4,1) oder von dort zurück nach Galiläa (4,14)" (182).]

30. *Glory of the Lord* VII, 400. [373–74.]

31. Ibid., 402, 403. [376, 377.]

32. *Two Sisters in the Spirit*, 461. ["Die Person ist durch die Gnadeneinwohnung Gottes in ihr geheimnisvoll sozialisiert, ohne als Person aufgehoben zu werden" (439).]

33. Ibid., 462. ["Etwas von der Relationalität der göttlichen Personen hat in der «Teilnahme an der göttlichen Natur» sich in die geschöpfliche Person eingesenkt und sie zu Abenteuern der Liebe in Bewegung gesetzt, von denen die natürlichen Subjekte keine Verstellung haben" (439).]

34. Von Balthasar, *Prayer*, 104.

35. Von Balthasar, *Christian Meditation*, 89.
36. Ibid.
37. Ibid., 90.
38. Ibid., 84.
39. Von Balthasar, *Theo-Drama* III, 17. [15.]
40. Ibid. [15.]
41. *A Theological Anthropology*, 285.
42. "There are two moments, which can be distinguished from each other but belong together, in which the event of the abandonment is 'accomplished,' in the double sense that it goes 'to the end' (Jn. 13.1) with no possibility of revocation, and that it now succeeds therein in attaining the form that is Jesus' own, bestowed by God, on the far side of himself. These are the Eucharist and the verbalising of Jesus' life in the sphere of the early Church. Both are the work of the *paradosis*: which is now understood not as the act of God who gives up the Son, nor as the act of the Church which hands on further what has been handed on to her, but as Jesus' handing over of himself (cf. 1 Pet 2.23; Heb 9.14), so that by the power of this handing over, he may become what he should be for God and humankind" (*Glory of the Lord* VII, 148). ["Es gibt zwei unterscheidbare, obschon zusammengehörige Momente, in denen sich das Ereignis der Überlassung «vollendet», im Doppelsinn, daß es ohne mögliche Rücknahme «bis ins Ende» (Jo 13,1) geht, und es darin nun eben «gelingt», jenseits seiner selbst die eigene, von Gott verliehene Form zu gewinnen: die Eucharistie und die Wortwerdung des Lebens Jesu im Raum der Urkirche. Beide ist Wirkung der Paradosis: diese nun nicht als Akt Gottes genommen, der den Sohn hingibt, oder als Akt der Kirche, die das ihr Überlieferte weitergibt, sondern als die Selbstübergabe Jesu (vgl. 1 Pt 2,23; Hb 9,14), um kraft dieser Übergabe zu dem zu werden, was er für Gott und die Menschen sein soll" (136).]
43. Von Balthasar, *Prayer*, 128.
44. We find a helpful analogy in the final stages of Bonaventure's classic *Journey of the Mind to God*. Bonaventure would have the contemplative caught up to a new level of ecstatic wonder in considering the marvelous union of opposites in the Incarnation—not just the supreme coincidence of opposites in the Trinity (consubstantiality and hypostatic plurality, coeternity and emanation, etc.), but the even more astonishing union of the first principle with the last, God with human being, eternity with time, and so on, which is found in Jesus Christ (VI, 3–7). And as a result of this overwhelming conjunction the soul is ravished into an ecstatic sabbath: "It now remains for the soul, by considering such things, to transcend and go beyond not only this sensible world, but even its own self. In this going beyond, Christ is the way and the door, Christ is the ladder and the conveyance" (Bonaventure, *The Works of St. Bonaventure*,

vol. 1, *Mystical Opuscula*, "The Journey of the Mind to God," (VII, 1), trans. José de Vinck [Paterson, New Jersey: St. Anthony Guild Press, 1960], 56).

45. *Mysterium Paschale*, 214.

46. Ibid.

47. Ibid., 220.

48. Ibid., 220–21.

49. "In this do resurrection and life consist: in further proclaiming the Good News, in carrying on the flame, in being a useful instrument in my hand that I may build up my kingdom in men's hearts, in letting my heart go on beating in yours" *(Heart of the World*, 160).

50. Von Balthasar, "The Absence of Jesus," in *New Elucidations*, 58–59.

51. *Mysterium Paschale*, 250.

52. Ibid.

53. Von Balthasar, *Parole et mystère chez Origène*, 51.

54. Ibid., 52: "La vie historique du Sauveur, si précieuse en soi, n'est pourtant que le prélude, l'exemple, le symbole d'une vie de Christ beaucoup plus vaste, celle de son corps mystique à travers l'histoire du monde. . . . La vie historique du Christ historique et la vie historique du Christ mystique ne sont donc pas deux vie distinctes, mais une seule vie sous deux aspects."

55. Against the idea of an incarnation in the totality of human nature in its patristic forms and also against post-Hegelian concepts of Jesus as a "universal human being" or the "central individual," von Balthasar asserts: "All this must be countered, in our view, by John Damascene's assertion that the definite profile of Jesus' divine Sonship makes him a very definite, individual human being [*einem sehr bestimmten einzelnen Menschen zu machen*] [*De fide orthod*. III, 7 (PG 94, 1009AB).]. Nor does this prevent him, thanks to the same Sonship and the universal mission with which he is entrusted, from extending the scope of his work and his being to the whole of human nature" *(Theo-Drama* III, 236–37. [216–18]).

56. Von Balthasar, *Theo-Drama* III, 38. [35.]

57. Ibid., 230–31. ["Ist diese Identität gesichert, so folgt daraus, daß in dem durch die Durchführung der Sendung eröffneten Spielraum sich auch das Ich des Gesendeten—in einer näher zu beschreibenden Weise—vergegenwärtigt und zum «Raum» wird, worin sich jene befinden, die durch die universale Sendung tangiert, verwandelt, neu angesiedelt werden" (211–212).]

58. In his insightful *Theology After Wittgenstein* (Oxford: Basil Blackwell, 1986), Fergus Kerr provides a description of Wittgenstein's understanding of the self which rather intriguingly sheds light on von Balthasar's

communal and historical understanding of the Incarnation: "What constitutes us as human beings is the regular and patterned reactions that we have to one another. It is in our dealings with each other—in how we *act*—that human life is founded: Wittgenstein's word *handeln*, conveniently enough, means dealing and trading as well as acting and doing. When the shopkeeper acts as he does in the story he necessarily acts with his customer: it is an exchange, a collaboration. Community is built into human action from the beginning" (65). Or again: "I discover myself, not in some pre-linguistic inner space of self-presence, but in the network of multifarious social and historical relationships in which I am willy-nilly involved" (69). In terms of von Balthasar on the Incarnation, as we have seen, it is Jesus' mission, which is utterly communal and historical, that constitutes him through his ultimate "dealings" with the Father and his people.

59. *Theo-Drama* III, 231. [". . . werden sie im theologischen Sinn «personalisiert», das heißt nicht nur negativ «erlöst», sondern positiv mit Sendungen («Charismen») begabt, die sie—innerhalb der Ur-Sendung Jesu—zu qualitativ bestimmten Personen macht" (212).]

60. Ibid., 241. [". . . daß Christi real-stellvertretende Sendung nicht nur . . . ein Tun und Leiden sein kann, das den andern die gerechte Strafe erspart, sondern ein Mit-Tun und Mit-Leiden mit den von Gott Entfremdung, um ihnen (als zweiter Adam) einen Raum christlicher Sendung zu eröffnen, in welchem sie *en Christoi*, an seinem heilsamen Tun und Leiden für die Welt erhalten können" (221–22).]

See also *Heart of the World*, 80–81: "I am the vine, you are the branches. . . . Are you then surprised if a drop of my Heart's blood trickles into your every thought and deed? Are you surprised if the thoughts of my Heart quietly infiltrate your worldly heart? If a whispering takes wing in you and day and night you perceive a low, beckoning call? To a love that wants to suffer, to a love that, together with mine, redeems? . . . And to complete in your own body what is still lacking to my sufferings, what must still lack as long as I have not suffered my Passion in all my branches and members? For to be sure, none of you is redeemed by anyone save myself; but I am the total Redeemer only united with each of you."

61. Von Balthasar, *A Theology of History*, 79, 80, 84.

8. THE HUMANITY OF CHRIST

1. Wolfhart Pannenberg, *Jesus—God and Man*, trans. Lewis L. Wilkins and Duane A. Priebe (Philadelphia: The Westminster Press, 1968), 34–35.

2. Von Balthasar, *A Theology of History*, 10–12.

3. Ibid., 10–11.

4. Von Balthasar, *Kosmische Liturgie: Das Weltbild Maximus des Bekenners*, 205: "... kein reines Negativum Gottes ist, also nicht einseitig durch mystische Auflösung in Gott, sondern—bei aller Erhebung zur Gott-Teilnahme, bei allem Absterben dieser Welt—doch nur in ausdrücklicher Bewahrung und Vollendung seiner Natur erlöst werden kann."

5. Ibid., 254.

6. Von Balthasar, *A Theology of History*, 11.

7. Donald M. MacKinnon, "The Relation of the Doctrines of the Incarnation and the Trinity," in *Themes in Theology. The Three-Fold Cord: Essays in Philosophy, Politics and Theology* (Edinburgh: T. & T. Clark, 1987), 159. (My emphasis.)

8. Ibid., 154.

9. Von Balthasar, *Mysterium Paschale*, 30.

10. Ibid., 28–29.

11. "We shall never know how to express the abyss-like depths of the Father's self-giving, that Father who, in an eternal 'super-Kenosis,' makes himself 'destitute' of all that he is and can be so as to bring forth a consubstantial divinity, the Son. Everything that can be thought and imagined where God is concerned is, in advance, included and transcended in this self-destitution which constitutes the person of the Father, and, at the same time, those of the Son and the Spirit. God as the 'gulf' (Eckhart: *Un-grund*) of absolute Love contains in advance, eternally, all the modalities of love, of compassion, and even of a 'separation' motivated by love and founded on the infinite distinction between the hypostases—modalities which may manifest themselves in the course of a history of salvation involving sinful humankind" (Von Balthasar, *Mysterium Paschale*, viii–ix).

12. Von Balthasar, "The Word, Scripture and Tradition," in *Explorations in Theology* I, 20–21.

13. Ibid., 93.

14. Von Balthasar, *Kosmische Liturgie: Das Weltbild Maximus des Bekenners*, 259: "Die Göttlichkeit seines Tuns hat ihres letzte Garantie in der unverkürzten und unversehrten Echtheit seiner Menschheit. Gerade sein Reden, Atmen, Wandern, sein Hungern, Essen, Dürsten, Trinken, Schlafen, Weinen, Sichängstigen ist der unterscheidende Ort der Erscheinung des Göttlichen. . . . Soweit das unterscheidend Menschliche sich durchhält, soweit erscheint Gott."

15. Von Balthasar, *Prayer*, 46–47.

16. Joseph de Guibert, S.J., *The Jesuits: Their Spiritual Doctrine and Practice*, 134–35.

17. *Glory of the Lord* VII, 143–44; *Herrlichkeit* III/2, 131–32.

18. *Heart of the World*, 50. ["Nicht ein blasses Abbild himmlischer Wahrheit spielt sich auf Erden, sondern das Himmlische selbst, übersetzt in die irdische Sprache. Wenn der Knecht hienieden müde und verbraucht von der Last seines Tages zu Boden sinkt und Gott anbetend sein Haupt die Erde berührt, dann faßt diese arme Gebärde alle Huldigung des unerschaffenen Sohns vor dem Throne des Vaters in sich. Und sie fügt dieser ewigen Vollkommenheit für immer hinzu die mühsam erschmerzte, unscheinbare, glanzlose Vollkommenheit einer menschlichen Demut" (32–33).]

19. See von Balthasar's own summary of what he set out to accomplish in *A Theology of History* and *A Theological Anthropology*: the former "begins by pointing exclusively to Christ's form of existence at the center of history, where the time of sin and reprobation is reintegrated into God's original time by virtue of Christ's loving obedience to the Father. This earthly obedience has as its terminus the Father's coming 'hour', which the Son awaits even while bending under the creaturely time common to all men, so that this attitude becomes the measure and norm of every temporal existence"; and the latter ends "with a sketch of a christological reintegration of man's fragmentary and concrete 'stages of life' into their final eschatological form" (Von Balthasar, "In Retrospect," in *The Analogy of Beauty*, 203–4).

20. *The Christian State of Life*, 192–93 (my emphasis). ["Er ist diese Idee nicht irgendwo jenseits der realen Welt und ihrer Geschichte, sondern gerade, indem er in diese Welt und ihre Geschichte eintritt und sie von innen her «in sich als dem Haupte zusammenfaßt» (Eph 1,10). . . . Das ist so wahr, daß der Einwand, er sei ja erst am Ende der Zeiten in die Welt eingetreten, kraftlos ist, denn der Weltprozeß wäre nicht von Stapel gelaufen, wenn dieser Augenblick in der Fülle der Zeit nicht vorausgesehen worden wäre. Und nochmals: dieses Realwerden der Weltidee in der Menschwerdung ist nur realisierbar geworden, weil seine Idee innerhalb der freien Möglichkeiten der ewigen Realität trinitarischen Lebens lag" (153).]

21. *Prayer*, 137.

22. Ibid.

23. Von Balthasar, *Explorations in Theology* I, 57 (my emphasis).

24. Again we can find some background illumination of von Balthasar's approach by noting the very similar structure of thought in Ignatius of Loyola. Commenting on Ignatius' own mystical life, Alois Haas suggests that there is more to Ignatius' emphasis on obedience than simply the need for service in the contemporary church: "The reverential love (*amor reverencial*) is rather a climate, given to redeemed man once for all through the God-Man, Jesus, of openness to the Father and to the most

Holy Trinity. In Jesus, the humble servant, this climate has for Ignatius received an unmistakable impress as a service of humility and reverence inspired by love. Ignatius comes to share, through this path of humility in the service of the servant of God, Jesus, in all the exalted trinitarian visions; and he himself, the more he appears in the raiment of his humble Lord, completes the final spiritualization of his attitude" (Adolf Haas, S.J., "The Mysticism of St. Ignatius According to His Spiritual Diary," in *Ignatius of Loyola: His Personality and Spiritual Heritage*, ed. Friedrich Wulf, S.J., [St. Louis: The Institute of Jesuit Sources, 1977], 190). The key imagery in relationship to von Balthasar would be the "climate" of love which Jesus creates, by participation in which one achieves "the final spiritualization."

25. Von Balthasar, *Mysterium Paschale*, 135.

26. *Heart of the World*, 120–21. [87.]

WORKS CITED

WORKS BY HANS URS VON BALTHASAR

The most comprehensive bibliography now available of all von Balthasar's writings is *Hans Urs von Balthasar. Bibliographie 1925–1990*. Edited by Cornelia Capol. Einsiedeln: Johannes Verlag, 1990. For ease of reference, the original German title of a work that has been cited in both the original and translation is given in brackets as part of the English translation entry.

"The Absence of Jesus." In *New Elucidations*. Translated by Sr. Mary Theresilde Skerry. San Francisco: Ignatius Press, 1986.

"Another Ten Years—1975." Translated by John Saward. In *The Analogy of Beauty: The Theology of Hans Urs von Balthasar*. Edited by John Riches, 222–33. Edinburgh: T. & T. Clark, 1986.

Christian Meditation. Translated by Sr. Mary Theresilde Skerry. San Francisco: Ignatius Press, 1989.

The Christian State of Life. Translated by Sr. Mary Frances McCarthy. San Francisco: Ignatius Press, 1983. [*Christlicher Stand*.]

Christlicher Stand. Einsiedeln: Johannes Verlag, 1977.

Au coeur du mystére Rédempteur. Paris: Editions C.L.D., 1980.

"La conscience de Jésus et sa mission." In *Nouveaux Points de Repère*. Paris: Librairie Arthème Fayard, 1980.

Elizabeth of the Trinity. Translated by Dennis Martin. In *Two Sisters in the Spirit: Thérèse of Lisieux and Elizabeth of the Trinity*. San Francisco: Ignatius Press, 1992. [*Schwestern im Geist*.]

"Experience God?" In *New Elucidations*. Translated by Sr. Mary Theresilde Skerry. San Francisco: Ignatius Press, 1986.

First Glance at Adrienne von Speyr. Translated by Antje Lawry and Sr. Sergia Englund, O.C.D. San Francisco: Ignatius Press, 1981.

Foi du Christ: Cinq approches christologiques. Paris: Aubier, 1968.

The Glory of the Lord. A Theological Aesthetics. Vol. I, *Seeing the Form*. Translated by Erasmo Leiva-Merikakis. Edinburgh: T. & T. Clark, 1982. [*Herrlichkeit* I.] Vol. III, *Studies in Theological Style: Lay Styles*.

Translated by Andrew Louth et al. Edinburgh: T. & T. Clark, 1986. [*Herrlichkeit* II/2.] Vol. V: The Realm of Metaphysics in the Modern Age. Translated by Oliver Davies et al. Edinburgh: T. & T. Clark, 1991. [*Herrlichkeit* III/1.] Vol. VII, *Theology: The New Covenant*. Translated by Brian McNeil, C.R.V. San Francisco: Ignatius Press, 1989. [*Herrlichkeit* III/2.]

"God Speaks as Man." In *Explorations in Theology* I: *The Word Made Flesh*. Translated by A. V. Littledale with Alexander Dru. San Francisco: Ignatius Press, 1989.

"The Gospel as Norm and Test of All Spirituality in the Church." *Concilium* 9 (1965): 7–23.

Heart of the World. Translated by Erasmo S. Leiva. San Francisco: Ignatius Press, 1979. [*Das Herz der Welt*.]

Herrlichkeit: Eine theologische Ästhetik. Vol. II/2, *Fächer der Stile: Laikale Stile*. 2d ed. Einsiedeln: Johannes Verlag, 1969. Vol. III/1, *Im Raum der Metaphysik: Neuzeit*. Einsiedeln: Johannes Verlag, 1965. Vol. III/2, *Theologie: Neuer Bund*. Einsiedeln: Johannes Verlag, 1969.

Das Herz der Welt. 3d ed. Zürich: Arche, 1959.

"The Holy Spirit as Love." In *Explorations in Theology* III: *Creator Spirit*. Translated by Brian McNeil, C.R.V. San Francisco: Ignatius Press, 1993.

"The Implications of the Word." In *Explorations in Theology* I: *The Word Made Flesh*. Translated by A. V. Littledale with Alexander Dru. San Francisco: Ignatius Press, 1989.

"In Retrospect." Translated by Kenneth Batinovich. In *The Analogy of Beauty: The Theology of Hans Urs von Balthasar*, ed. John Riches, 194–221. Edinburgh: T. & T. Clark, 1986.

Kosmische Liturgie: Des Weltbild Maximus des Bekenners. 2d ed. Einsiedeln: Johannes Verlag, 1961.

Love Alone: The Way of Revelation. London: Sheed and Ward, 1968.

The Moment of Christian Witness. Translated by Richard Beckley. New York: Newman Press, 1968.

Mysterium Paschale. Translated by Aidan Nichols, O.P. Edinburgh: T. & T. Clark, 1990.

"Obedience in the Light of the Gospel." In *New Elucidations*. Translated by Sr. Mary Theresilde Skerry. San Francisco: Ignatius Press, 1986.

Parole et mystère chez Origène. Paris: Ed. du Cerf, 1957.

Prayer. Translated by A. V. Littledale. New York: Paulist Press, 1967.

Présence et pensée. Essai sur la philosophie religieuse de Grégoire de Nysse. Paris: Beauchesne, 1942.

Schwestern im Geist: Therese von Lisieux und Elisabeth von Dijon. Einsiedeln: Johannes Verlag, 1970.

"Spirituality." In *Explorations in Theology* I: *The Word Made Flesh*. Translated by A. V. Littledale with Alexander Dru. San Francisco: Ignatius Press, 1989.

Theo-Drama: Theological Dramatic Theory. Vol. III, *The Dramatis Personae: The Person in Christ*. Translated by Graham Harrison. San Francisco: Ignatius Press, 1992. [*Theodramatik* II/2.]

Theodramatik. Vol. II/2, *Die Personen des Spiels: Die Personen in Christus*. Einsiedeln: Johannes Verlag, 1978.

A Theological Anthropology. New York: Sheed and Ward, 1967.

"Theologie und Spiritualität." *Gregorianum* 50 (1969): 571–87.

Theologik II. Einsiedeln: Johannes Verlag, 1985.

"Theology and Sanctity." In *Explorations in Theology* I: *The Word Made Flesh*. Translated by A.V. Littledale with Alexander Dru. San Francisco: Ignatius Press, 1989. ["Theologie und Heiligkeit." *Skizzen zur Theologie* I: *Verbum Caro*. Einsiedeln, 1960. This was an expansion of a much earlier form of the essay which first appeared in 1948; it is entirely distinct from "Theologie und Spiritualität."]

A Theology of History. 2d ed. New York: Sheed and Ward, 1963.

Thérèse of Lisieux: The Story of a Mission. Translated by Donald Nicholl. New York: Sheed and Ward, 1954. [*Schwestern im Geist*.]

"The Word, Scripture and Tradition." In *Explorations in Theology* I: *The Word Made Flesh*. Translated by A. V. Littledale with Alexander Dru. San Francisco: Ignatius Press, 1989.

"Zur Ortsbestimmung Christlicher Mystik." In *Grundfragen der Mystik*. With Werner Beierwaltes and Alois M. Haas. Einsideln: Johannes Verlag, 1974.

"Zwei Glaubensweisen." In *Skizzen zur Theologie* III: *Spiritus Creator*. Einsiedeln: Johannes Verlag, 1967.

SECONDARY WORKS

Barth, Karl. *Church Dogmatics*. Edited by G. W. Bromiley and T. F. Torrance. Vol. I/2, *The Doctrine of the Word of God*. Edinburgh: T. & T. Clark, 1956. Vol. IV/2, *The Doctrine of Reconciliation*. Edinburgh: T. & T. Clark, 1958.

Bonaventure. *The Journey of the Mind to God*. In *The Works of St. Bonaventure*. Vol. I, *Mystical Opuscula*. Translated by José de Vinck. Paterson, New Jersey: St. Anthony Guild Press, 1960.

Buckley, Michael J. *At the Origins of Modern Atheism*. New Haven: Yale University Press, 1987.

Burrows, Ruth. *Before the Living God*. London: Sheed and Ward, 1975.

de Guibert, Joseph, S.J. *The Jesuits: Their Spiritual Doctrine and Practice.* Translated by William J. Young, S.J. Chicago: The Institute of Jesuit Sources, 1964.

Egan, Harvey, S.J. *Ignatius Loyola the Mystic.* Wilmington, Delaware: Michael Glazier, 1987.

Eicher, Peter. *Offenbarung. Prinzip neuzeitlicher Theologie.* Munich: Kösel-Verlag, 1977.

Farrer, Austin. "Incarnation." In *The Brink of Mystery*, ed. Charles C. Conti, 19–21. London: SPCK, 1976.

———. "Very God and Very Man." In *Interpretation and Belief*, ed. Charles C. Conti, 126–37. London: SPCK, 1976.

Garrigues, Juan-Miguel, O.P. "La Personne composée du Christ d'après S. Maxime." *Revue Thomiste* 74 (April 1974): 181–204.

Greiner, Maximilian. "The Community of St. John: A Conversation with Cornelia Capol and Martha Gisi." In *Hans Urs von Balthasar: His Life and Work*, ed. David L. Schindler, 87–101. San Francisco: Ignatius Press, 1991.

Haas, Adolf, S.J. "The Mysticism of St. Ignatius According to His Spiritual Diary." In *Ignatius of Loyola: His Personality and Spiritual Heritage*, ed. Friedrich Wulf, S.J. St. Louis: The Institute of Jesuit Sources, 1977.

Heinz, Hans-Peter. *Der Gott des Je-mehr: der christologische Ansatz Hans Urs von Balthasar.* Bern: Herbert Lang, 1979.

Henrici, Peter. "Hans Urs von Balthasar: A Sketch of His Life." In *Hans Urs von Balthasar: His Life and Work.* Edited by David L. Schindler, 7–43. San Francisco: Ignatius Press, 1991.

Ignatius of Loyola. *The Spiritual Exercises of Saint Ignatius.* Translated by George E. Ganss, S.J. Chicago: Loyola University Press, 1992.

John of the Cross. *The Ascent of Mount Carmel.* In *John of the Cross: Selected Writings.* Edited and translated by Kieran Kavanaugh, O.C.D. The Classics of Western Spirituality. New York: Paulist Press, 1987.

Kehl, Medard. "Hans Urs von Balthasar: A Portrait." Tranlated by Robert J. Daly and Fred Lawrence. In *The Von Balthasar Reader.* Edited by Medard Kehl and Werner Löser, 3–54. New York: Crossroad, 1982.

Kerr, Fergus. *Theology After Wittgenstein.* Oxford: Basil Blackwell, 1986.

Löser, Werner. "The Ignatian *Exercises* in the Work of Hans Urs von Balthasar." In *Hans Urs von Balthasar: His Life and Work*, ed. David L. Schindler, 103–20. San Francisco: Ignatius Press, 1991.

Maximus the Confessor. *Liber Ambiguorum 7.* In *Patrologiae cursus completus: Series Graeca* 91. Paris: Jacques Paul Mígne, 1857–66.

MacKinnon, Donald. "The Relation of the Doctrines of the Incarnation and the Trinity." In *Themes in Theology. The Three-Fold Cord: Essays in Philosophy, Politics and Theology.* Edinburgh: T. & T. Clark, 1987.

McCabe, Herbert, O.P. *God Matters.* London: Geoffrey Chapman, 1987.

McGinn, Bernard. "Resurrection and Ascension in the Christology of the Early Cistercians." *Cîteaux: Commentarii Cisterciences* 30 (1979): 5–22.

McNeil, Brian, C.R.V. "The Exegete as Iconographer: Balthasar and the Gospels." In *The Analogy of Beauty: The Theology of Hans Urs von Balthasar.* Edited by John Riches. Edinburgh: T. & T. Clark, 1986.

Meyendorff, John. *Christ in Eastern Christian Thought.* 2d ed. Crestwood, New York: St. Vladimir's Seminary Press, 1975.

Mooney, Hilary A. *The Liberation of Consciousness: Bernard Lonergan's Theological Foundations in Dialogue with the Theological Aesthetics of Hans Urs Von Balthasar.* Frankfurt: Verlag Josef Knecht, 1992.

Newman, John Henry. "The Humiliation of the Eternal Son." In *Parochial and Plain Sermons,* 578–87. San Francisco: Ignatius Press, 1987.

O'Collins, Gerald. *Interpreting Jesus.* London: Geoffrey Chapman, 1983.

O'Donnell, John J., S.J. "God and World in Trinitarian Perspective." In *The Mystery of the Triune God.* New York: Paulist Press, 1989.

O'Hanlon, Gerald F., S.J. *The Immutability of God in the Theology of Hans Urs von Balthasar.* Cambridge: Cambridge University Press, 1990.

Pannenberg, Wolfhart. *Jesus—God and Man.* Translated by Lewis L. Wilkins and Duane A. Priebe. Philadelphia: Westminster Press, 1968.

Rahner, Hugo, S.J. *Ignatius the Theologian.* Translated by Michael Berry. San Francisco: Ignatius Press, 1990.

———. *The Spirituality of St. Ignatius of Loyola: An Account of Its Historical Development.* Translated by Francis John Smith, S.J. Chicago: Loyola University Press, 1980.

Rahner, Karl. *Karl Rahner in Dialogue: Conversations and Interviews, 1965–1982.* Edited by Paul Imhof and Hubert Biallowons. New York: Crossroad, 1986.

Riou, Alain. *Le monde et l'église selon Maxime le Confesseur.* Paris: Beauchesne, 1973.

Roberts, Louis. "The Collision of Rahner and Balthasar." *Continuum* 5 (1968): 755–57.

Schleiermacher, Friedrich. *The Christian Faith.* 2d ed. Edinburgh: T. & T. Clark, 1986.

Temple, William. *Readings in St. John's Gospel.* Wilton, Connecticut: Morehouse Barlow, 1985.

Williams, Rowan. "Balthasar and Rahner." In *The Analogy of Beauty: The Theology of Hans Urs von Balthasar*. Edited by John Riches. Edinburgh: T. & T. Clark, 1986.

————. *The Wound of Knowledge*. 2d ed. Boston: Cowley Publications, 1991.

Index

ABOUT THE AUTHOR

Mark A. McIntosh is Assistant Professor of Systematic Theology and Spirituality at Loyola University of Chicago and is currently at work on a study exploring the relationship between spirituality and theology in the modern era.